T&T Clark Studies in Systematic Theology

Edited by

John Webster
Ian A. McFarland
Ivor Davidson

Volume 9

B L O O M S B U R Y

LONDON • NEW DELHI • NEW YORK • SYDNEY

LETTERS OF THE DIVINE WORD

The Perfections of God in Karl Barth's Church Dogmatics

Robert B. Price

BLOOMSBURY

LONDON · NEW DELHI · NEW YORK · SYDNEY

Bloomsbury T&T Clark
An imprint of Bloomsbury Publishing Plc

50 Bedford Square	175 Fifth Avenue
London	New York
WC1B 3DP	NY 10010
UK	USA

www.bloomsbury.com

First published by T&T Clark International 2011
Paperback edition first published 2013

British Library Cataloguing-in-Publication Data
A catalogue record for this book is available from the British Library.

ISBN: HB: 978-0-567-07543-7
PB: 978-0-567-01271-5

Library of Congress Cataloging-in-Publication Data
A catalog record for this book is available from the Library of Congress

Typeset by Newgen Imaging Systems Pvt Ltd, Chennai, India

CONTENTS

CONTENTS

ACKNOWLEDGEMENTS

The problem of where to begin with Barth is a real one. I faced it when I finally came to the realisation that Karl Barth was a theologian whose acquaintance I could no longer avoid. The sheer shelf-space so commandingly occupied by the innumerable volumes of the *Church Dogmatics* made the prospect of genuine acquaintance seem so remote as to be unattainable. A good friend, however, was ready with providential encouragement. 'Start with II/1', he said. The years since then have not carried me much further afield. CD II/1 contains the account of the perfections of God on which this study is based. CD II/1 is also dedicated in part to the University of Aberdeen (though, oddly, the English translation omits this dedication). Who could have known?

It was a gift of stunning generosity that the Lord should even have allowed us to embark on the dream of pursuing doctoral studies abroad. That he in unstinting kindness has now carried us to the final, happy stages of this adventure is yet greater cause for wonder, for thanks, and for rejoicing. What indeed shall we render to the Lord for all his benefits to us? To him belongs eternal praise!

It is a great privilege to be able to acknowledge a few of the many other debts of gratitude which have accumulated over the years. Thanks to Aaron Kleist, who for over 15 years now has modelled to me a life of deep Christian faith and academic excellence, and who was the first to encourage me to pursue doctoral studies. Fred Sanders introduced me to theology proper and, particularly, to the work of Karl Barth. Peter and Patricia Anders spoke from first-hand experience of John Webster's expertise as a supervisor and of the many pleasures of living in the UK.

Thanks especially to John Webster, whose Christian witness, timely encouragement, enduring patience, wise guidance, and sparkling sense of humour have so wonderfully eased the burden of research and sped its progress, and who has set a standard for the pursuit of a truly theological theology within both church and academy. Brian Brock, Francesca Murphy, Nick Thompson, Pete Williams, Don Wood and Phil Ziegler immeasurably enriched our four wonderful years in Aberdeen by their friendship, counsel, encouragement and instruction. Thanks to that anonymous foundation which so generously housed us rent-free in a lovely flat for the duration of our stay. Dominic Smart and Gilcomston South Church proclaimed to us the gospel of Jesus Christ with a passion and clarity, a joy and seriousness which we will never forget, and surrounded us with such a warmth of Christian fellowship as truly to have made Aberdeen feel like home. Clint Arnold, Mike Wilkins, Alan Gomes and others at Talbot School of Theology launched us on our little adventure, gave us hope of having a job on completion, and then received us upon our return.

Thanks go also to our parents, Bob and Linda Price and Walt and Sherry Harrah, who prayed for us, financed us, cheered for us, and alternately visited us or brought us home for visits. Finally, the deepest thanks go to my wife, Mindy, joyful as her beauty, my comfort and my delight, who has with untiring interest and irrepressible good cheer followed the course of my studies and teaching. To her this project is most affectionately and gratefully dedicated.

ABBREVIATIONS

CD   Karl Barth, *Church Dogmatics* ed. G. W. Bromiley and
         T. F. Torrance; (Edinburgh: T&T Clark, 1956–1975).

KD   Karl Barth, *Die kirchliche Dogmatik* (Munich: Chr. Kaiser,
         1932; Zürich: Evangelischer Verlag Zürich, 1938–1967).

ChrL   Karl Barth, *The Christian Life: Church Dogmatics IV/4,*
         Lecture Fragments, trans. G. W. Bromiley (Grand Rapids:
         Eerdmans, 1981)

INTRODUCTION

Plan of the Present Study

In the introduction to his elegantly career-capping commentary on the Acts of the Apostles, Jaroslav Pelikan rehearses his long-standing insistence on the fundamental role played by Scripture, and hence by Scripture commentary, in the Christian theological tradition. He then quotes an author who chides post-modernism for promoting 'the idea that commentary is in some way a benighted activity, a secondary or tertiary activity rather than a primary one' – an activity which historically has constituted one of the 'great intellectual opportunities for originality...of thought'.[1] The present study is an exercise in the genre of commentary. It is an attempt at a close reading and analysis of a single text, rather than an endeavour to argue a specific thesis. These more limited aims do not make it any less prone to failure. For while arguing a thesis on the basis of Barth's text 'risks merely using Barth for ends extrinsic to his theology', then, certainly, the kind of analysis attempted here risks mere repetition of its text.[2] In fact, a significant proportion of this study is devoted precisely to setting forth Barth's argument. As often as possible, this is done using Barth's own words, for one of the strategies of successful commentary is to remain transparent to its text. In so doing, this study often simply confirms generally acknowledged features of Barth's theology, but from a less frequently studied locus of the *Dogmatics*. The primary aim of commentary, however, is interpretation. Thus, even in tracing Barth's argument, this study attempts that combination of observation and clarification and argumentation which ultimately directs attention back to its text. 'As always in Barth, summarizing the main moves is a relatively simple affair, but penetrating to the fundamentals and re-articulating them is no easy matter....The sum of the interpreter's wisdom is probably: take and read.'[3]

---

[1] Jaroslav Pelikan, *Acts*, Brazos Theological Commentary on the Bible (Grand Rapids: Brazos, 2005), 25.

[2] James J. Buckley, 'Christian community, baptism, and the Lord's Supper', in *The Cambridge Companion to Karl Barth*, ed. John Webster (Cambridge: Cambridge University Press, 2000), 196.

[3] John Webster, '"Eloquent and Radiant": The Prophetic Office of Christ and the Mission of the Church', in *idem, Barth's Moral Theology: Human Action in Barth's Thought* (Grand Rapids: Eerdmans, 1998), 126.

1

Barth's own exposition of the divine perfections in *Church Dogmatics* II/1 is broken down into four sections: §28 on the identity of the God whose perfections are to be described; §29 on the proper way to go about a doctrine of the divine perfections; §30 on what Barth categorises as 'the perfections of the divine loving'; and §31 on what Barth categorises as 'the perfections of the divine freedom'. In good commentarial style, chapters one, two, three, and four of the present study analyse these respective sections of Barth's exposition. Each proceeds, as it were, verse-by-verse, following the development of Barth's argument, with occasional excursuses into the directly relevant secondary literature or into issues in broader scholarship on Barth. The fifth and final chapter identifies some of the key theological decisions which govern Barth's exposition as a whole. While this concluding chapter does not attempt to assess the adequacy of Barth's exposition, it argues that such adequacy is largely a matter of the validity or invalidity of these key theological decisions, and that assessment must therefore begin with these. This chapter also suggests paths for further research by glancing ahead at a surprising twist in Barth's handling of the attributes later in the *Church Dogmatics*.

The Context of Barth's Doctrine of the Perfections

In the spring of 1951, while on holiday in Locarno, Switzerland, Karl Barth had a dream. Having just completed his doctrine of creation with *Church Dogmatics* III/4, his thoughts turned to the doctrine of reconciliation, on which he was to begin lecturing in the summer. But what would provide the structure for his exposition of 'this centre of all Christian knowledge'?[4] In a letter to his son Christoph, Barth excitedly recounts his visions in the night:

> I dreamed of a plan. It seemed to go in the right direction. The plan now had to stretch from christology to ecclesiology together with the relevant ethics. I woke at 2 a.m. and then put it down on paper hastily the next morning.[5]

The elegance and multi-layered complexity of Barth's doctrine of reconciliation (*CD* IV/1–3) bears witness to a moment of true inspiration.

Although on a smaller scale, the plan of Barth's doctrine of the divine attributes (or 'perfections') in *Church Dogmatics* II/1 displays a comparable

---

[4] *CD* IV/1, ix.

[5] Letter to Christoph Barth, 2 June 1951; quoted in Eberhard Busch, *Karl Barth: His Life from Letters and Autobiographical Texts*, trans. John Bowden (Grand Rapids: Eerdmans, 1994), 377. Barth summarises the main features of this plan in the heading to §58, 'The Doctrine of Reconciliation (Survey)' (*CD* IV/1, 79).

elegance. And what it lacks by way of a precipitating dream Barth supplies from long practice with the doctrine. When Barth began lecturing in the summer semester of 1937 on the material which would be published as CD II/1,[6] he had already twice before delivered complete lecture-cycles on dogmatics, including accounts of the divine perfections.

Barth's first lectures on the divine perfections came in November and December 1924, as part of his Göttingen/Münster dogmatics lectures of 1924–1926.[7] These lectures anticipate many of the features of Barth's doctrine of the divine attributes as it appears in the Church Dogmatics. Similarities include Barth's insistence on revelation as an event; on the manifold simplicity of the divine nature; on the identity of each attribute with the others and with the entire divine nature; on the inseparability of divine transcendence and immanence; on the necessity of a twofold ('dialectical') division of the attributes; and on the necessity of treating what he calls the attributes of personality before the attributes of aseity, in accordance with the intrinsic order of revelation.[8] On the other hand, in the Göttingen lectures, trinitarian and christological categories figure much less prominently in the formulation of individual attributes. It is only in his account of the divine blessedness, for example, that Barth speaks explicitly of the relations between Father, Son, and Spirit;[9] and it is only in his account of the divine righteousness that Barth makes extended reference to Jesus Christ.[10] The Göttingen lectures also evince a particular methodological preoccupation which Barth would later eschew: the attempt to derive the attributes of personality by way of eminence and those of aseity by way of negation.[11]

The second of Barth's accounts of the divine perfections came in the summer semester of 1927 (part of the Münster dogmatics lectures of 1926–1928).[12] According to Eberhard Busch, these lectures were 'not, in fact, a mere repetition of the first course, but a completely new version which preserved the old structure'. In Barth's own estimate, 'hardly one stone

---

[6] Barth finished these lectures in summer semester 1939. See Busch, Karl Barth, 284, 292. It was during the 1938–1939 winter semester that Barth did the majority of his lecturing on the divine perfections. See Jan Štefan, 'Gottes Vollkommenheiten nach KD II/1', in Karl Barth im europäischen Zeitgeschehen (1935–1950): Widerstand – Bewährung – Orientierung, ed. Michael Beintker, Christian Link, and Michael Trowitzsch (Zürich: Theologischer Verlag Zürich, 2010), 85.

[7] Štefan, 'Gottes Vollkommenheiten nach KD II/1', 85.

[8] Karl Barth, The Göttingen Dogmatics: Instruction in the Christian Religion, vol. 1, ed. Hannelotte Reiffen, trans. Geoffrey W. Bromiley (Grand Rapids: Eerdmans, 1991), 351–439.

[9] Barth, Göttingen Dogmatics, 425–6.

[10] Barth, Göttingen Dogmatics, 419–20.

[11] Barth, Göttingen Dogmatics, 399–400. Happily, Barth is rather half-hearted in this attempt.

[12] Štefan, 'Gottes Vollkommenheiten nach KD II/1', 85.

remains on another'.[13] Amy Marga, on the other hand, says the Münster lectures 'are essentially a rewrite' of Göttingen, though she acknowledges 'some marked differences'.[14] It remains to be seen precisely how far Barth's doctrine of the divine perfections from Münster advances over that from Göttingen. For while the first semester's worth of these lectures (the 'Münster prolegomena') appeared as *Die christliche Dogmatik im Entwurf* in 1927,[15] the lectures from the following two semesters remain unpublished.

With all this practice behind him, it is small wonder that, when Barth turned a third time to the doctrines of the knowledge, nature and attributes of God, he produced a volume that has been described as 'one of the most splendidly developed in the *Church Dogmatics*, and one of the most useful'.[16] *CD* II/1 appeared in 1940 and contains the first half of Barth's doctrine of God.[17] Like the doctrine of God in his Göttingen lectures, it begins with an account of the knowledge of God (*CD* II/1, §§25–7). The intervening years, however, had witnessed at least two fierce conflicts over the source or sources of human knowledge of God. The first was Barth's famous falling-out with Emil Brunner over the issue of natural theology.[18] The second was the coalescence (and ultimate dissolution) of the confessing church movement around *inter alia* the political implications of the rejection of natural theology (172–8).[19] These conflicts galvanised Barth's position, and so when in *CD* II/1 he re-enters the fray over the knowledge of God, he issues a vigorous manifesto on the exclusivity of God's self-revelation as a source of human knowledge of God: 'God is known through God and through God alone' (44). This account also

---

[13] Busch, *Karl Barth*, 172–3.

[14] Amy Marga, *Karl Barth's Dialogue with Catholicism in Göttingen and Münster: Its Significance for His Doctrine of God* (Tübingen: Mohr Siebeck, 2010), 91. Štefan ('Gottes Vollkommenheiten nach KD II/1', 85) suggests the two accounts are fairly similar.

[15] Karl Barth, *Die christliche Dogmatik im Entwurf*, vol. 1, *Die Lehre vom Worte Gottes: Prolegomena zur christlichen Dogmatik, 1927*, Karl Barth Gesamtausgabe 14, ed. Gerhard Sauter (Zürich: Theologischer Verlag Zürich, 1982).

[16] Robert W. Jenson, *Alpha and Omega: A Study in the Theology of Karl Barth* (1963; reprint Eugene: Wipf and Stock, 2002), 68–9.

[17] Barth's doctrine of revelation in *CD* I/1 (1932) includes his account of God's triunity.

[18] Emil Brunner and Karl Barth, *Natural Theology: Comprising 'Nature and Grace' by Professor Dr. Emil Brunner and the reply 'No!' by Dr. Karl Barth*, trans. Peter Fraenkel, with an introduction by John Baillie (1946; reprint Eugene: Wipf and Stock, 2002). The same issue also contributed to Barth's break with Tillich's theology of correlation and Bultmann's existentialism. See Bruce L. McCormack, *Karl Barth's Critically Realistic Dialectical Theology: Its Genesis and Development 1909–1936* (New York: Oxford University Press, 1995), 322–3, 410–11; Eberhard Busch, *The Great Passion: An Introduction to Karl Barth's Theology* (Grand Rapids: Eerdmans, 2004), 72; Christophe Chalamet, *Dialectical Theologians: Wilhelm Herrmann, Karl Barth and Rudolf Bultmann* (Zürich: Theologischer Verlag Zürich, 2005), 105–6, 257–8.

[19] Busch, *Karl Barth*, 246–8. In-text page references to *CD* II/1 will be given throughout in brackets.

provides Barth the occasion to engage in a truly epic piece of sustained theological polemic against natural theology. The heat of Barth's angry 'No!' to Brunner may have subsided, but his polemic had lost none of its relentless intensity in the calamitous years leading to the Second World War.

Controversy abates, as it were, as Barth transitions from the knowledge of God into his account of the divine perfections (*CD* II/1, §§28–31). Here Barth sketches a more serene portrait of the divine identity, centred upon his identification of God as 'the One who loves in freedom'. Barth groups the perfections in dialectically balanced pairs. These paired perfections comprise in turn two dialectically balanced series. First are the perfections of the divine loving (grace and holiness, mercy and righteousness, patience and wisdom). Second are the perfections of the divine freedom (unity and omnipresence, constancy and omnipotence, eternity and glory).[20] Throughout, Barth has his eye fixed on Scripture's testimony to Jesus Christ, who is the definitive revelation of the divine identity.

Here we do in fact observe a shift in Barth's thought – if only one of emphasis – from earlier in the 1930s. It was spurred on by the reorientation of his doctrine of election, which began in the summer of 1936. In his doctrine of the divine perfections, Barth speaks of revelation less in terms of the here-and-now events in which God encounters the individual, and more in terms of God's ultimate act of self-revelation in Jesus Christ.[21] As regards the theological tradition on the divine perfections, Barth gratefully appropriates the insights particularly of the Protestant scholastics where these are governed by Christology, and charitably but no less decisively rejects those that are not. Barth insists, for example, on a multiple divine simplicity, a lively immutability, and a limited omnipotence. The pastoral warmth and kerygmatic urgency of this typically abstract and philosophical locus are remarkable, as is also its elegant joining of form to content. Here, too, Barth gives substantial dogmatic grounding to a theme he will continue to unfold through the rest of the *Dogmatics*: God is in himself precisely as he reveals himself to be in Jesus Christ, for what God reveals in Christ is his very being. God's freedom finds its ultimate expression not in withdrawal from humanity but in his love for humanity: God's deity, as Barth famously described it, includes his humanity.[22] Understandably, many of these striking features of Barth's portrait of the divine identity have (in that most sincere form of flattery) been

---

[20] Though Hans Urs von Balthasar was conspicuously fond of *CD* II/1 (Busch, *Karl Barth*, 302), the prominence of dialectic in it is strangely unaccounted for by his thesis that Barth left dialectic largely behind him with the early 1930s. Hans Urs von Balthasar, *The Theology of Karl Barth: Exposition and Interpretation*, trans. Edward T. Oakes (San Francisco: Ignatius, 1992).

[21] McCormack, *Dialectical Theology*, 253–6, 461.

[22] Karl Barth, 'The Humanity of God', in *idem*, *The Humanity of God*, trans. Thomas Wieser and John Newton Thomas (Atlanta: John Knox, 1960), 46.

taken up by subsequent theologians into their own accounts of the divine perfections.[23] Such breadth of appreciation was not to attend the following volumes of the *Dogmatics*.

CD II/2, which appeared in 1942, contains the second half of Barth's doctrine of God, remarkable for its inclusion of Barth's monumental doctrine of election, which has proved no less controversial than his rejection of natural theology.[24] One expositor from among Barth's defenders has said of his doctrine of election, 'When the history of theology in the twentieth century is written from the vantage point of, let us say, one hundred years from now, I am confident that the greatest contribution of Karl Barth to the development of church doctrine will be located in his doctrine of election.'[25] Barth's contribution consists, not surprisingly, in the christological focus he gives to the doctrine. According to Barth, it is Christ himself, that is, God the Son as already determined to be incarnate, who is both the subject and the object of election. As the electing God, the subject of election, Christ himself already constitutes God's reconciling will toward humanity and so elects himself and all of humanity to salvation. And as the elect man, the object not only of election but also of reprobation, Christ himself and Christ alone endures God's absolute rejection of sinful humanity. Barth thus radically reconfigures the concept of double predestination around Christ himself, rather than around two separate groups of humanity.

With such famous neighbours on either side – the attack on natural theology before and the doctrine of election after – and the raging of a world war to muffle its publication in 1940, it is hardly surprising that Barth's doctrine of the divine perfections has received little public attention.[26] The same neighbourly celebrity has also cast its shadow over the doctrine, as such. The doctrine of the divine perfections (or attributes) is traditionally paired with the doctrine of the Trinity to comprise the doctrine of God. Yet, while the history of the doctrine of the Trinity has enjoyed its share of the

---

[23] For example, Otto Weber, *Foundations of Dogmatics*, 2 vols., trans. Darrell L. Guder (Grand Rapids: Eerdmans, 1981–1983), 1.397–460; Donald G. Bloesch, *God the Almighty: Power, Wisdom, Holiness, Love* (Carlisle: Paternoster, 1995); Colin E. Gunton, *Act and Being: Towards a Theology of the Divine Attributes* (London: SCM, 2002); Daniel L. Migliore, *Faith Seeking Understanding: An Introduction to Christian Theology*, 2nd ed. (Grand Rapids: Eerdmans, 2004), 82–7. See further Štefan, 'Gottes Vollkommenheiten nach KD II/1', 103–4.

[24] Cf. David Gibson, *Reading the Decree: Exegesis, Election and Christology in Calvin and Barth* (London: T&T Clark, 2009).

[25] Bruce McCormack, 'Grace and Being: The Role of God's Gracious Election in Karl Barth's Theological Ontology', in *The Cambridge Companion to Karl Barth*, ed. John Webster (Cambridge: Cambridge University Press, 2000), 92.

[26] A signal of things to come, the only early English-language review of *KD* II/1 devotes over twice as many words to 'The Knowledge of God' as it does to the much longer chapter on the divine perfections. See Sydney Cave, review of *Die kirchliche Dogmatik II/1, Die Lehre von Gott*, by Karl Barth, *The Congregational Quarterly* 19.2 (1941): 170–1.

spotlight,[27] the same cannot be said for the history of the doctrine of the divine attributes. Wolf Krötke laments that no adequate history of the doctrine has yet been written, and Richard Muller notes the very uneven consideration given to this doctrine in standard accounts of the history of doctrine.[28] What scholarly attention has filtered through to the development of the doctrine of the divine attributes and to Barth's exposition of it in particular has typically been very selective. No full-scale study of either has been published.

That is not to say, however, that there is not a growing body of scholarly literature on Barth's doctrine of the attributes, from book reviews[29] and summaries of Barth's *Dogmatics*[30] to the relevant sections of comparative studies,[31] thematic studies,[32] and interpretations of Barth's thought as a

---

[27] For example, Ferdinand Christian Baur, *Die christliche Lehre von der Dreieinigkeit und Menschwerdung Gottes in ihrer geschichtlichen Entwicklung*, 3 vols. (Tübingen: Osiander, 1841–1843); J. Lebreton, *Histoire du dogme de la Trinité*, 2 vols. 7th ed. (Paris: Beauchesne, 1927–1928); Bertrand de Margerie, *The Christian Trinity in History*, trans. Edmund J. Fortman, Studies in Historical Theology 1 (Still River: St. Bede's, 1982); Franz Courth, *Trinität: In der Schrift und Patristik*, *Trinität: In der Scholastik*, and *Trinität: Von der Reformation bis zur Gegenwart*, Handbuch der Dogmengeschichte II.1a-c, ed. Michael Schmaus et al. (Freiburg: Herder, 1985–1996).

[28] Wolf Krötke, *Gottes Klarheiten: Eine Neuinterpretation der Lehre von Gottes »Eigenschaften«* (Tübingen: Mohr Siebeck, 2001), 34 n. 1. Richard A. Muller, *Post-Reformation Reformed Dogmatics: The Rise and Development of Reformed Orthodoxy, ca. 1520 to ca. 1725*, vol. 3, *The Divine Essence and Attributes* (Grand Rapids: Baker Academic, 2003), 23–4, with honourable mention to the historical material in Barth's account (*ibid.*, 24–5). Muller offers a very full survey of the doctrine of the divine existence, essence, and attributes from the twelfth through the eighteenth centuries (*ibid.*, 21–150).

[29] The fullest is Meinrad Benz, review of *Die kirchliche Dogmatik, Die Lehre von Gott*, by Karl Barth, *Divus Thomas: Jahrbuch für Philosophie und spekulative Theologie* 3.21 (1943): 213–23, esp. 219–22.

[30] For example, F. W. Camfield, 'Development and Present Stage of the Theology of Karl Barth', in *idem*, ed., *Reformation Old and New: A Tribute to Karl Barth* (London: Lutterworth, 1947), 47–71; Geoffrey W. Bromiley, *Introduction to the Theology of Karl Barth* (Edinburgh: T&T Clark, 1979), 69–83.

[31] For example, Mitchell Grell, *Der ewig reiche Gott: Die Erkenntnis, Gewinnung und Bestimmung der Eigenschaften Gottes nach Isaak August Dorner, August Hermann Cremer und Karl Barth mit besonderer Berücksichtigung des Einflusses der Theologie Dorners und Cremers auf die Gotteslehre Barths* (Ph.D. diss., University of Tübingen, 1992); Claus-Dieter Osthövener, *Die Lehre von Gottes Eigenschaften bei Friedrich Schleiermacher und Karl Barth*, Theologische Bibliothek Töpelmann 76 (Berlin: de Gruyter, 1996); Cornelis van der Kooi, *As in A Mirror: John Calvin and Karl Barth on Knowing God: A Diptych*, trans. Donald Mader (Leiden: Brill, 2005), 317–62; Christopher R. J. Holmes, *Revisiting the Doctrine of the Divine Attributes: In Dialogue with Karl Barth, Eberhard Jüngel, and Wolf Krötke* (New York: Peter Lang, 2007).

[32] For example, Wilfried Härle, *Sein und Gnade: Die Ontologie in Karl Barths Kirchlicher Dogmatik* (Berlin: de Gruyter, 1975); Gotthard Oblau, *Gotteszeit und*

whole.[33] A number of doctoral theses have also touched on aspects of Barth's doctrine of the divine perfections.[34] Perhaps the finest overview to date is that of Jan Štefan.[35] These studies have variously instructed, gratified, challenged, shocked, and baffled the present author; reference to them will be made as appropriate throughout the present work.

Menschenzeit: Eschatologie in der Kirchlichen Dogmatik von Karl Barth (Neukirchen-Vluyn: Neukirchener Verlag, 1988; E. P. Meijering, *Von den Kirchenvätern zu Karl Barth: Das altkirchliche Dogma in der 'Kirchlichen Dogmatik'* (Amsterdam: Gieben, 1993), 159–204; George Hunsinger, '*Mysterium Trinitatis*: Karl Barth's Conception of Eternity', in *idem, Disruptive Grace: Studies in the Theology of Karl Barth* (Grand Rapids: Eerdmans, 2000).

[33] For example, Otto Weber, *Karl Barth's Church Dogmatics: An Introductory Report on Volumes I:1 to III:4*, trans. Arthur C. Cochrane (Philadelphia: Westminster, 1953), 82–92; Colin E. Gunton, *The Barth Lectures*, ed. P. H. Brazier (London: T&T Clark, 2007), 97–109.

[34] For example, Charles Edward Raynal, III, *Karl Barth's Conception of the Perfections of God* (Ph.D. diss., Yale University, 1973); Terry L. Cross, *The Use of Dialectic in Karl Barth's Doctrine of God as Found in Church Dogmatics, II/1* (Ph.D. diss., Princeton Theological Seminary, 1991); published as *Dialectic in Karl Barth's Doctrine of God* (New York: Peter Lang, 2001); Todd Pokrifka-Joe, *Redescribing God: The Roles of Scripture, Tradition, and Reason in Karl Barth's Doctrines of Divine Unity, Constancy, and Eternity* (Ph.D. diss., University of St. Andrews, 2002).

[35] Štefan, 'Gottes Vollkommenheiten nach KD II/1'.

1

THE BEING OF GOD AS THE ONE WHO LOVES IN FREEDOM (§28)

The task of a doctrine of the divine attributes is to describe God. Its sister component in Christian theology is the doctrine of the Trinity, which attempts to give an account of the way in which Father, Son and Spirit, as operative in the economy of salvation, are also one God in eternity. In a similar fashion, a doctrine of the divine attributes attempts to delineate various characteristics of this same God on the basis of some aspect of his relation to the created order. Precisely how this delineation proceeds, and precisely which aspects of God's relation to the created order are thought to warrant such a doctrine, are naturally matters of debate.

Edward Farley has classified the two dominant positions in this debate as, respectively, the rational 'attribute tradition', which he identifies particularly with classical Roman Catholic thought on the divine attributes, and the mystical 'anti-attribute tradition', which he identifies particularly with Jewish theology of God.[1] The attribute tradition takes its start from the God-world relationship and proceeds by way of logical, 'theophilosophical' deduction. On the assumption of 'the necessary superiority of explanatory causes', God the Creator, as world-cause, is argued to be 'the perfection, the realisation and the perfect instance of all the relative perfections of created being'.[2] Such attribution by way of eminence is not, however, without its negative aspect, an attendant acknowledgement of the indirectness (at best) with which human concepts can fittingly describe the divine being. The anti-attribute tradition, on the other hand, takes its start not from creation and the generic God-world relation, but from redemption and the specific identity of God as manifest in his actions through the course of Israel's history.

---

[1] Edward Farley, *Divine Empathy: A Theology of God* (Minneapolis: Fortress, 1996), 82–9.

[2] Farley, *Divine Empathy*, 83–4.

The anti-attribute tradition is less rational and more existential, concerned with the personal encounter between God and human persons and, thus, with the problem of ethics. Its more strongly negative character arises not from 'the philosophically based awareness of God's metaphysical transcendence', but from a jealous defence of God's utter uniqueness and the consequent fear of idolatry.[3] The anti-attribute tradition, finally, asserts that only God can enable human language to bespeak him properly.

Surprisingly, on these terms Barth's exposition – setting aside its confidence in revelation and consequent readiness to make metaphysical claims – would actually take its place more squarely in Farley's anti-attribute tradition. Barth is convinced, for example, that God is to be known in his historical particularity rather than by means of a generic concept of deity; that God's presence to his community confronts it more urgently with the problem of ethics than with the problem of systematic explanation; and that proper bespeaking of God is something which God himself must enable, and not an inherent capacity of human reason and language.

As noted, however, Barth does not fit Farley's categories neatly. The reason for this can be illustrated by reversing the comparison and asking how Farley's categories might be fitted into Barth's own exposition. In Barth's terms, Farley's 'attribute tradition' might be said to give greater dogmatic weight to what is thought to be the divine freedom. Farley's 'anti-attribute tradition', on the other hand, might be said to give greater dogmatic weight to what is thought to be the divine loving. Barth does not fit Farley's categories because Barth insists that God's freedom is just as central to his identity as is his loving. God is, according to Barth, 'the One who loves in freedom', and though there is an intrinsic order to this loving and this freedom, the two are ineffaceable and mutually constitutive aspects of God's identity.

Interestingly, one of the tendencies of interpreters of Barth is, in effect, to try to make him fit more neatly into either Farley's 'attribute' or 'anti-attribute' tradition. That is, despite what Barth clearly affirms in his exposition of the divine attributes, there is a lingering temptation to isolate the divine loving and the divine freedom from each other and then to privilege one or the other in Barth's thought. Some interpreters claim that love (abstracted from the divine freedom) is in fact the dominant, controlling attribute in Barth's account, as we will see. Others, such as 'Claus-Dieter' Osthövener, claim that something like the divine freedom (abstracted from the divine love) is actually the driving concept for Barth. This privileging of either love or freedom in Barth is one way of reading the present debate surrounding by Bruce McCormack's proposal that Barth should have realised (or realised more clearly) that God's triunity must be the logical consequence of election.[4] McCormack's proposal

---

[3] Farley, *Divine Empathy*, 88–9.

[4] Bruce McCormack, 'Grace and Being: The Role of God's Gracious Election in Karl Barth's Theological Ontology', in *The Cambridge Companion to Karl Barth*, ed. John

might be said to represent an overemphasis on the divine loving (God's love for us) and a compromising of the divine freedom, which objectors have sought to reaffirm.[5] This debate itself takes its place within the broader debate over 'Rahner's Rule', with those who affirm a strict equivalence between immanent and economic Trinity representing, from the perspective of Barth's exposition of the divine attributes, the privileging of the divine loving, and those who attempt to qualify this strict equivalence representing either the safeguarding or even the privileging of the divine freedom.[6]

Of the relatively scant attention which Barth's doctrine of the divine perfections has received, most has understandably been devoted to its foundational opening section, 'The Being of God as the One Who Loves in Freedom' (§28). Here, Barth lays out in brief the basic dogmatic convictions which will guide the entire subsequent exposition: God has his being in his act of self-revelation in Jesus Christ, and this act shows him to be one who loves in freedom. It is thus to this section that Barth will either allude or explicitly refer, in later volumes of the *Dogmatics*, as shorthand for the whole of his doctrine of the perfections.[7] Barth also hints here in §28 at some of the implications of these dogmatic convictions for his method of exposition – implications which he will detail explicitly in §29. Secondary concepts such as the personhood of God and what Barth calls the 'divinity' of the divine attributes are introduced here, both to serve and to receive further development in accounts of individual attributes. Even the expository structure of this introductory section – an iterative pattern of increasingly specific and ultimately christological description – anticipates what is to follow. Reading this section with some familiarity with the exposition as a whole reveals both how central are its themes to Barth's thinking as well as how much substantive dogmatic description still lies outwith the scope of these substantial introductory remarks.

The title of this section, 'The Being of God as the One Who Loves in Freedom', neatly outlines what is to follow: a treatment first of God's being (§28.1), then of God's love (§28.2), and finally of God's freedom (§28.3). The thesis elaborates:

> God is who he is in the act of his revelation. God seeks and creates fellowship between himself and us, and therefore he loves us. But he is this

Webster (Cambridge: Cambridge University Press, 2000), 92–110.

[5] For example, Paul D. Molnar, *Divine Freedom and the Doctrine of the Immanent Trinity: In Dialogue with Karl Barth and Contemporary Theology* (Edinburgh: T&T Clark, 2002), 61–4.

[6] Fred Sanders, *The Image of the Immanent Trinity: Rahner's Rule and the Theological Interpretation of Scripture* (New York: Peter Lang, 2005).

[7] For example, CD II/2, 3; IV/1, 213; IV/2, 755; IV/3.1, 412; cf. IV/2, 751–83 (§68.2, 'The Basis of Love').

loving God also without us as Father, Son and Holy Spirit, in the freedom of the Lord, who has his life from himself. (257 rev.; *KD* 288)

First, in other words, it is only in his act of self-revelation that we can know who God is – a reiteration of the point secured in the previous chapter of the *Church Dogmatics*. Second, this self-revelation shows God to be, in his seeking and creating fellowship with us, one who loves. Third, God's self-revelation shows that God has his being also without us, in himself, and therefore in freedom. The three sub-sections which follow elaborate and explain these basic affirmations about God's being, God's love and God's freedom.

Barth also refers both here in his thesis – where presumably his words may be understood to have been chosen with care – as well as throughout his exposition, to the being of God as Father, Son and Spirit. This should make it clear that, in describing God as the one who loves in freedom, Barth has in no way reverted to a non-trinitarian concept of the divine essence, but both presupposes the triunity of God's essence and further expounds its implications. Barth says back in *CD* I/1, 'In a dogmatics of the Christian church we cannot speak correctly of God's nature and attributes unless it is presupposed that our reference is to God the Father, the Son and the Holy Spirit.'[8] A telling comment in the following section makes the trinitarian presupposition strikingly explicit: 'God is Father, Son and Holy Spirit, i.e., loves in freedom' (323). Gunton explains:

> God's revelation as Father, Son and Holy Spirit is the event in which he creates fellowship with man, and it is in doing that that he reveals that he is love. But this is a love that is given freely, for the mode of revelation makes it clear that, first, he is Father as well as Son, and, second, that he is Father, Son and Spirit independently of his relation to man.[9]

This point requires emphasis because a number of interpreters charge Barth with being insufficiently trinitarian in his account of the attributes. Mitchell Grell, for example, knows that 'when [Barth] identifies God as the One who loves in freedom, he is speaking of the triune God'. He claims nevertheless that generally in Barth's account 'talk of God as triune is excluded, or at best appears on the margins'.[10] This claim represents a failure to understand

---

[8] *CD* I/1, 312.

[9] Colin E. Gunton, *Becoming and Being: The Doctrine of God in Charles Hartshorne and Karl Barth*, 2nd ed. (London: SCM, 2001), 187–8, cf. 198; cf. Stephen R. Holmes, *God of Grace and God of Glory: An Account of the Theology of Jonathan Edwards* (Edinburgh: T&T Clark, 2000), 64.

[10] Mitchell Grell, *Der ewig reiche Gott: Die Erkenntnis, Gewinnung und Bestimmung der Eigenschaften Gottes nach Isaak August Dorner, August Hermann Cremer und*

'love' and 'freedom' in the way in which the present section makes perfectly clear Barth intends them to be understood: as aspects of the eternal, triune life as manifest in God's history with his people and ultimately in Jesus Christ.[11] Every time Barth speaks of the divine loving or of the divine freedom, he is appealing to trinitarian categories.

§28.1. The Being of God in Act

In light of all that was said in the previous chapter of the *Dogmatics* about the knowledge of God, Barth begins his exposition of 'The Reality of God' with the deceptively simple statement, 'God is' (257). Yet the exegesis of this statement, according to Barth, constitutes 'the hardest and at the same time the most extensive task of church dogmatics [and] Christian preaching', for this task is to describe God himself (257). Dogmatics and preaching have in fact 'no other *raison d'être* than to serve the Word of God' and therefore to say, whether directly or indirectly, that 'God is' (258). All other statements which dogmatics or preaching might wish to make have their 'common truth' in this statement (259). Thus, says Barth, it was a first 'act of rashness' when Philipp Melanchthon, preoccupied with how Christ blesses believers, attempted to 'hurry over the statement that "God is"' in his first *Loci* of 1521.[12] It was a second and more 'disastrous' act of rashness when Melanchthon then took up the doctrine of God in later editions without reference to the very '*beneficia Christi*' to which he had earlier so quickly turned (259).

Barth cites Melanchthon's errors because they raise the pivotal question of the relationship between God's being and his *beneficia*. Is God the same in himself as he appears to be in his beneficent dealings with humanity? Barth's entire exposition of the divine perfections will constitute his resounding but nuanced yes in answer to this question. As Barth sees matters, the 'older

---

Karl Barth mit besonderer Berücksichtigung des Einflusses der Theologie Dorners und Cremers auf die Gotteslehre Barths (Ph.D. diss., University of Tübingen, 1992), 270.

[11] As Grell elaborates his claim, it becomes clear that, at another level, it represents a common but misdirected criticism of Barth's doctrine of the Trinity. That is, critics of Barth often assume that a truly operative doctrine of the Trinity necessarily involves distinct roles for Father, Son and Spirit in the immanent actuality of every divine perfection. When these critics find no such distinctions in Barth's exposition, they charge Barth with being insufficiently trinitarian. Such charges will be addressed below.

[12] Colin Gunton notes that this act was frequently cited as justification for disregard of God's being by theologians from the nineteenth century through Bultmann, who 'may be in Barth's sights' at this point. See Colin Gunton, 'Salvation', in *The Cambridge Companion to Karl Barth*, ed. John Webster (Cambridge: Cambridge University Press, 2000), 153. Joseph L. Mangina, *Karl Barth: Theologian of Christian Witness* (Aldershot: Ashgate, 2004), 64, suggests that the real target is Kant.

13

theology', in its concern to safeguard the divine transcendence, tends to *separate* God's being from his dealings with humanity, as did Melanchthon. Modern theology, on the other hand, with its emphasis on divine immanence, tends to *reduce* God's being to his dealings with humanity. Barth naturally wants to preserve what he considers the valid insights of each. In a crucial and definitive passage, Barth clearly explains how he understands the relation between God's being and his act of revelation:

> God is who he is in his works. He is the same even in himself, even before and after and over his works, and without them. They are bound to him, but he is not bound to them. They are nothing without him. But he is who he is without them. He is not, therefore, who he is *only* in his works. Yet in himself he is not another than he is in his works. (260 rev.; *KD* 291)

Against the tendency of the older theology, Barth insists that God is in himself 'the same' as and 'not another' than he is in his dealings with humanity, that is, 'in his works'. Against the tendency of modern theology, Barth insists that God is 'not bound' to his works but is who he is even 'without them'. God works freely, but in a way that is true to himself and not arbitrary. The picture God presents of himself in his works is reliable. Barth's concern for the simultaneous freedom and reliability of God in revelation thus leads him back to one of the basic claims of the previous chapter: 'God is known through God and through God alone' (44). 'This means that we cannot discern the being of God in any other way than by looking where God himself gives us himself to see, and therefore by looking at his works', that is, at 'God's act in his revelation' (261).

Barth here mentions the work of two theologians who stand as exemplars of the respective tendencies of the 'older' and modern theology regarding the relation between God's being and his works. While Barth has high regard for both, he wants to distance himself explicitly from what he sees as their respective errors. Representing the trend in modern theology is Hermann Cremer's 1897 study, *Die christliche Lehre von den Eigenschaften Gottes*, an 'extraordinarily informative book', but one which succumbs to modern theology's 'revulsion against the idea of being as such', that is, against talk of God's being in himself (260).[13] *Contra* Cremer, Barth maintains that 'God is not swallowed up in the relation and attitude of himself to the world and us' (260). Representing the trend in the older theology is Barth's predecessor

---

[13] Hermann Cremer, *Die christliche Lehre von den Eigenschaften Gottes*, ed. Helmut Burkhardt (Gießen: TVG Brunnen, 2005). Cremer's theology is analysed in Grell, *Der ewig reiche Gott*, 84–128; parallels between Cremer and Barth are detailed throughout. Grell, 170–336.

at the University of Basel, Amandus Polanus (1561–1610).[14] Polanus is the first of the Protestant orthodox theologians whom Barth cites in this chapter and, for all the disagreement between them, perhaps also the one Barth most respects – judging both from citation frequency (Polanus is effectively cited in reference to every single perfection[15]) and from the fact that it is Polanus's encomium of the divine glory which Barth judged the fitting conclusion of his own exposition (677).[16] When Polanus comes to speak of the perfections of the divine essence, Barth finds a fatal abstraction from 'God's act in his revelation' and, therefore, from the doctrine of the Trinity (261). *Contra* Polanus – at least in the execution of his doctrine of the perfections, if not its intent[17] – Barth states, 'In all the considerations that are brought before us in this chapter we must keep vigorously aloof from this tradition, remembering that a church dogmatics derives from a doctrine of the Trinity, and therefore that there is no possibility of reckoning with the being of any other God...than that of the Father, the Son and the Holy Spirit as it is in God's revelation and in eternity' (261; cf. 268). Barth's entire subsequent exposition is guided by this twofold concern, both to speak appropriately of God's being in himself and, thus, to do so strictly on the basis of his triune self-revelation.[18]

As Barth has already hinted, what unites this twofold concern for God's being and his revelation is the concept of act. 'God is who he is', that is, God

---

[14] Rinse H. Reeling Brouwer, 'The Conversation between Karl Barth and Amandus Polanus on the Question of the Reality of Human Speaking of the Simplicity and the Multiplicity of God', in *The Reality of Faith in Theology: Studies on Karl Barth: Princeton-Kampen Consultation 2005*, ed. Bruce McCormack and Gerrit Nevin (New York: Peter Lang, 2007), 51–2.

[15] Brouwer, 'The Conversation between Karl Barth and Amandus Polanus', 81–2, 84.

[16] Cf. Robert Letham, 'Amandus Polanus: A Neglected Theologian?' *Sixteenth Century Journal* 21.3 (1990): 463–76. It is perhaps not accidental that it is again to Polanus that Barth turns, in a climactic description of the passion of Christ, for an example of 'how fearlessly and unequivocally the older orthodoxy' could speak of 'the heart of the New Testament message' (*CD* II/1, 398). Cf. Barth's commendation of the role Polanus assigns to the divine glory in the interpretation of Scripture: *CD* I/2, 721–2.

[17] It would indeed constitute a 'major misunderstanding' of Polanus and the Reformed orthodox tradition if it were assumed that their 'discussion of the divine essence and attributes is a matter for "natural theology" whereas the doctrine of the Trinity belongs to "supernatural theology."' See Richard A. Muller, *Post-Reformation Reformed Dogmatics: The Rise and Development of Reformed Orthodoxy, ca. 1520 to ca. 1725*, vol. 3, *The Divine Essence and Attributes* (Grand Rapids: Baker Academic, 2003), 159. Barth, however, does not make any such assumption. His point here is that, by deferring the doctrine of the Trinity until after that of the divine attributes, traditional expositions of the attributes, though expressly intended and to some degree also executed as a matter of 'supernatural theology', nevertheless fell easier prey to natural-theological influence.

[18] Cf. Gotthard Oblau, *Gotteszeit und Menschenzeit: Eschatologie in der Kirchlichen Dogmatik von Karl Barth* (Neukirchen-Vluyn: Neukirchener Verlag, 1988), 84.

has his being, 'in the act of his revelation' (262). This, says Barth, is what he had hoped to capture by entitling this chapter 'The Reality [*Wirklichkeit*] of God', which, for this purpose, might have been better translated as 'The Actuality of God' (262).[19] *Wirklichkeit* 'holds together being and act' (262).[20] Revelation, as act, is an 'event', a 'happening' whose temporal character is not only one of 'historical completeness' but also of 'full contemporaneity', and which yet remains 'truly future' (262). Barth is not saying that God possesses merely punctiliar existence, coming into being for as long as it takes him to act and then vanishing back into non-being like light switched on and off. Rather, this act is 'once for all'; it is ultimate and 'cannot be transcended or surpassed or dispensed with' because it is God's self-revelation in Jesus Christ. Barth does not restrict this act to the cross or to that moment when faith encounters the Crucified, as might have been his tendency earlier in his career.[21] Rather, this act is comprehensive: it is 'always the birth, death and resurrection of Jesus Christ, always his justification of faith, always his lordship in the church, always his coming again, and therefore himself as our hope' (262).[22] How then is this comprehensive act of God in Jesus Christ also his eternal being? Hinting at the way in which he will later affirm the divine constancy or immutability, Barth explains, 'To its very deepest depths God's Godhead consists in the fact that it is an event...the event of his action, in which we have a share in God's revelation' (263). That is, 'God's being is *life*' (263), the eternally eventful life of Father, Son and Spirit which is also revealed to us.[23]

Barth's talk of God's being-in-act is often described as a particularly clear example of his 'actualism' or 'actualist ontology', his preference for speaking in terms of 'occurrence, happening, event, history, decisions and act' rather than in terms of static and non-relational essences.[24] Not that Barth eschews ontology. As ought to be clear from his rejection of modern theology's

---

[19] T. F. Torrance, *Karl Barth: An Introduction to his Early Theology 1910–1931*, new ed. (Edinburgh: T&T Clark, 2000), 151 n. 1; George S. Hendry, 'The Freedom of God in the Theology of Karl Barth', *Scottish Journal of Theology* 31.3 (1978): 231 n. 2; Gunton, *Becoming and Being*, 186–7.

[20] Cf. F. W. Camfield, 'Development and Present Stage of the Theology of Karl Barth', in idem, ed., *Reformation Old and New: A Tribute to Karl Barth* (London: Lutterworth, 1947), 47; Cornelis van der Kooi, *As In A Mirror: John Calvin And Karl Barth On Knowing God: A Diptych*, trans. Donald Mader (Leiden: Brill, 2005), 322.

[21] Bruce L. McCormack, *Karl Barth's Critically Realistic Dialectical Theology: Its Genesis and Development 1909–1936* (New York: Oxford University Press, 1995), 245–63.

[22] Cf. Robert W. Jenson, *God After God: The God of the Past and the God of the Future, Seen in the Work of Karl Barth* (Indianapolis: Bobbs-Merrill, 1969), 125–6.

[23] Wilfried Härle, *Sein und Gnade: Die Ontologie in Karl Barths Kirchlicher Dogmatik* (Berlin: de Gruyter, 1975), 49–50.

[24] George Hunsinger, *How to Read Karl Barth: The Shape of His Theology* (Oxford: Oxford University Press, 1991), 30.

aversion to the concept of being, Barth 'does not shy away from making ontological statements'.[25] But Barth is by no means concerned strictly with ontology when he describes God's being (or for that matter of man's being[26]) as a being-in-act. At one level, by linking God's being to his act of revelation in Christ, as (on Barth's account) the older theology often failed to do, Barth shows his concern also to secure the integral place of ethics within dogmatics: 'the act of God's revelation carries with it the fact that by the Word of God in the Holy Spirit, with no other confidence but this unconquerable confidence', man is met by God 'as the source of his life, as comfort and command' (262), and as the one who grants knowledge, creates fellowship, and inspires worship (263). More importantly, Barth's concern in speaking of God's being-in-act is with the particularity of this act and, hence, with what might more helpfully be designated an 'actualist epistemology'. Human knowledge of God's being can be found only in his act.[27]

> The action of God that takes place in revelation is a particular action, different from any other happening, even in contradiction to it. *Actus purus* is not sufficient as a description of God. To it there must be added at least '*et singularis*'. (264)

Thus, if God's being is itself an incomparably singular act, and if it is revealed in a correspondingly singular act, then no other event can convey knowledge of God. As Barth will later explain, God's 'ontic absoluteness' implies his 'noetic absoluteness', his knowability strictly in the act of revelation (310–12). Not only does this rule out more obviously natural-theological means to the knowledge of God such as logical extrapolation based on observation of the created order. It also means that even familiar biblical concepts – and these particularly – cannot be treated as familiar. They must be allowed to take their content afresh from revelation itself. If, for example, Scripture describes God as living, 'we have to admit that generally and apart from him we do not know what this is' (264), for (in Polanus's words) '*Propriissime solus Deus vivere dici potest*' (263). Clearly, the particularity of God's being-in-act does not exclude all possible connection and relation to human concepts. In that case there could be no knowledge of God (cf. 224–5). Such connection and relation, however, can only

---

[25] Eberhard Jüngel, *God's Being Is In Becoming: The Trinitarian Being of God in the Theology of Karl Barth: A Paraphrase*, trans. John Webster (Grand Rapids: Eerdmans, 2001), 76.

[26] For example, *CD* I/2, 793: 'As we will, we are; and what we do, we are. It is not as if man first exists and then acts. He exists in that he acts.' Cf. Eberhard Busch, *The Great Passion: An Introduction to Karl Barth's Theology*, trans. Geoffrey W. Bromiley (Grand Rapids: Eerdmans, 2004), 164–6.

[27] Härle, *Sein und Gnade*, 19–22.

be established by God's 'saving contradiction' and 'undialectical transcendence' of human concepts in his act of revelation (264–5; cf. 75–6).[28] Barth therefore attempts to fill out from revelation the concepts he uses to describe God. Because Barth tends to do so descriptively and at length rather than in terse, formal definitions, the interpreter of Barth must likewise beware of treating as familiar the various concepts to which Barth has given distinctive content.

What Barth has said so far of the act in which God has his being sounds remarkably, and potentially disturbingly, like one of the major themes in the thought of Hegel. As Barth once put it, the 'key to everything' in Hegel is that:

> reason, truth, concept, idea, mind, [even] God himself are understood as an *event*, and, moreover, only as an event. They cease to be what they are as soon as the event, in which they are what they are, is thought of as interrupted, as soon as a state is thought of in its place. Essentially reason and all its synonyms are life, movement, process. God is God only in his divine action, revelation, creation, reconciliation, redemption; as an absolute act, as *actus purus*.[29]

In light of the similarities to what Barth has said, it is important to note again that, unlike Hegel, Barth affirms that God's act, and thus his being, is independent of the created order. God is 'the same even in himself, even before and after and over his works, and without them' (260). Barth also emphasises that the divine act within the created order is utterly unique: it is *actus purissimus et singularis* (263–4). Barth thus affirms an independence and a uniqueness, a freedom and a particularity of the divine being and act, which Hegel does not. On the other hand, Barth may well have found in Hegel a fuller appreciation of the tradition's own insight into the activity and livingness of the divine being.

A more precise definition of God's 'undialectical transcendence' of human concepts rounds out this sub-section (265–72). However, as Barth goes to expound God's transcendence and freedom – what he refers to as God's 'spirituality' – Barth finds that, if he is to avoid regrettable misunderstanding, he must first give an account of God's 'saving contradiction' of the human concepts of 'spirit' and 'nature' so dear to the tradition of liberal theology (269–70).[30] That is, Barth must win back what he considers the

---

[28] Cf. Terry L. Cross, *Dialectic in Karl Barth's Doctrine of God* (New York: Peter Lang, 2001), 174–5.

[29] Karl Barth, *Protestant Theology in the Nineteenth Century: Its Background and history*, new ed., trans. Brian Cozens and John Bowden (London: SCM, 2001), 384–5.

[30] Cf. Terry Pinkard, *German Philosophy 1760–1860: The Legacy of Idealism* (Cambridge: Cambridge University Press, 2002), 175–80.

biblical concept of 'spirit' from its distortion in much modern thought. Barth uses the term 'spirit' to indicate that which is self-determining, free from external limitation, and 'wholly self-sufficient' (268). By 'nature', Barth indicates that which is determined, concrete, historical and perceptible.[31] Thus, the particularity of God in his revelation clearly cannot be identified with any so-called 'absolute spirit' that is opposed to 'nature' (265). Therefore, if the concepts of spirit and nature are to be salvaged for theological use, their mutual opposition must be contradicted. Scripture's many anthropological and hence 'natural' descriptions of God, therefore, have a rightful place in theology and must not be 'arbitrarily translated into something spiritual' (266). 'The divine being must be allowed to transcend both spirit and nature, yet also to overlap and comprehend both, as attested in his revelation according to the testimony of Holy Scripture' (266).

Thus contradicted, the concepts of spirit and nature can serve to elucidate 'the specific freedom of the event, act and life of God in his revelation and in eternity' (267). It is with a decisive and programmatic assertion of this divine freedom, over against what he sees as the errors of liberal theology, that Barth concludes his opening sub-section. The divine freedom, according to Barth, is 'the freedom of the spirit...of a knowing and willing I', the freedom of a person (267). If God's being is considered to exist 'in the unity of spirit and nature' (267), 'due superiority' must be accorded its spirituality over its naturalness (268). God's being, as spirit, is 'an act of his omnipotence'; it is 'self-moved being' and not what Barth considers the man-moved deity of liberal theology (269).[32] 'The fact that God's being is event...means that it is his own conscious, willed and executed decision...executed once for all in eternity, and anew in every second of our time' (271).[33] While Barth can say that God himself 'decides...what his nature shall be', this decision must not be understood as 'the production of his being but the confirmation of the being which he always has' (cf. 305–7).[34] This is the divine freedom,

---

[31] Osthövener, *Gottes Eigenschaften*, 164–5, suggests that Barth here uses 'nature' to refer to that which is perceptible but incomprehensible, and 'spirit' to refer to that which is comprehensible but imperceptible. Cf. *CD* II/1, 543: 'Nature' indicates 'extended, multiple, finite and visible being'.

[32] Cf. Barth, *Protestant Theology*, 386–7.

[33] At this point, an egregious English translation error has Barth suggest that God's triunity is to be aligned not with the divine 'spirituality' but with the subordinate divine 'naturalness'. The offending sentence reads: 'Being in its own, conscious, willed and executed decision, and therefore personal being, is the being of God in the *nature* [*Seinsweisen!*] of the Father and the Son and the Holy Spirit' (271; *KD* 304–5). A correct translation would indicate that Father, Son and Spirit are not part of the divine being in the 'inferiority of its naturalness' (268), but rather *modes of being* of that free decision which constitutes the divine 'spirituality'.

[34] Robert W. Jenson, *Alpha and Omega: A Study in the Theology of Karl Barth* (1963; reprint Eugene: Wipf and Stock, 2002), 70, 70–1 n. 4. Cf. George Hunsinger, 'Election

personality and spirituality, beside which there can exist only 'secondary', created forms. As God alone may properly be said to live, so God alone may properly be said to be a person. God's being is 'eminently personal act'.[35] Thus, 'It is not God who is a person by extension, but we' (272).[36] As Barth says in his account of the divine unity:

> It is he alone who lives. It is he alone who loves. He alone is gracious, merciful and wise. He alone is holy, righteous and patient. And he alone is also free, with all that this involves. To be one and unique is true only of him in the sense proper to him. For it is only in him that everything (including uniqueness) is essential, original, proper, and for this reason also creative, so that now it can all belong to other forms of being also in a created, dependent, derived and improper way. (442–3)

In everything that is to be said of God in his perfections, there can be 'no evasion of this act and decision of the living quality of God...because alone in his act he is who he is' (272). 'If we keep this clearly in mind', says Barth with a final glance at Feuerbach (cf. 292–3),[37] 'if all our thoughts are always grasped by God's action, because in it we have to do with God's being, we may be sure that they cannot err and become either openly or secretly thoughts about ourselves' (272).

§28.2. The Being of God as the One Who Loves

Having argued that God's being is in his act of self-revelation, Barth now turns to a more precise description, in three stages, of who this self-revelation shows God to be. First, Barth argues that, in the act of seeking and creating fellowship with us, God shows himself to be one who loves (272–5). Second, since this loving is the particular act (and thus essence) of God himself, it is distinct from general concepts of love (275–84). Third, it is the loving in which God has his being which shows God to be a person (284–97).

---

and the Trinity: Twenty-Five Theses on the Theology of Karl Barth', *Modern Theology* 24.2 (2008): 185–6.

[35] Gunton, *Becoming and Being*, 190; cf. 191. Härle, *Sein und Gnade*, 60: 'For Barth, personality is not ultimately a human attribute, but a divine one.'

[36] *Contra* Raynal, *The Perfections of God*, 85, Barth does not deduce the personality of God from the fact that God acts in the unity of nature and spirit. Rather, Barth presupposes it. Cf. *CD* I/1, 136–9; Karl Barth, *The Knowledge of God and the Service of God According to the Teaching of the Reformation: Recalling the Scottish Confession of 1560*, trans. J. L. M. Haire and Ian Henderson (London: Hodder and Stoughton, 1938), 30–1.

[37] Cf. Barth, *Protestant Theology*, 521–2.

Barth begins by explaining in more detail the content of God's self-revelation.

> God is he who, without having to do so, seeks and creates fellowship between himself and us. He does not have to do it, because in himself without us, and therefore without this, he has that which he seeks and creates between himself and us. It implies so to speak an overflow of his essence that he turns to us. We must certainly regard this overflow as itself matching his essence, belonging to his essence. But it is an overflow which is not demanded or presupposed by any necessity, constraint, or obligation.... On the contrary, in itself and as such it is again rooted in himself alone. (273)

What Barth affirms here once again is that God's seeking and creating of fellowship with us is both utterly free and yet not arbitrary. God 'does not have to do it', yet when he does, it is an act 'matching his essence, belonging to his essence...rooted in himself'. The link between God's essence and his establishing of fellowship with us is God's triunity. Because God 'seeks and creates fellowship...in his eternal essence' (274), his seeking and creating of fellowship with us is an act 'matching his essence'; its 'paradigm is the event of election'.[38]

On what grounds then does Barth venture to name God as the One who freely seeks and creates fellowship with us? The task of a doctrine of the divine attributes, that of describing God, has often been aided by a consideration of the biblical names for God. Here Barth takes up this tradition, in what may seem a highly presumptuous attempt to give God a new name. Yet this naming of God is simply an obedient response to revelation. This name captures precisely who the entire scope of creation, reconciliation and redemption shows God to be. 'What God does in all this, he is' (274). In words which anticipate the exquisitely crafted prelude to his doctrine of reconciliation,[39] Barth explains that, 'in all this', 'he wills to be ours, and he wills that we should be his....He wills as God to be for us and with us who are not God' (274). However, because this involves not merely creatures, but sinful creatures, God's seeking and creating of fellowship often assumes what seems to be the 'very opposite' form of judgement, death and hiddenness (274). It is, therefore, no simple matter to specify what this seeking and creating of fellowship will look like. 'We shall have to learn ever and again what it really means to say that God seeks and creates fellowship between himself and us' (274–5). The reason, again, is that this seeking and creating of fellowship bears all the uniqueness of the divine essence itself.

---

[38] Gunton, *Becoming and Being*, 192.
[39] *CD* IV/1, §57.1, 'God With Us' (3–21).

> As and before God seeks and creates fellowship with us, he wills and completes this fellowship in himself. ... Therefore what he seeks and creates between himself and us is in fact nothing else but what he wills and completes and therefore is in himself. (275)

Barth's intention in claiming that God 'wills and completes' the fellowship of Father, Son and Spirit is not to suggest that this fellowship, God's very nature, is the logical result of the divine will, nor that it is ever incomplete in itself. Rather, Barth wants to indicate that this fellowship is an act, an event, something which God does. For sinful creatures, the revelation of this event means salvation, a blessing 'than which there is no greater blessing', because in creating fellowship with us, that is, 'in giving himself, he has given us every blessing' (275). Barth is now in a position to specify more closely what this act of God means, namely, that 'he is the One who loves' (275).[40]

> That he is God – the Godhead of God – consists in the fact that he loves, and it is the expression of his loving that he seeks and creates fellowship with us. It is correct and important in this connexion to say emphatically his *loving*, i.e., his act as that of the One who loves. (275)

What we see of God in his self-revelation in creation, reconciliation and redemption is that he seeks and creates fellowship with us. This is what it means to affirm that God loves or that 'God is love' (1 Jn 4:8) (275).

The second stage of Barth's argument (275–84) elaborates four aspects of the ultimacy of the divine loving as distinct from general ideas of love.[41]

First, God's loving is unique in its primacy or ultimacy (276–8). 'God's loving is concerned with a seeking and creation of fellowship for its own sake' (276). The reason for this lies in the trinitarian character of this loving, which is its own basis. 'It is the fellowship [i.e. the Spirit] of the One who loves [i.e. the Father] with the loved himself [i.e. the Son]' (276). By way of distinction, 'God is not ... the Good first, and then the One who loves. ... God is the One who loves, and as such the Good' (276). That is, *contra* Thomas, God's love is not the *desire* to confer upon the beloved some good, even the *summum bonum* (277).[42] Rather, God's love is *itself* the conferring of good upon the beloved: 'Loving us, God does not give us something, but himself; and giving us himself, giving us his only Son, he gives us everything' (276).

Second, because God's loving is itself ultimate, it is neither caused nor sustained by any worthiness or capacity of its object (278–9). Now if the object of the divine loving is understood to be the human creature, 'alien and hostile' to God, such a claim is hardly unexpected. It is only after the

---

[40] Cf. CD I/2, 377–80.
[41] Cf. Grell, *Der ewig reiche Gott*, 171–96.
[42] Cf. Grell, *Der ewig reiche Gott*, 172–4: Barth's criticism of Thomas parallels Dorner's.

human creature has been loved by God in Christ, only after 'the justification of the ungodly', that the creature becomes (again in Christ) lovable.[43] Barth, however, speaks not only of the human objects of the divine loving, but also of God the Son. The Father, according to Barth, loves the Son too, without regard to worthiness or capacity. While this may suggest that the Son has no capacity or worthiness to be loved by the Father, Barth's point is rather that the Father's love is not evoked by something in the Son, and therefore logically secondary to it.

> Certainly God is *objectum amabile* to himself. But he is not eternal love because he finds himself worthy of love. He is worthy of love, and blessed in himself, because in his life as Father, Son and Holy Spirit, he is eternal love. (279)

Unlike the human objects of the divine loving, God the Son is in fact lovable and worthy of such love. The divine loving, however, does not follow upon the lovability of the Son. It is not the logical result of the divine will, but the eternal event of the triune life.

Third, and again because God's loving is itself ultimate, it has no other goal than itself (279–80). This includes even God's desire to be glorified in and through the created order.

> Certainly in loving us God wills his own glory and our salvation. But he does not love us because he wills this. He wills it for the sake of his love. (279)

Simply put, 'God loves because he loves; because this act is his being, his essence and his nature' (279). Surprisingly, Osthövener sees here a problematic abstraction of love from other aspects of the divine identity, and wonders how God can seek and create fellowship for its own sake if he actually does everything for love's sake.[44] The solution would seem a simple one. Just because God's loving is not subordinated to other aspects of his character does not mean that it is unrelated to them. And only if God's seeking and creating of fellowship is something separate from his loving could there exist any tension between them. Osthövener's begrudging concession of the relevance of Barth's appeal to 'the love of the Father, the Son and the Holy Spirit' (279) actually belies the existence of any such tension. God's love is

---

[43] Grell, *Der ewig reiche Gott*, 177, points out the parallel to Luther's proof to his 28th thesis at the Heidelberg Disputation: 'Therefore sinners are attractive because they are loved; they are not loved because they are attractive.' See Martin Luther, *Luther's Works: American Edition*, ed. Jaroslav Pelikan and Helmut T. Lehmann (St. Louis: Concordia, 1957–86), 31.57.

[44] Osthövener, *Gottes Eigenschaften*, 167.

his fellowship. On Barth's account, God could no more have fellowship with us without loving us than God could have fellowship with himself without being himself love.

Fourth and finally, the divine loving is thus both necessary with respect to itself and also free with respect its object (280–3; cf. 591). This is 'the ever-wonderful twofold dynamic' of God's love. On the one hand, the internal necessity of the divine loving means that God 'would still be the One who loves without us and without the world' (280), yet this would not make his existence 'pointless, motionless and unmotivated, nor would it be any less majestic' (281). This is what the older theology referred to as the divine blessedness (283). On the other hand, though God was free to do otherwise, in fact he 'has not withheld himself from us', but has taken us up 'into the fellowship of his eternal love' (280) to share in his eternal blessedness (283). If there is thus 'an eternal correlation between God and us', it is one which 'grounded in God alone' (281). That is, over against the 'pious blasphemies' of much of liberal Protestant theology (281–2),[45] God does not need the existence of humanity in order for his love to have an object, for as the triune God he 'is sufficient in himself...as object of his love' (280).[46] This, then, is the uniqueness, the ultimacy, the 'mystery' of the divine loving, both in itself and in its overflow to us (283).

The third and final stage of Barth's argument takes up again the contested issue of God's personhood (284–97; cf. 267–72).[47] With typically penetrating historical insight and dramatic flair, if not a little self-congratulation (293–4), Barth details the controversy surrounding the personhood of God in an extended excursus (287–97; cf. 370) which concludes this stage. As Barth tells the story – at times in a confrontational tone which reaches prophetic pitch (e.g. 290) – the doctrine of the Trinity first drifted to the margins of the older theology and then was made problematic by the application of modern ideas of 'person' to Father, Son, and Spirit (287–8, 296–7). As this occurred, traditional, impersonal talk of God as 'perfect being' or 'highest good' was transformed, particularly in Hegelian thought right up to Barth's own day, into the outright denial that God is a person (288–9).

In light of this history, and in light of the further and primary specification of the act of God as the act of his loving, Barth moves to 'repeat and underline' the subordinate truth that God – 'in his own way!' – acts as a

---

[45] Cf. Barth, *Göttingen Dogmatics*, 424–5.

[46] Cf. Grell, *Der ewig reiche Gott*, 185.

[47] Cf. Grell, *Der ewig reiche Gott*, 196–207. Barth's return to the concept of the person-hood of God (both here as well as in his discussion of the divine omnipotence) is no indication that 'Barth was obviously...not entirely satisfied' with his initial discussion in §28.1 (*ibid.*, 196), but rather part of a deliberate rhetorical strategy of emphasis to convince his readers of a point he deems essential to theologically responsible description of God. Cf. the editors' comments on Barth's method of exposition in *CD* I/2, vii–viii.

person (284, 296). 'To be a person means...to be what God is, to be, that is, the One who loves in God's way' (284). Barth will go on to explain that the personality of God must be defended if theology is to be able to affirm, for example, an 'affective aspect' of God's love, a real 'movement of the heart of God' such as the divine mercy (370). Barth is not saying of God that it is 'exclusively from the revelation of his love'[48] that we know him to be a person. We know him to be a person, and we know what it is to be a person, from his self-revelation as such, which includes also the revelation of his freedom (271).[49] It is God himself in his self-revelation – not 'absolute man'[50] – who is *the* person, the benchmark of personhood (284), 'not the personified but the personifying person' (285). Man 'is not a person, but he becomes one' and 'finds what a person is when he finds it in the person of God' (284).[51] he anhypostasis of Christ's human nature is a case in point: 'The One, the person, whom we really know as a human person, is the person of Jesus Christ, and even this is in fact the person of the Son of God, in which humanity, without being or having itself a person, is caught up into fellowship with the personality of God' (286).

This primacy, even exclusivity, of the personhood of God has three implications for human talk of God. These recall Barth's discussion of analogy in the previous chapter (224–43) and anticipate his brief comments on the topic in the following section (§29). First, Scripture's description of God as personal 'is not in any way childish or naïve or anthropomorphic', but rather 'corresponds absolutely' to who God is (286).[52] Second, the fact that God's personhood 'surpasses all our concepts and ideas of person' does not mean either that God is in fact 'the impersonal absolute' behind his appearance of personhood or that we cannot know God's personhood itself 'on the basis of his revelation' (286). Third, there is no paradox in the fact that God's personhood both transcends human concepts and yet can be truly described by them (286–7). That is, God's nature is not (as Barth himself had once argued) some paradoxical combination of personhood with impersonal absolute (287).[53] 'No: the (to us) inexplicable paradox of the nature of God is the fact that he is primarily and properly all that our terms seek to mean, and yet of themselves cannot mean, that he has revealed himself to us in his

---

[48] Grell, *Der ewig reiche Gott*, 197; cf. 204–5. Grell implicitly qualifies these statements, *ibid.*, 206, 211.

[49] Cf. *CD* I/1, 138: God's Word is 'God's speaking person, *Dei loquentis persona*'.

[50] Barth, *Protestant Theology*, 22–3.

[51] Cf. Van der Kooi, *As in a Mirror*, 325.

[52] Cf. *CD* I/1, 138–9.

[53] Cf. Christophe Chalamet, *Dialectical Theologians: Wilhelm Herrmann, Karl Barth and Rudolf Bultmann* (Zürich: Theologischer Verlag Zürich, 2005), 233; Katherine Sonderegger, 'The Absolute Infinity of God', in *The Reality of Faith in Theology: Studies on Karl Barth: Princeton-Kampen Consultation 2005*, ed. Bruce McCormack and Gerrit Nevin (New York: Peter Lang, 2007), 39–42.

original and proper being, thus remaining incomprehensible to us even in his revelation, yet allowing and commanding us to put our concepts into the service of knowledge of him, blessing our obedience, being truly known by us within our limits' (287). The real paradox is thus 'the paradox of the combination of his grace and our lost condition' (287).[54]

§28.3. The Being of God in Freedom

Thus far in his exposition, Barth has frequently emphasised the utter uniqueness of the divine being, act and loving. Now comes his chance not merely to assert, but to give dogmatic precision to the description of the divine uniqueness. Barth does this in two stages. He begins with an initial explanation of the divine freedom or aseity (297–310). Barth then elaborates on the divine freedom in terms of what he calls God's primary and secondary absoluteness (310–21). It is God's freedom as his secondary absoluteness which grounds the immense variety of his interactions with his creatures (314–16) and which finds its order and unity in Jesus Christ (316–21). The complexity of these themes and the terminology Barth introduces to explain them make for a challenging read.[55]

First, and fittingly, because God's being, act and loving are unique (297–8), it will only be with 'difficulty' (298) that the freedom of this being, act and loving can be described. Barth thus begins with a warning. God's uniqueness, that divine evasion of human conceptual generalities, poses serious challenges to theological use of these same human concepts. Since this pursuit of the divine otherness also presents a great temptation to devalue God's self-revelation (because of its perceived familiarity) and to enquire elsewhere, that is, to indulge in a little natural theology, no small measure of 'doubtfulness' hangs over the enterprise (298–9). Success will depend on whether 'now as before we do not enquire in disregard of God's revelation, but with our attention concentrated upon it and only upon it' (299–300).

It is precisely such concentrated attention on God's self-revelation which yields, as a specifying description of the divine uniqueness, the concept of freedom (300–1). 'God's being as he who lives and loves is being in freedom' (301).

> Freedom is, of course, more than the absence of limits, restrictions, or conditions. This is only its negative and to that extent improper aspect....But freedom in its positive and proper qualities means to be grounded in one's own being, to be determined and moved by oneself. (301)

---

[54] Cf. Cross, *Dialectic*, 176–8.
[55] Härle, *Sein und Gnade*, 63.

26

Thus, God's freedom is, positively, his lordship, his sovereignty, or what the early church termed his aseity (301–2). Barth will later speak of this positive aspect of the divine freedom as God's 'primary absoluteness' (317). What revelation shows is that, 'without sacrificing his distinction and freedom, but in the exercise of them, he enters into and faithfully maintains communion with this reality other than himself' (303). As regards his relation to the creature, God's freedom is thus a freedom *for* before it is a freedom *from*. It therefore represented a fatal inversion of dogmatic order when theology came to speak of God's freedom primarily in terms, not of aseity or self-sufficiency, but of independence or infinitude or transcendence, for these latter terms suggest that God is to be understood chiefly 'in opposition to the reality distinct from himself' (302–4).[56]

God's freedom in its primary, positive aspect is thus his freedom 'to begin with himself' rather than with his difference from the created order (304). Beginning with himself, God is able to be entirely himself in his revelation to a reality utterly distinct from himself, and thus, as Anselm taught,[57] to prove his own existence (304–5). 'Without reserving the secret possibilities of a being beyond that which he is' in his self-revelation, God can be 'recognised' and 'apprehended' by man in faith (304). 'This is the freedom of his incarnation in Jesus Christ foreshadowed in his election and rule of Israel, the freedom of his Word, the freedom of his Spirit, the freedom of his grace' (304).

God's freedom in its secondary, negative aspect is his freedom from both internal and external constraints. Internally, it means that God 'does not "need" his own being in order to be who he is' (306). It is not the case that God is somehow compelled to exist and so 'creates, produces or originates himself' or 'lifts himself, as it were, out of non-existence' (306). There is no sense in which God's being may be said to be caused, even in the sense of God as *causa sui*. While God is not 'free' *not* to exist and so can be said to exist in some sense necessarily, this cannot be understood in any way that would suggest constraint or obligation on God's part (30–57; cf. 280).[58]

Externally, just as God's loving is not evoked by any prior worthiness or lovability on the part of the beloved (278–9), so God, in his freedom, is 'free from all origination, conditioning or determination from without' (307–8). Once again, Barth issues a warning that, if theology is not to misconstrue God's relation to the world in competitive or oppositional terms, God's freedom must be 'primarily and fundamentally defined as God's freedom in

---

[56] Cf. Camfield, 'Development', 49.

[57] Cf. Karl Barth, *Anselm: Fides Quaerens Intellectum: Anselm's Proof of the Existence of God in the Context of his Theological Scheme*, trans. Ian W. Robinson (London: SCM, 1960), 97–100.

[58] Cf. Osthövener, *Gottes Eigenschaften*, 174–5; Grell, *Der ewig reiche Gott*, 226–7.

himself, and only from that point of view understood as his independence of the world' (309).

Moving to his second stage of argument, Barth expands his description of the divine freedom in terms of what he calls the divine absoluteness (310–21). The primary aspect of God's freedom, according to which God is free in himself, and the secondary aspect of God's freedom, according to which God is free in relation to the created order and thus free from external limitation, constitute, respectively, God's 'primary' and 'secondary' absoluteness. Having drawn this distinction, it is only God's 'secondary' absoluteness which Barth develops here at any length. This secondary absoluteness (God's freedom with respect to the created order) has first a noetic dimension: 'There exists no synthesis in which the same attribute, whether being, spirit, life or love, can be predicated in the same sense both of God and of something else' (310). In other words, there is no parity or univocity of meaning in terms as applied to God and to creatures (cf. 224). Furthermore, 'Because *Deus non est in genere*, every theological method is to be rejected as untheological in which God's self-revelation is apparently recognised, but in fact is subsumed beneath a higher term' (311). God's secondary absoluteness has also an ontic dimension, itself the basis of its noetic dimension. God exists, according to Barth, 'in supreme and utter independence', 'at an infinite distance' from all other beings (311). 'Every relationship into which God enters with that which is not himself must be interpreted...as eventuating between two utterly different partners' (312).[59]

On its own, this stark assertion of God's secondary absoluteness might seem to pull against what Barth has said of the divine loving.[60] It does – but by way of dialectical complement, not careless contradiction. Barth now draws out a highly counterintuitive[61] implication of this divine freedom.

> It is just the absoluteness of God properly understood which can signify not only his freedom to transcend all that is other than himself, but also his freedom to be immanent within it, and at such a depth of immanence as simply does not exist in the fellowship between other beings. No created being can be inwardly present to another, entering and remaining in communion with it in the depths of its inner life...seriously leading and governing it, binding itself to the other and the other to itself in eternal faithfulness and whole-hearted devotion. (313 rev.; *KD* 352)

---

[59] Cf. Barth, *Fides Quaerens Intellectum*, 44–53, on Anselm's concepts of ontic and noetic rationality and necessity.
[60] Busch, *The Great Passion*, 106–7.
[61] Härle, *Sein und Gnade*, 66–7.

This is the real turning-point in the argument of this sub-section, and it prepares the way both for Barth's crowning account of that ultimate exercise of the divine life, love, and freedom in Jesus Christ (316–21), as well as for his doctrine of election in *CD* II/2.[62] Here Barth explains how it is that God's freedom *for* the creature and his freedom *from* the creature are actually one and the same freedom.[63] It is precisely God's transcendence of external limitation which allows him to be savingly immanent to his creatures. This bursts any lingering suspicion that God's freedom might ultimately be a matter of opposition to the creature. Barth's exposition of the divine freedom provides no basis for 'the accusation of authoritarianism' in his theology, but rather for grateful acknowledgement of the gracious lordship of God.[64] In this unique freedom, God 'can be so internal to'[65] the creature that he can sustain and guide it 'infinitely…more deeply' than could any other being. Crucially, this occurs 'not in dissolution but in confirmation of his own divine singularity, and again not in dissolution but in confirmation of the singularity of the creature' (314).[66]

This pivotal definition of God's freedom as freedom for communion with the other, as a freedom which does not exist except as it is directed toward 'eternal faithfulness and whole-hearted devotion' to the other, Barth will maintain through the whole of his theology.[67] Thus it is entirely to miss the point to claim that, according to Barth, 'the strongest possible affirmation of God's freedom is the declaration that the sovereign free being is inaccessible to others except on terms it establishes itself'.[68] It is true that the divine freedom, for Barth, captures God's inaccessibility. But that is only its negative aspect. What Barth is most keen to affirm is that what God does with his freedom is the exact opposite of remaining inaccessible. As Barth later put it,

---

[62] John Webster, *Barth's Ethics of Reconciliation* (Cambridge: Cambridge University Press, 1995), 44–7.

[63] Cf. Karl Barth, 'The Gift of Freedom', in *idem, The Humanity of God*, trans. Thomas Wieser and John Newton Thomas (Atlanta: John Knox, 1960), 71–5.

[64] Busch, *The Great Passion*, 121–4.

[65] The English (*CD* II/1, 313–14; *KD* 353) translates '*inseitig sein*' as 'indwell' (twice), '*der Geber seines Seins*' as 'the Giver of its life', and '*bewegen*' as 'inspire and guide', thus making the role of the Spirit more explicit than it is in Barth's text. Grell, *Der ewig reiche Gott*, 232–3, notes the parallels to Augustine, *Confessions* 3.6.11 (trans. Henry Chadwick (Oxford: Oxford University Press, 1991), 43): 'You were more inward than my most inward part and higher than the highest element within me.'

[66] Cf. Christopher A. Franks, 'The Simplicity of the Living God: Aquinas, Barth, and Some Philosophers', *Modern Theology* 21.2 (2005), 295–6: 'Barth claims that what is most revealing of God's freedom is the freedom God has not to be bound by that freedom.'

[67] John Webster, 'Freedom in Limitation: Human Freedom and False Necessity in Barth', in *idem, Barth's Moral Theology: Human Action in Barth's Thought* (Grand Rapids: Eerdmans, 1998), 104–7.

[68] Robert Brown, 'On God's Ontic and Noetic Absoluteness: A Critique of Barth', *Scottish Journal of Theology* 33.6 (1980): 544.

'The freedom of which we talk is God's freedom to disclose himself to men, to make men accessible to himself, and so to make them on their part free for him.'[69] The very 'starting-point of Barth's thought' – not just in *CD* II/1 – is that God's freedom 'is primarily freedom for the recipient'.[70] Freedom for Barth is a directed, purposeful freedom, one ordered toward a specific goal. 'From the very beginning, [Barth] is concerned to insist that the God who is Lord, who is free, is the very one who brings salvation and life out of decay, sin and death; that the one who is free relates himself to us and is in himself the basis of this relation.'[71]

A second implication of God's secondary absoluteness is that God is not bound always to act in the same way toward his creatures (314–16).[72] God is not 'inflexible', but works in his creation 'in the most varied ways' (314). God is free 'even to become a creature himself' and 'to die…in utter abandonment and darkness' (314–15).[73]

> This is how he meets us in Jesus Christ. His revelation in Jesus Christ embraces all these apparently so diverse and contradictory possibilities. They are all his possibilities. (315)

Moreover, this richness in the variety of God's ways arises not merely in response to the 'varying characteristics' of the creatures with whom God deals, but also from 'the demands of his own intention with regard to the creature' (315).

> There is not only the infinite individual variation of the divine action *ad extra*,…but as its ground in the being and will of God, in his decrees, there is a whole hierarchy of his decisions and acts. (315)

This, again, is no 'speculation' but simply what it means for God to have his being in act (316). The variety God exhibits in his act of self-revelation is the variety of his very own eternal being. In saying this, Barth is preparing the reader for the introduction of the formal concept of divine perfections in

---

[69] Karl Barth, *Evangelical Theology: An Introduction* (Grand Rapids: Eerdmans, 1979), 53; cf. Härle, *Sein und Gnade*, 63–4.

[70] Hendry, 'The Freedom of God', 233.

[71] Hans Frei, *The Doctrine of Revelation in the Thought of Karl Barth, 1909 to 1922: The Nature of Barth's Break with Liberalism* (Ph.D. diss., Yale University, 1956), 107–8; quoted in John Webster, '"Life from the Third Dimension": Human Action in Barth's Early Ethics', in *idem, Barth's Moral Theology*, 38.

[72] Cf. Osthövener, *Gottes Eigenschaften*, 177–9.

[73] Grell, *Der ewig reiche Gott*, 234, voices the common complaint that Barth's treatment of the attributes does not devote sufficient attention to the cross. To his credit, Grell also acknowledges that, had Barth done so, his exposition as it stands would not have been invalidated, but deepened.

§29. As Barth will elaborate, both in §29 as well as in his discussion of the divine unity in §31, the unity and simplicity of God's being do not exclude, but include, the rich multiplicity of the divine life.

This rich multiplicity is not multiplicity 'of any and every kind' because it has its 'very definite centre' in Jesus Christ (316–17). Jesus Christ is 'not merely the focus and the crown of all relationship and fellowship between God and the world, but also their basic principle, their possibility and pre-supposition in the life of the Godhead' (317–18). Here Barth clarifies how it is that God has variety in his own eternal being:

> Before all worlds, in his Son he has otherness in himself from eternity to eternity. But because this is so, the creation and preservation of the world, and relationship and fellowship with it, realised as they are in perfect freedom, without compulsion or necessity, do not signify an alien or contradictory expression of God's being, but a natural, *the* natural expression of it *ad extra*. (317; cf. 499–502)

God the Son is, thus, the 'original truth' of God's secondary absoluteness or freedom with respect to the created order, just as God's triunity is the basis of God's primary absoluteness or freedom in himself (317).

Because the Son is the basis of God's freedom with respect to the created order, and thus the basis of divine revelation, the Son himself must be the guiding reality in both exegesis and theology.[74] This is simply to repeat the claim that 'we know God in Jesus Christ alone' (318; cf. 44). God's freedom, says Barth, 'will not confuse us by its manifoldness, but will comfort, warn and cause us to rejoice if we see that it derives from Jesus Christ the Son of God, attesting him, serving him and leading to him' (318 rev.; *KD* 357–8).

> Christology, therefore, must always constitute the basis and criterion for the apprehension and interpretation of the freedom of God in his immanence. The legitimacy of every theory concerning the relation-ship of God and man or God and the world can be tested by considering whether it can be understood also as an interpretation of the relation-ship and fellowship created and sustained in Jesus Christ. (320; cf. 148–50)[75]

In fact, Barth will return to Christology, he will perform this christological 'test', in his treatment of each of the divine attributes. All of the divine per-fections 'are present completely and perfectly and in all their plenitude in

---

[74] Cf. CD I/2, 866.

[75] Cf. Osthövener, *Gottes Eigenschaften*, 179–80. Osthövener typically downplays the immanent character of the divine otherness by suggesting that its elaboration is to be found in the doctrine of election rather than in the doctrine of the Trinity.

Christ...in a way which can be neither transcended nor supplemented'.[76] This includes even such attributes as omnipresence, constancy and eternity, which have traditionally formed an uneasy alliance at best with Christology.

In Barth's judgement, the tradition sooner fails this christological 'test' with God's so-called incommunicable or metaphysical attributes than with his communicable or moral attributes. It is probably this which explains why Barth's most extended discussion of Jesus Christ in §28 comes not as part of the description of God's loving (§28.2), but here as part of the description of God's freedom. As Barth sees it, there is a deeper error to correct in the tradition's handling of the incommunicable attributes. It is these which have tended to wander further from Christology and which need to be summoned home more urgently.

> God is free. Because this is the case, we must say expressly in conclusion that the freedom of God is the freedom which consists and fulfils itself in his Son Jesus Christ. In him God has loved himself from all eternity. In him he has loved the world. He has done so in him, in the freedom which renders his life divine, and therefore glorious, triumphant, and strong to save. (321)

There is also a certain elegance to Barth's having placed his brief statement of Christology at the very end of §28. Barth's opening statement, 'God is' (257), is first elaborated as 'God is the one who loves in freedom' and then resolved, in praise, to the simple but climactic claim, 'God is Jesus Christ and Jesus Christ is God' (318). Barth concludes by reminding his readers that this robust Christology lays claim not only to the theologian's task, but also to the church's tasks of evangelism and discipleship. 'For this reason Jesus Christ alone must be preached to the heathen as the immanent God, and the church must be severely vigilant to see that it expects everything from *Jesus Christ*, and from Jesus Christ *everything*; that he is unceasingly recognised as *the* way, *the* truth, and *the* life (Jn 14:6)' (319–20).

---

[76] *CD* IV/4, 118.

2

THE PERFECTIONS OF GOD (§29)

Having given in §28 his first-order sketch of God as the one who loves in freedom, Barth now introduces, in §29, the concept of divine perfections. For all of its methodological preoccupation, it is a powerful section, rich even by Barth's standards in broad historical analysis, and decisive in its formulation of the task of a doctrine of the divine perfections. It is in this section that Barth anticipates, as explicitly as anywhere else in the *Church Dogmatics*, the logic of Karl Rahner's famous rule concerning the relation between the immanent and economic Trinity.[1] It is also here that Barth identifies what distinguishes the whole of his doctrine of the divine attributes from its various predecessors in the Christian tradition.

Following his introductory comments (322), Barth's exposition proceeds in three stages: the identification of the task of a doctrine of the divine perfections (323–7); a closer specification of this task in terms of the relation between the one God and his multitude of perfections (327–35); and a discussion of the ways in which the divine perfections are derived and how they should be ordered in a systematic presentation (335–50).

Barth begins by identifying the two poles around which exposition will turn: God's perfections and God himself. The two are in fact identical. 'God lives his perfect life in the abundance of many individual perfections', each of which 'is nothing else but God himself' (322). Theology, nevertheless, distinguishes between God's being and his perfections because God's being is not something that can be grasped statically and in its entirety. It is grasped, rather, in the course of a history along which 'we are confronted by his richness'. God's rich abundance of perfections is not merely a feature of this history with us, however, only to be found along 'the way which in the

---

[1] Karl Rahner, *The Trinity*, trans. Joseph Donceel (New York: Herder and Herder, 1970), 21–2; cf. Fred Sanders, *The Image of the Immanent Trinity: Rahner's Rule and the Theological Interpretation of Scripture* (New York: Peter Lang, 2005), 50–60, 147–8.

presence of the living God we must tread'. God's richness is the richness of his own, eternal being.

> The real God is the one God who loves in freedom, and as such is *der «ewig reiche Gott»*.[2] To know him means to know him again and again, in ever new ways...in the abundance, distinctness and variety of his perfections. (322; *KD* 362)

Robert Jenson explains:

> God *lives* his being. Our knowledge of him is therefore a matter of following the way he goes, of tracing after a history. Our knowledge is therefore discursive; it is a *succession* of apprehensions.[3]

Exposition of a series of divine perfections is thus aimed at capturing this succession of apprehensions of God's being; though the individual concepts employed can only partially describe the divine being, the series represents an effort to indicate the whole. The first two stages of Barth's argument spell out in detail the nature of this relationship between God's being and his perfections.

Before proceeding, one further feature of this opening description deserves comment: In the midst of what may appear a rather abstruse theological point, Barth's tone is anything but distant. For Barth – as his allusion to Rinkart's hymn indicates – the knowledge of God is also a matter of joyful astonishment, of wonder.[4] As we know God, that is, as God draws us into his presence, we discover 'in ever new ways' the richness of his perfections. God thus shows himself able 'to meet every real need' and to fill 'every real lack' (322) and grants us, in Rinkart's line, 'an ever joyful heart'. These are the perfections of *our* God, of the God who seeks and creates fellowship with *us*.

Barth's first stage of argument, then, takes up the 'problem' or 'task' of a doctrine of the divine attributes (323–7). Before explicitly defining this task, Barth insists that in speaking of the divine attributes 'our primary affirmation must be that here too it is a question of nothing else but of God himself' (323). That is, the divine attributes are nothing other than

---

[2] Eberhard Busch, *Karl Barth: His Life from Letters and Autobiographical Texts*, trans. John Bowden (Grand Rapids: Eerdmans, 1994), 487 n., records that 'Barth was particularly fond of the phrase "*der ewig reiche Gott*"' from Martin Rinkart's hymn *Nun danket alle Gott* (ca. 1636; ET 1856 by Catherine Winkworth, 'Now Thank We All Our God').

[3] Robert W. Jenson, *God After God: The God of the Past and the God of the Future, Seen in the Work of Karl Barth* (Indianapolis: Bobbs-Merrill, 1969), 134.

[4] Karl Barth, *Evangelical Theology: An Introduction* (Grand Rapids: Eerdmans, 1979), 63–73.

God himself. God's unity, God's oneness, does not relegate the multiplicity of his attributes to some less-than-divine realm. Rather, it is precisely this multiplicity, this richness, which is the 'confirmation and glorification' of the divine unity (323).

> He is who he is and what he is in both unity and multiplicity....The One is he who loves in freedom. The many are his perfections – the perfections of his life. (323)

This peculiarity of the divine unity, namely, that it is also a divine multiplicity, explains Barth's express preference for the term 'perfections' rather than 'attributes', even though he continues to use the latter. 'The fact that God's being has attributes is something which it has in common with the being of others' (322), while 'perfections' are 'his own exclusively' (323). In other words, to speak of the divine unity, for example, as a divine 'perfection' (rather than merely a divine 'attribute') points to its difference from that unity which may fittingly describe beings other than God.

Granted, then, that God's attributes are God himself – that 'Since God is Father, Son, and Holy Spirit, i.e., loves in freedom, *every* perfection exists *essentially* in him' (323; *KD* 363) – Barth can now proceed to define 'the special task of the doctrine of God's attributes' (324). This task is 'to grasp and understand [the] connexion' between God's perfections as we encounter them in his revelation and God's own, eternal being. 'For as the triune God, both in regard to his revelation and to his being in itself, he exists in these perfections, and these perfections again exist in him and only in him as the One who, both in his revelation and in eternity, is the same' (323–4).

The success of a doctrine of the divine attributes is therefore compromised if God's 'glory' (God's revealed perfection) is not understood as that of 'the Lord' (God's being in himself) (324–5). Where God's being and his revelation are separated, two opposing fates await a doctrine of God's perfections. On the one hand, God can be portrayed as acquiring 'abundance of life, vividness and palpable reality only as he enters into relation with us'. But since, behind this vividness, God remains all the while 'slender', 'impoverished' and 'spectral' in himself, 'his glory cannot be accepted strictly', that is, the believer cannot fully rely upon God's perfections:

> It is dangerous and ultimately fatal to faith in God if God is not the Lord of *glory*, if it is not guaranteed to us that in spite of the analogical nature of the language in which it all has to be expressed God is actually and unreservedly as we encounter him in his revelation: the Almighty, the Holy, the Righteous, the Merciful, the Omnipresent, the Eternal, not less but infinitely more so than it is in our power to grasp, that is, in actuality, and therefore not only for us but in himself. (325 rev.; *KD* 365)

35

Faith requires the revelation of God himself. On the other hand, God's glory can be understood to have no Lord at all (325–6). By 'God's glory', Barth means the 'mighty potencies' in which man 'on the basis of revelation' believes himself to be 'confronted by the divine'. By 'having no Lord', Barth means that these potencies are understood not as 'concentrated, gathered up and unified in God himself', but as independent, mutually contradictory, almost demonic forces. This second fate compromises a doctrine of the divine perfections even more severely than the first, for in this case man finds himself, not merely disappointed by empty 'perfections', but surrounded by a 'chaos [of] hypostatised principles' (326). If, as Barth will go on to explain, the former fate is that of nominalism, the latter is that of an unbridled realism: making 'God's perfections substantial so that they are independent entities within, or even above, the being of God'.[5] Once again, it is 'dangerous and ultimately fatal to faith if God is not the *Lord* of glory', that is, if the multiplicity of the divine perfections is not seen as having a 'very definite centre' in the Lord Jesus Christ (316–7). In other words, a doctrine of God's attributes can never be 'concerned merely with these attributes or perfections as such, but with them *as his*, and therefore always directly with himself' (326; *KD* 367). Thus, in light of the danger that threatens from both directions, 'to attest and expound this biblical unity of the Lord with his *glory*' and of 'all glory with its *Lord*' 'is the business of the doctrine of the divine perfections' (325, 326).

Barth concludes this first stage of exposition by noting the parallel here with the doctrine of the Trinity (326–7). Just as Father, Son and Spirit cannot be understood modalistically as mere figments of the economy, neither can God's perfections be understood as mere figments of the economy. God's perfections are those of his essence. And just as Father, Son, and Spirit cannot be understood tritheistically, that is, as of independent interest, neither can God's perfections be understood in their own right. God's perfections are those of the one Lord. Barth explains:

> The attributes or perfections of God are as it were the letters of the divine Word. It becomes a Word only through the sequence and unity of these letters. But again, it is only in this sequence and unity that the letters can constitute the Word. (327)[6]

One might say that the task of a doctrine of the divine perfections is to spell out, by means of God's many perfections, the one perfection of God's triune loving in freedom.

---

[5] Stephen R. Holmes, *God of Grace and God of Glory: An Account of the Theology of Jonathan Edwards* (Edinburgh: T&T Clark, 2000), 67.

[6] Cf. *CD* III/3, 159: Barth speaks of God's will 'to declare and make manifest his own being in a Word – and that *in suis operibus*, in the works of creation, which in some sense form, therefore, the consonants and vowels of this Word and thus serve the revelation of himself'.

The second stage of Barth's exposition takes up again the explanation of the task to hand, this time with greater historical and dogmatic precision and in light of the dogmatic tradition on divine simplicity (327–35).[7] In this light, the problem may be seen as one of the very 'legitimacy...of speaking here of perfections (in the plural)' of the one and simple divine essence (327). Until the nineteenth century, according to Barth, the tradition had denied this legitimacy with a stringency which varied depending on whether God himself or his revealed perfections were in view (327–30). That is, whether explicitly denying a plurality of perfections in God himself (the strict nominalism of, for example Occam and Biel) or affirming this plurality merely in his relation to us (the moderate nominalism of, for example, Thomas, Calvin and Protestant orthodoxy), the simplicity of the divine essence was thought ultimately to exclude any multiplicity of perfections. Though there are to be found those happy inconsistencies in the tradition which Barth is always glad to point out,[8] the thought of plurality in God was generally regarded as 'something of an embarrassment'.[9] On either the strict or the moderate account, the tradition opted for a 'spectral' Lord whose glory is not really his own.

> The fact that the life of God was identified with the notion of pure being, the fact that the idea of God was not determined by the doctrine of the Trinity, but the latter was shaped by a general conception of God (that of ancient Stoicism and Neo-Platonism), was now avenged at the most sensitive spot. Starting from the generalised notion of God, the idea of the divine simplicity was necessarily exalted to the all-controlling principle, the idol, which, devouring everything concrete, stands behind all these formulae. As a result it was impossible to make proper use of what Augustine had so happily indicated with his phrase *multiplex simplicitas* or *simplex multiplicitas*: the triumphant unity in God of the Lord with glory and of glory with the Lord. (329)[10]

---

[7] Cf. Charles Edward Raynal, III, *Karl Barth's Conception of the Perfections of God* (Ph.D. diss., Yale University, 1973), 6–10; Cornelis van der Kooi, *As In A Mirror: John Calvin And Karl Barth On Knowing God: A Diptych*, trans. Donald Mader (Leiden: Brill, 2005), 334–5.

[8] Richard A. Muller, *Post-Reformation Reformed Dogmatics: The Rise and Development of Reformed Orthodoxy, ca. 1520 to ca. 1725*, vol. 3, *The Divine Essence and Attributes* (Grand Rapids: Baker Academic, 2003), 287 n. 324, claims that it was not merely by happy inconsistency but by consensus that Reformed orthodoxy affirmed a multiplicity of distinguishable perfections in the divine essence itself. Cf. John Webster, *Holiness* (Grand Rapids: Eerdmans, 2003), 38.

[9] Jenson, *God After God*, 133.

[10] Augustine's happy phrase finds an echo in Barth's talk of the God 'whose simplicity is abundance itself and whose abundance is simplicity itself' (*CD* II/1, 406).

Acknowledging the pioneering work of 'certain German theologians' of the previous century (F. H. R. Frank, G. Thomasius and Dorner), Barth makes clear his intention to make a clean break at this point with the older dogmatic tradition (330).

The dogmatic entailments of such a break can be sketched, according to Barth, in 'three explanatory propositions' concerning the unity, simplicity, and particularity of the divine essence. That is – recalling the thesis statement of §29 (322) – God's perfections are those of his one, simple, distinctive (*einen, einfachen, eigenen*) being (330–5; *KD* 372–7).[11] First, 'the multiplicity, individuality and diversity of the divine perfections are those of the *one* divine being' (331–2). God's perfections, in other words, are not accidental, but essential. God does not *possess* his perfections; he *is* his perfections. 'God is in essence all that he is' (331). Second, God's perfections 'are those of his *simple* being' (332–3). God's unity and simplicity include multiplicity and diversity.[12] In fact, 'every individual perfection in God is nothing but God himself and therefore nothing but every other divine perfection' (333).

> If God is the God who is rich in himself, and if he is the one true God even in his works *ad extra*, we cannot emphasise either his *simplicitas* or his *multiplicitas* as though the one or the other *in abstracto* were the very being of God, as though the one inevitably precluded the other. (333)

Exactly how both of these can be true of God Barth does not say. According to Balthasar, 'the more the aspects of God are differentiated, the more they reciprocally interpenetrate'.[13] Todd Pokrifka-Joe aptly notes that 'Barth's concept of simplicity retains a quality of mystery', citing Barth's parallel appeal in *CD* I/1 to the *mysterium trinitatis*.[14] Third, God's perfections 'are

---

[11] Cf. Raynal, *The Perfections of God*, 11–18.

[12] While Barth understands the divine simplicity not to exclude a multiplicity of other perfections, it is hardly correct to claim that simplicity is 'the foundation upon which constancy, eternity, omnipresence, omnipotence and glory are built'. See Richard H. Roberts, 'Karl Barth's Doctrine of Time: Its Nature and Implications', in *idem, A Theology on its Way: Essays on Karl Barth* (Edinburgh: T&T Clark, 1991), 25.

[13] Hans Urs von Balthasar, *The Glory of the Lord: A Theological Aesthetics*, trans. Erasmo Leiva-Merikakis, ed. Joseph Fessio and John Riches (Edinburgh: T&T Clark, 1982–1989), 6.54.

[14] Todd Pokrifka-Joe, *Redescribing God: The Roles of Scripture, Tradition, and Reason in Karl Barth's Doctrines of Divine Unity, Constancy, and Eternity* (Ph.D. diss., University of St. Andrews, 2002), 155–6 (cf. 131); cf. *CD* I/1, 366–8. Cf. also *CD* II/1, 40–2; Jenson, *God After God*, 134–5; George Hunsinger, *How To Read Karl Barth: The Shape of His Theology* (Oxford: Oxford University Press, 1991), 34; Mitchell Grell, *Der ewig reiche Gott: Die Erkenntnis, Gewinnung und Bestimmung der Eigenschaften Gottes nach Isaak August Dorner, August Hermann Cremer und Karl Barth mit beson-*

rooted in his *own* [distinctive] being' (333–5). God's perfections do not reflect his participation in 'power, goodness, knowledge, will, etc. in general': 'God does not borrow what he is from outside' (334). Rather, these concepts only have their reality in God, and created being participates in them only insofar as God enables it to do so.[15]

Barth's third stage of argument takes up 'the problem of the derivation and distribution of the divine attributes', that is, the methodological questions surrounding the ways in which a divine perfection may be defined and in which an assortment of perfections should be ordered in a systematic exposition (335–50). Barth immediately notes the apparent superficiality of such concerns. If 'each of the divine perfections is materially identical with each of the others and with the fulness of them all, indeed with God himself', what could the exposition of a series of divine perfections be but the reiteration of the divine identity (335)? The solution to this quandary comes from revelation itself – a solution which, as Barth formulates it here, stands as a forceful apologia for the whole enterprise of dogmatics:

It is also written that God not only appears but *is* almighty, eternal, just, wise, merciful – not merely for us but in himself. And although in all this he is concealed from us in so far as these words are our words and not his own Word about himself, yet it remains true that we are invited and authorised by his revelation to name him with these words of ours in the confidence that in this way we are moving in the sphere of truth and not of falsehood so long as we are always willing to allow him to be himself the interpreter of these human words which he has placed on our lips. (335–6)[16]

In other words, God in his self-revelation 'invites and authorises' – he places on our lips – the confession of an abundance of perfections, a confession which 'has to be expressed in words' (336; cf. 61–2). Barth expresses here his understanding of the task of theology as *Nachdenken*: 'Knowledge of God consists for human beings in a following-after and a thinking-after the movement of God in his Self-revelation.'[17] In revealing himself, God 'takes from us the pretext of our incapacity' and commands us to give him 'the

---

derer Berücksichtigung des Einflusses der Theologie Dorners und Cremers auf die Gotteslehre Barths (Ph.D. diss., University of Tübingen, 1992), 267–8.

[15] Cf. CD III/1, 5.

[16] Cf. Karl Barth, *The Epistle to the Romans*, trans. Edwyn C. Hoskyns (Oxford: Oxford University Press, 1968), 273.

[17] Bruce L. McCormack, *Karl Barth's Critically Realistic Dialectical Theology: Its Genesis and Development 1909–1936* (New York: Oxford University Press, 1995), 270; cf. 273–4. Cf. Terry L. Cross, *Dialectic in Karl Barth's Doctrine of God* (New York: Peter Lang, 2001), 189.

honour which belongs to him, to the very best – no less – of our ability, i.e., the ability which he himself gives us' (336).

Thus, when it comes to the derivation and distribution of the divine attributes, and despite the fallibility of the human theological endeavour of *Nachdenken*, revelation itself is sufficiently clear as to have engendered 'a classical, and to some extent ecumenical line of theological reflection', in light of which 'there are a number of errors which we have to avoid and reject' (337). Revelation, and thus God himself, is the principle of the derivation and distribution of the divine attributes. Thus, a doctrine of the divine attributes cannot be ordered by a bias either for or against what are deemed psychological attributes; nor according to the religious self-consciousness of man (Schleiermacher's 'religio-genetic' principle); nor on the basis of Jesus' own personal consciousness (the 'historical-intuitive' approach) (337–40).[18] A common fault of these approaches is their lack of concern for what Barth refers to as the divine freedom or aseity. 'There is, however, another and better way', a 'classical line of approach' which finds expression in the typical Reformed division between incommunicable and communicable attributes and in the typical Lutheran divisions between absolute and relative, immanent and transcendent, metaphysical and moral attributes (340–1). A common thread runs through these various paired categories:

> On the one hand it is a question of the moment of God's aseity, absoluteness or freedom: of God in the exaltation proper to him in himself, as against all that is not himself. And on the other hand it is a question of the moment of the love of God, of the activity of his personal being. (341)

Barth's categories will follow this same insight. If theology is truly to be a *Nachdenken* about the God who loves in freedom, says Barth, 'we shall have to enquire into the perfections of the divine loving and those of the divine freedom' (340). With this announcement, Barth brings his exposition thus far to its denouement. Suddenly, everything Barth developed in §28 about God's being-in-act and his loving in freedom beautifully coalesces. And the broad logic of everything Barth will go on to say in §§30–1 about God's individual perfections begins to make sense. The elegance of the structure of Barth's exposition stands forth here for the first time in all its clarity. Though readers will of course have been prepared for this by having scanned the table of contents, by various hints along the way (e.g. 302), and no less by the accumulating force of Barth's argument itself, it is only here that the plan

---

[18] Cf. Grell, *Der ewig reiche Gott*, 272–5. Raynal, *The Perfections of God*, 95 (cf. 131–2), nevertheless makes the baffling assertion that 'the concept of God as person…is the principle of the derivation and distribution of the attributes of God'.

of the whole, with its exact mirroring of dogmatic content in analytic form, begins to emerge for consideration in its own right.

It is important to note that Barth arranges the attributes as he does out of dogmatic necessity, and not because it will make for convenient appropriation from the 'classic' twofold approach. It is the 'two fundamental features of the being of God – his love and his freedom in their unity and diversity' which require an exposition of the divine attributes a corresponding twofold series (344). Love and freedom are simply conceptual shorthand for aspects of God's identity. They possess no independent function. It is therefore misleading to claim that, in Barth's account, 'love operates as a kind of "control attribute" that regulates the other divine perfections',[19] or, far worse, that according to Barth 'all the attributes of God are subordinate to the one attribute of love or grace'.[20] As Barth states, no concept can be 'given the position of a supreme governing principle in the whole doctrine of attributes, because there can be no such overriding principle where God himself is all' (338; cf. 311, 375, 407, 448, 526).

One aspect of God's self-revelation, about which Barth has remained silent since the previous chapter (e.g. 16–17, 215, 234–6), he now reintroduces as a way of explaining the relationship between the love and freedom of God and therefore the form of the following exposition (§§30–1). It is the dialectic of veiling and unveiling in revelation (341–3).

> A fully restrained and fully alive doctrine of God's attributes will take as its fundamental point of departure the truth that God is for us fully revealed and fully concealed in his self-disclosure. We cannot say partly revealed and partly concealed, but we must actually say wholly revealed and wholly concealed at one and the same time. We must say wholly revealed because by the grace of revelation our human views and concepts are invited and exalted to share in the truth of God and therefore in a marvellous way made instruments of a real knowledge of God (in his being for us and as he is in himself). We must say wholly concealed because our human views and concepts...have not in themselves the smallest capacity to apprehend God. (341–2)

Though Barth avoids using the term 'analogy' here, presumably because of what he sees as its misuse in natural theology, the idea of a 'similarity,

---

[19] Kevin J. Vanhoozer, 'Introduction: The Love of God – Its Place, Meaning, and Function in Systematic Theology', in *idem*, ed., *Nothing Greater, Nothing Better: Theological Essays on the Love of God* (Grand Rapids: Eerdmans, 2001), 15.

[20] Cornelius Van Til, *Christianity and Barthianism* (Philadelphia: Presbyterian and Reformed, 1962), 76; cf. 76–7: Grace is 'supreme above all other attributes' and 'the central attribute of God'.

partial[21] correspondence and agreement' between human concepts and divine reality is clearly what he has in mind (225). Barth is quick to clarify that this simultaneous veiling and unveiling in revelation cannot be understood to imply that 'in [God's] self-unveiling we have grounds for knowing him, and in his self-concealment for not knowing him' (342). It is not so simple as that. Rather, God is also 'completely recognisable' in his hiddenness, and he is also 'completely unknowable' in his self-disclosure. Every instance of God's self-disclosure demands both 'the obedience of knowledge and the humility of ignorance' (342). It will become crucial to recall this point when Barth goes on to explain the relation between this dialectic of unveiling and veiling and the dialectic between God's love and his freedom. 'At every point, therefore, we have to be silent, but we have also to speak' (342). A doctrine of the divine attributes which follows God's self-revelation is therefore bound to give due emphasis to both the unity of and the distinction between God's self-disclosure and self-concealment.

Barth then draws a rather stark parallel, which has understandably derailed many an unwary interpreter:

> This unity and this distinction corresponds to the unity and distinction in God's own being between his love and his freedom. God loves us....As such he is completely knowable to us. But he loves us in his freedom....He is therefore completely unknowable to us. That he loves us and that he does so in his freedom are both true in the grace of his revelation. (343)

These lines are easily misread as implying that it is *strictly* in God's love that he is knowable and *strictly* in his freedom that he is unknowable. Christophe Chalamet takes such a position: 'God's veiling is reflected in his freedom, in his unknowability, whereas his unveiling is reflected in his love and in the fact that he gives himself to be known.'[22] But this does not appear to be what Barth actually affirms. For just as God's self-disclosure is also unknowable to us, and just as his hiddenness is also completely recognisable by us, so God's loving is also unknowable to us and his freedom completely recognisable. What Barth does affirm here is that the dialectic of revelation (unveiling and veiling) must be faithfully expressed in a doctrine of the divine attributes,

---

[21] As Barth explained earlier (233), though 'our words about God' do not possess such correspondence on their own, they 'receive analogy to God's being' in the event of revelation. This analogical knowledge of God nevertheless remain partial even as God is 'wholly revealed' because of God's incomprehensibility.

[22] Christophe Chalamet, *Dialectical Theologians: Wilhelm Herrmann, Karl Barth and Rudolf Bultmann* (Zürich: Theologischer Verlag Zürich, 2005), 241; cf. 241–3.

and that the dialectic between love and freedom of God can be a means to this end, a way of indicating the element of the unknown in every moment even of true human knowledge of God. But while the dialectics (love and freedom, unveiling and veiling) correspond to each other, their individual elements do not:

> The unity of self-disclosure and concealment, of the knowability and unknowability of God, constitutes the biblical idea of the revelation of God, just as the unity of love and freedom constitutes the biblical idea of the being of God....Therefore, explicitly or implicitly, when we speak of the love of God we shall have to speak also of his freedom, when we speak of his freedom we shall have to speak also of his love, and when we speak of one individual aspect we shall have to speak also of all the others. (343)

Thus, 'when we speak of the love of God' – that is, when Barth expounds the divine grace, mercy and patience – these do represent God as he unveils himself. And when Barth says that, in doing so, 'we shall have to speak also of his freedom' – that is, when Barth addresses the holiness, righteousness, and wisdom of God – these capture something of the veiled aspect (the particularity, the 'divinity') of God's grace, mercy and patience. But the logic works the other way round when it comes to the perfections of the divine freedom. So, 'when we speak of his freedom' – that is, when Barth expounds the divine unity, constancy and eternity – these now represent God as he unveils himself. And when Barth says that, in doing so, 'we shall have to speak also of his love' – that is, when Barth addresses the omnipresence, omnipotence and glory of God – these now represent something of the veiled aspect (again, the particularity, the 'divinity') of God's unity, constancy and eternity. Thus, every divine perfection is itself both unveiled and veiled: 'God is gracious not only in his unveiling, but also in his veiling' (236). The correspondence between the dialectic of God's revelation (unveiling and veiling) and the dialectic of his being (love and freedom) which Barth intends to capture here is this: each perfection is unveiled when considered on its own and veiled when considered in light of its unity with its counterpart and with the other perfections. It is crucial to realise, however, that there remains a distinction between the two dialectics, and that it is the dialectic of God's being (love and freedom), and not the dialectic of his revelation (veiling and unveiling), which orders Barth's exposition. The reason is that the dialectic of revelation is operative strictly at the economic level. God is never veiled to himself. 'God is not hidden from himself but is open to himself' (68).[23] The dialectic of revelation therefore cannot be operative within the triune life – a point

---

[23] Cf. CD II/1, 16. Barth describes God's primary objectivity as immediate, direct and naked. Presumably, this excludes any veiling in God's knowledge of himself, particularly

which Barth had long since emphasised over against the implications of his earlier theology.[24] To structure a doctrine of the divine perfections on the basis of God's unveiling and veiling in revelation would give to the knowing human subject as determinative a role in the formulation of the doctrine as had Schleiermacher. Barth would not have conceded to this.

It is also crucial to note here that Barth does not conceive of God's knowability and unknowability, or of God's love and freedom, as in any sort of competitive relationship. Barth emphasises that God is 'wholly revealed and wholly concealed at one and the same time' (341). Therefore God is not less revealed the more he is concealed; he is wholly both. 'The paradox that in his self-disclosure God becomes ever more manifest as the Incomprehensible One must retain its full vigour.'[25] Likewise God is not less loving the more he is free; he is wholly both. 'If we do not wish to deviate from Scripture, the unity of God must be understood as this unity of his love and freedom which is dynamic and, to that extent, diverse' (343). There is thus a 'complete reciprocity' between God's love and freedom, such that 'each of the opposing [sich gegenüberstehenden] ideas not only augments but absolutely fulfils the other, yet it does not render it superfluous or supplant it' (343; KD 386). Love and freedom, while positionally opposed (i.e. paired) in the structure of Barth's exposition, do not materially contradict or limit each other, but rather fulfil each other. 'It is only in conjunction with the other...that each can describe the Subject, God' (343).[26] It is therefore simply not the case that, as Wolf Krötke charges, 'Time and again God's freedom emerges [in Barth's exposition] as a restriction of what we can say about him on the basis of his revelation in Christ.'[27] Barth has made it abundantly clear that Jesus Christ

---

as Barth contrasts this with that secondary objectivity in which God is known mediately, indirectly and as 'clothed under the sign and veil of other objects'.

[24] In response to similar charges in Erik Peterson's 1925 article, 'What is Theology?', Barth made clear that, because theology is 'theology after the fall', it is therefore 'conditioned in its basic assumptions by human misery'. Thus, 'The fragmentariness, the paradox, the continual need of radical completion, the essential inconclusiveness of all its assertions are not to be denied. The revelation of which theology speaks is not dialectical, not paradox. That hardly needs to be said. But when theology begins, when we men think, speak, or write,...then there is dialectic.' See his 'Church and Theology', in idem, Theology and Church: Shorter Writings 1920–1928, trans. Louise Pettibone Smith (New York: Harper and Row, 1962), 286–306 (299); cf. CD II/1, 663, 665; McCormack, Dialectical Theology, 6–7, 367–71.

[25] Balthasar, The Glory of the Lord, 6.54.

[26] John Webster, Barth's Ethics of Reconciliation (Cambridge: Cambridge University Press, 1995), 45.

[27] Wolf Krötke, Gottes Klarheiten: Eine Neuinterpretation der Lehre von Gottes »Eigenschaften« (Tübingen: Mohr Siebeck, 2001), 28. Following Krötke's claim that Barth understands the concepts of love and freedom as materially opposed and thus mutually limiting, C. Holmes argues that Barth's clear affirmation of the unity and coinherence of the perfections is compromised, rather than confirmed, by the structure

does not reveal to us something substantive about the divine loving, only to have theological recollection of the divine freedom mischievously sneak in to limit or negate this. 'The great reciprocal qualification and expansion of the two leading ideas of the love and freedom of God' is not intended to 'postulate a cleavage and dualism in God', but rather 'to respect the unity of God in the clearness and fulness of his revelation and being' (358–9). It a device not only for following after the sequence of revelation, but also for constantly turning our thoughts back to God himself, resisting the isolation and abstraction to which our inadequate human concepts tend – even those concepts rightly used in describing God. 'It is not possible to say everything at once, at least for those who live and work "where a word has both a beginning and an ending."'[28]

Before turning to exposition of individual perfections, Barth identifies three points at which he will part ways with more traditional accounts (344–50). First, the perfections of the divine loving are not to be thought of as expressing exclusively God's fellowship with the world, or his modes of immanence within, nor are the perfections of the divine freedom to be thought of as expressing exclusively God's transcendence of the world (344–6). Put differently, the world, even in so far as God relates to it, cannot provide a doctrine of the divine attributes with its structure.

> [Where this occurs] the essential being of God will probably be decisively sought in his sovereign freedom and the perfections proper to it, eternity, omnipotence and so on, while the love of God and its perfections, holiness, justice, mercy and so on, are treated nominalistically or semi-nominalistically as a question of mere economy, as non-essential, as perhaps merely noetic determinations, so that the final and decisive word in our doctrine of God is the affirmation of God as the impersonal absolute. (345)

---

of his account. See Christopher R. J. Holmes, *Revisiting the Doctrine of the Divine Attributes: In Dialogue with Karl Barth, Eberhard Jüngel, and Wolf Krötke* (New York: Peter Lang, 2007), 223–4. Mitchell Grell, on the other hand, suggests at one point that it is not the unity of the divine perfections which is compromised in Barth's account, but rather their distinction. He feels it legitimate to ask of Barth's more theoretical discussion in §29, if not of the actual exposition of the perfections themselves, whether there is any real difference between God's freedom and his love. Grell, *Der ewig reiche Gott*, 275. As already noted, it is only if 'love' and 'freedom' are abstracted from the divine reality to which they refer that – perhaps in light of Barth's assertion of their material identity (e.g. 322, 335) – they could be misunderstood as lacking mutual distinction.

[28] Fred Sanders, 'The Trinity', in *The Oxford Handbook of Systematic Theology*, ed. John Webster et al. (Oxford: Oxford University Press, 2007), 38; citing Augustine's account of his visionary experience in *Confessions* 9.10.24. Barth discusses this passage of Augustine in *CD* II/1, 10–12.

Moreover, as Barth has already indicated (302–5), it is precisely God's freedom 'which he discloses and exercises in his fellowship with the world' (344). It is not merely God's love, Barth points out, but also his eternity, which God has 'implanted...utterly in our hearts' (345; cf. Eccl. 3:11). On the other hand, God's loving is first and foremost a matter of the triune life, even apart from the world. Barth summarises in an epigram this peculiarity of the divine loving and freedom: 'What he is there in the heights for us, here in the depths he is also in himself' (345 rev.; *KD* 388).

Second, on the basis of a false identification of God's freedom with his transcendence and of God's love with his immanence, the tradition has often employed correspondingly false methods of defining God's perfections. It has attempted, on the one hand, to define the perfections of God's freedom by transcending or negating concepts which describe the world, and, on the other, to define the perfections of the divine loving 'by expanding, elevating and enriching' these same concepts (346–8).[29] Robert Jenson illustrates this way of thinking in its more modern guise using the example of time: 'If God is the religious projection into infinity of our dissatisfaction with time, then the more complete the abstraction from our temporality, the more perfect the conception of God.'[30] This, too, must be avoided. For neither the negation of creaturely realities and concepts (apophaticism, the *via negationis*, in which 'we make our limits the object of an apotheosis' (304)), nor their intensification (kataphaticism, the *via eminentiae*), provides any sure pathway to the description of divine realities (347). While Barth is happy to make use of the 'specific though limited services' of these methods, they clearly cannot play a major role in a doctrine of the divine attributes.

Third and finally, the intrinsic order of divine revelation requires that, contrary to the *de facto* consensus of the tradition, a doctrine of the divine perfections must treat the perfections of the divine loving first, and only then the perfections of the divine freedom (348–50).[31] The reason is simple, and the reason is dogmatic:

> God's revelation is first and last a gospel, glad tidings, the word and deed of divine grace....Only through the power of the gospel does there arise for us a divinely binding and authoritative law, and a knowledge of our sin, and therefore of our creatureliness, our distance from God, and therefore the recognition of God's transcendence in himself and over against all that he is not. (349)

---

[29] Barth himself was once part of this very tradition. *The Göttingen Dogmatics: Instruction in the Christian Religion*, vol. 1, ed. Hannelotte Reiffen, trans. Geoffrey W. Bromiley (Grand Rapids: Eerdmans, 1991), 399-400.

[30] Jenson, *God After God*, 134.

[31] Barth had already come to this realization in his first dogmatics lectures. See Karl Barth, *Göttingen Dogmatics*, 394.

According to Barth, the problem with the traditional sequence (e.g. incommunicable then communicable, metaphysical then moral), is that in failing to follow the order of divine revelation it implies 'that God is first and properly the impersonal absolute, and only secondarily, inessentially and in his relationship *ad extra* the personal God of love with the attributes of wisdom, justice, mercy, etc.' (349).[32] Contrary to the position he maintained in his second *Romans*,[33] Barth now insists that revelation (logically) is first of all love, disclosure and gospel, and only then freedom, concealment and law. Therefore, 'a knowledge of [God's] being and attributes which is to be faithful to the intrinsic character of his revelation must adhere to this sequence' (349). Wary of committing the opposite error, Barth makes clear that this sequence reflects no devaluing of the perfections of the divine freedom. 'This order obtains even in the full reciprocity' between the two series of perfections (350).

With this, the stage is set for exposition of the individual perfections. Following the richness and order of God's self-revelation, and in the confidence that what is revealed is also the order and richness of God's own life, Barth will lay out these perfections in two series: those of the divine loving (§30) and those of the divine freedom (§31). A large part of Barth's objective in these sections will be to show how each particular perfection, as manifest in the economy of salvation, is also a perfection of God's own, immanent life. No abstract concept of divine simplicity, nor any nominalistic hesitation can be allowed either to obscure the clarity of God's self-unveiling in revelation or to restrain the full, unqualified affirmation that these perfections are truly those of God's very essence. On the other hand, God's self-veiling in revelation, and hence the strangeness of each perfection, must somehow also be indicated. In reality, each perfection is itself the essence, the entire essence, of God and thus identical with every other perfection. However, because human thinking can at best capture only partially the reality of any given perfection, only an obedient unfolding of an entire sequence of perfections can hope to grasp 'what are the upper and lower aspects, the right and the left, the contours' of God's being (336).

---

[32] Cf. Karl Rahner, 'Remarks on the Dogmatic Treatise "*De Trinitate*"', in *idem*, *Theological Investigations*, vol. 4, trans. Kevin Smyth (Baltimore: Helicon, 1966), 83–4. Polanus, at least, crafted his traditional sequence to reach its climactic resolution in God's personal, saving attributes. See Brouwer, 'The Conversation between Karl Barth and Amandus Polanus', 78–9. Presumably Barth would be less unhappy with a traditional sequence provided it were so constructed as to accent God's saving love.

[33] Chalamet, *Dialectical Theologians*, 226–7.

3

THE PERFECTIONS OF
THE DIVINE LOVING ($30)

An account of the divine perfections must begin with the perfections of the divine loving. While Barth often places his decisions regarding the form or structure of dogmatics under the proviso, '*methodus est arbitraria*' (352), with the attributes this is not the case.

> God is he who in his Son Jesus Christ loves all his children, in his children all men, and in men his whole creation.....Since our knowledge of God is grounded in his revelation in Jesus Christ and remains bound up with it, we cannot begin elsewhere. (351)

Since God himself eternally is and therefore in time reveals himself to be 'the One who loves in freedom', an account of God's being, if it is drawn from revelation, must begin with a description of God's loving. It must follow the logic of God's revelation, which is the logic of God's own life. This claim, introduced in §29, is an implicit critique of traditional accounts of the divine attributes which begin with what Barth calls the perfections of the divine freedom. One of Barth's aims is to correct this tradition, but not to over-correct it. He insists that the necessity of treating the perfections of the divine loving first must not be taken to imply that these perfections possess any intrinsic superiority, any deeper reality than the perfections of the divine freedom. 'God's freedom is in fact no less divine than his love' (351). The sequence is rather a matter of obedient following of 'the order of the divine life', and it involves keeping constantly in mind the perfections of the divine freedom while expounding those of the divine love, and vice versa (351–2).

While Barth has already explained that the divine perfections must be treated in two series, those of the divine loving and those of the divine freedom, we come to find here in §30 that this love-freedom dialectic is also replicated at a second level, in Barth's treatment of the attributes in pairs. Barth's exposition has been aptly described as 'a sort of Renaissance

49

building: each determinant of God's being grows out of and leads to all the others, and the whole is deliberately and perfectly symmetrical'.[1] Generally speaking, in §30 the first attribute of the pair indicates some aspect of the divine loving, while the second indicates some aspect of the divine freedom. The love-freedom dialectic is one of the most prominent and intricate features of Barth's account and can occasionally be found, most notably in the treatment of omnipotence, at even lower levels of exposition.

It is important to note that Barth's intention in structuring his exposition in this way is not merely aesthetic. The reason one must keep God's freedom in mind even when considering his love (and vice versa) is that 'There is no love of God in itself and as such, just as there is no freedom of God in itself and as such' (352). Rather, only as all the attributes are viewed together, as letters of the one divine Word, do they convey what Barth calls the 'divinity', that is, the particular essence of God as distinct from all created being (353). Lest we 'suppose that we ought to seek the divinity of the divine being much rather in the freedom of God' (351), Barth insists that God's freedom is never other than his freedom to love. The pairing of the attributes provides an inescapable reminder of this.

> The aim of this elaborate patterning is to secure from the beginning a point of critical importance about Christian belief in God, namely that God's lordship or absoluteness is to its very depths specified by a turning to humanity. Thus the formal structure of the account of the perfections of God expresses the same point made more substantively by the doctrines of election and covenant: God *is* God for us.[2]

Barth's intention with this 'elaborate patterning' is dogmatic: he wants to keep as securely as possible before his readers the full reality of the being of God by constantly pointing to yet other aspects of this being. As Barth once explained in commendation of Calvin's comparable approach to theology, theology must 'remain humble':

> There has to be constant reference back to a first and original thing that cannot be put in any one statement but that simply stands creatively and critically behind all statements. In other words, all statements can only point to an inexpressible center, and to do so they must turn into apparently opposing statements.[3]

---

[1] Robert W. Jenson, *God After God: The God of the Past and the God of the Future, Seen in the Work of Karl Barth* (Indianapolis: Bobbs-Merrill, 1969), 135.

[2] John Webster, *Barth's Ethics of Reconciliation* (Cambridge: Cambridge University Press, 1995), 46.

[3] Karl Barth, *The Theology of John Calvin*, trans. Geoffrey W. Bromiley (Grand Rapids: Eerdmans, 1995), 169.

No one statement will suffice as a description of God because God is inexpressibly richer in himself than any single affirmation can capture (cf. 335–6). The love-freedom dialectic is thus intended both to express and to safeguard dogmatic convictions about God himself. The apparently 'unavoidable systematisation is only a means to an end' – the end of identifying God (352–3; cf. 442); what beauty it possesses can only be a reflection of the beauty of its object (657). Thus the formal intricacy of Barth's account is no grounds for the charge of formalism,[4] for 'whether it is correct and satisfactory, a significant and serviceable attempt and suggestion, is a question which can be answered...only by the presentation itself, or its relation to the biblical witness to God' (442).

One potential ambiguity in this dialectic, at least as Barth explains it here at the beginning of §30, concerns the precise function of the second of each pair of attributes. It is clear that the first of each pair (grace, mercy and patience) is an attribute of the divine loving. It is not immediately clear, however, whether their counterparts (holiness, righteousness and wisdom) are also intended as attributes of the divine loving, since their function in the dialectic is to remind readers of the divine freedom. Are holiness, righteousness and wisdom attributes of the divine loving or of the divine freedom? In fact, they are both. Late in §30 lies buried the following unambiguous explanation:

> In God wisdom is related to patience as holiness to grace, and righteousness to mercy. All these ideas express and translate the love of God. But the second set of ideas – holiness, righteousness and wisdom – express with greater distinctness than the first (grace, mercy and patience) the fact that it is his free and therefore distinctively divine love. (422)

Thus, 'Both members within the three pairs are said to manifest the divine love, but the second member of each pairing manifests love in a way that points backwards toward the divine freedom.'[5] The converse holds for the perfections of the divine freedom: unity, constancy, and eternity each display purely an aspect of God's freedom; and omnipresence, omnipotence and glory, which are primarily perfections of the divine freedom, also, secondarily, indicate the divine loving (441).

---

[4] So Mitchell Grell, *Der ewig reiche Gott: Die Erkenntnis, Gewinnung und Bestimmung der Eigenschaften Gottes nach Isaak August Dorner, August Hermann Cremer und Karl Barth mit besonderer Berücksichtigung des Einflusses der Theologie Dorners und Cremers auf die Gotteslehre Barths* (Ph.D. diss., University of Tübingen, 1992), 277–8 n. 144.

[5] William Stacy Johnson, *The Mystery of God: Karl Barth and the Postmodern Foundations of Theology* (Louisville: Westminster John Knox, 1997), 52.

51

This point is missed by Colin Gunton, who sees in §30 'three perfections of the divine loving (grace, mercy and patience) which are dialectically paired with…perfections of the divine freedom (holiness, righteousness and wisdom)', and, conversely, in §31 three attributes of the divine freedom paired with three attributes of the divine love.[6] Admittedly, Barth's initial discussion is not without ambiguity.[7] But Barth does say here:

> Thus the divinity of his love consists and confirms itself in the fact that it is grace, mercy and patience and in that way and for that reason it is also holiness, righteousness and wisdom. These are the perfections of his love. (352)

Here all six attributes of §30 are named, and Barth says of all of them, 'These are the perfections of his love'. This merely recapitulates the thesis of §30: 'The divinity of the love of God consists and confirms itself in the fact that in himself and in all his works God is gracious, merciful and patient, and at the same time holy, righteous and wise' (351). All six perfections are announced as perfections of the love of God. Holiness, righteousness and wisdom must therefore be understood, once again, as primarily attributes of the divine loving which secondarily indicate the divine freedom. That this is the right reading of Barth's intentions becomes even clearer throughout §30 and from his corresponding description of the attributes of the divine freedom in §31.

This point is worth underscoring because it is partly on the basis of misunderstanding here that Gunton claims to find 'the key both to the structure of Barth's treatment of the attributes and to its chief weakness'.[8] According to Gunton, the second attribute of each pair indicates either strictly the divine freedom (in §30) or strictly the divine love (in §31). It is this which (in part) allows him to claim that the love-freedom dialectic of Barth's exposition is actually just a rehearsal in a different key of the Son-Father dialectic of unveiling and veiling introduced in *CD* I.

---

[6] Colin E. Gunton, *Act and Being: Towards a Theology of the Divine Attributes* (London: SCM, 2002), 99–100; cf. Colin E. Gunton, *The Barth Lectures*, ed. P. H. Brazier (London: T&T Clark, 2007), 103–7; likewise Charles Edward Raynal, III, *Karl Barth's Conception of the Perfections of God* (Ph.D. diss., Yale University, 1973), 101, and Cornelis van der Kooi, *As In A Mirror: John Calvin And Karl Barth On Knowing God: A Diptych*, trans. Donald Mader (Leiden: Brill, 2005), 335–6.

[7] The opening sentence of Barth's exposition of grace could be rendered, 'We begin our consideration of the divine love with the concept of grace, as it stands in direct confrontation by the freedom of God in the controlling and clarifying concept of holiness' (353 rev.; *KD* 396). By dropping the reference to the freedom of God, the English translators may have been attempting to ameliorate this ambiguity.

[8] Gunton, *Act and Being*, 102.

In sum, the polarity of love and freedom in the doctrine of the divine perfections corresponds to the Son-Father duality in the preceding volume [of the *Church Dogmatics*]. That it is in a twofold pattern that Barth takes up the theme of the divine perfections is therefore not an accident and suggests that the doctrine of the Spirit is not determinative for the treatment of the attributes.[9]

To begin with, countless passages in Barth belie Gunton's assumption that love and freedom can be neatly mapped onto the Son and the Father. A few examples should suffice:

We are concerned with the relationship of the love of the Father for the Son, with which 'thou hast loved me before the foundation of the world' (Jn 17:23–26), and above all of the love which is event in the triune God himself to all eternity...he is worthy of love, blessed in himself, because in his life as Father, Son and Holy Spirit, he is eternal love. (279)

Here love is identified, not with the Son, but both with the Father and with the triune God himself. Consider the following passage:

The freedom of God...has its truth and reality in the inner trinitarian life of the Father with the Son by the Holy Spirit. It is here, and especially in the divine mode as the Son who is the 'image of the invisible God' (Col 1:15),...that the divine freedom in its aspect of communion with the other...has its original truth. (317)

Here freedom is identified, not with the Father, but both with the Son (as the image of the Father) and with the triune God himself.[10] However, even granting Gunton's assumption that love equals Son and freedom equals Father, once it is recognised that the second attribute of each pair indicates *both* love and freedom, the facile identification of these attributes with *either* the Father *or* the Son appears even less convincing.

Before Barth begins his account of the divine grace, he raises one further introductory question: Why precisely these six attributes (352–3)? Here, method is in fact arbitrary. Barth's selection represents a fairly traditional and a fairly complete sample of the communicable attributes. Truthfulness and goodness are among the few traditional attributes which Barth does

---

[9] Gunton, *Act and Being*, 103.

[10] In more generous moments, Gunton acknowledges an 'assumed pneumatology' which materially determines Barth's work. See Colin E. Gunton, 'Introduction', in Karl Barth, *Protestant Theology in the Nineteenth Century: Its Background and history* (Grand Rapids: Eerdmans, 2002), xvii–xviii.

not treat here.[11] Had he done so, the love-freedom dialectic would have required the inclusion of two further attributes of the divine freedom in order to maintain symmetry. Though Barth claims no direct scriptural precedent for his selection and exclusion (352; cf. 441), he does cite (407), in support of his decision to identify God as 'gracious, merciful and patient [gnädig, barmherzig und geduldig]' (351), a series of biblical passages which either report or recall God's declaration of his name to Moses in Exodus 34:6: 'herr, herr, Gott, barmherzig und gnädig und geduldig'. Barth concedes nevertheless that his selection can have 'the basic character only of a trial and proposal' (352).

§30.1 Grace and Holiness

Barth begins his exposition of the perfections of the divine loving with grace as 'controlled and clarified' by holiness (353 rev.; KD 396).[12] Why grace and holiness together? Barth locates the 'common factor linking the biblical concepts of the grace and the holiness of God' in the way they characterise God's relation to the other: God's grace is his turning in goodwill toward the other; God's holiness is his maintaining his own will and identity in doing so

---

[11] See, however, Barth's brief discussion of God's triune truthfulness, CD II/1, 68–9. Barth's discussion of the divine glory (CD II/1, 640–77) also makes mention of the divine truthfulness, and the connection between glory and truth is further elaborated in CD IV/3.1, §70.1, 'The True Witness' (368–434). Five of the six perfections of the divine loving are mentioned together in Heinrich Heppe, Reformed Dogmatics, ed. Ernst Bizer, trans. G. T. Thomson (1857; reprint Grand Rapids: Baker, 1978), §5.32 (95–7).

[12] The English translation of the opening paragraphs Barth's exposition of the divine grace is problematic at several points (CD II/1, 353; KD 396–7). First, the rendition of erläuternden as 'purified' can wrongly suggest a partly oppositional rather than entirely complementary relationship between the divine grace and the divine holiness. Second, das Sein und Sichverhalten Gottes is twice rendered as God's 'distinctive' or 'inner' 'mode of being' (rather than, e.g. 'God's being and conduct'). To readers familiar with the parallel rendering of Barth's well-known Seinsweise, grace as a 'mode of being' can sound like a fourth hypostasis. Third, in the passages of Scripture which Barth quotes, the English three times renders as 'mercy' what in German is a form of Gnade. Not a single instance of these is a matter of loyalty to the Authorised Version, with the possible exception of Psalm 89:2. As, however, the English also incorrectly follows the German versification ('89:3'), it would seem doubtful that the translators relied on the AV for this verse. The effect is disastrous for those wondering what possible relevance these 'mercy' passages have for a discussion of God's grace. Note also the rendition here of Friedens as 'order' (despite AV 'peace') in the allusion to 1 Cor 14:33 (353; KD 396); and of Gnade as, once again, 'mercy' (with the AV) in the quotation from Ps 103 (356; KD 400). II/1 may well be 'one of the worst translated' volumes of the Church Dogmatics; see Robert W. Jenson, Alpha and Omega: A Study in the Theology of Karl Barth (1963; reprint Eugene: Wipf and Stock, 2002), 68–9 n. 1.

(360). Both also have particular reference to God's transcendence over the creature, particularly the sinful creature.

> To say grace is to say the forgiveness of sins; to say holiness, judgement upon sins. But since both reflect the love of God, how can there be the one without the other, forgiveness without judgement or judgement without forgiveness? (360)

Thus, God's grace overcomes (353) and his holiness annihilates (359) opposition.

In placing grace first, not only of its pair but of the entire sequence of perfections, Barth's determination to avoid the nominalising tendency of the tradition meets one of its greatest challenges.[13] The orthodox Christian tradition at least in the West has never really doubted the full, essential divine reality of God's holiness, righteousness and wisdom, or of any of the perfections of the divine freedom. It is only attributes like grace, mercy and, occasionally, patience which have traditionally suffered from nominalising qualification, and of these grace plays arguably the most central dogmatic role. Thus Calvin, for example, says that grace, mercy and patience (Ex. 34:6) describe God 'not as he is in himself, but as he is toward us' (328).[14] A doctrine of the attributes which is not to prove 'dangerous and ultimately fatal to faith' (325) must leave no room for doubt that God himself is fully, essentially, and eternally gracious.

Grace

Given, then, this strategic role accorded grace in Barth's exposition of the perfections, it is indeed odd that, of all the perfections, grace should receive the briefest treatment. It amounts to barely five pages, while 85 pages are devoted to omnipotence (522–607). Barth's account of the divine grace does spill over into the ensuing expositions of both holiness and mercy,[15] but this does little to augment the few brusque comments officially devoted to it. At one level, this might be expected, since the first of Barth's iterative developments of any given theme is typically the shortest. A hint of explanation may

---

[13] It is certainly not the case that Barth places grace first because it is somehow a privileged perfection, more basic than the others, as Cross suggests. See Terry L. Cross, *Dialectic in Karl Barth's Doctrine of God* (New York: Peter Lang, 2001), 185, 187.

[14] John Calvin, *The Institutes of the Christian Religion*, 2 vols., ed. John T. McNeill, trans. Ford Lewis Battles, Library of Christian Classics (Philadelphia: Westminster, 1960), 1.10.2 (1.97). Barth knows, of course, that the 'nominalistic…tendency' (328) he sees in this line of Calvin is not Calvin's intent, and that Calvin in the same passage affirms that God's attributes are those of his essence (323). Cf. Benjamin B. Warfield, 'Calvin's Doctrine of God', *The Princeton Theological Review* 7 (1909): 400–3.

[15] Cf. *CD* IV/1, §58.1, 'The Grace of God in Jesus Christ' (79–92); *CD* IV/3.1, 173–80.

also be found in the fact that an early survey of his theology could aptly (despite Barth's subsequent objections) describe the whole as *The Triumph of Grace*.[16] If 'The archetypal form of God's gift of grace lies in the incarnation of his Word, the unity of God and man in Jesus Christ' (354), then a full exposition of grace can hardly avoid drawing in at least the major themes of election (*Gnadenwahl*) and Christology. Barth simply has too much to say on the matter, and so he says very little. Wary of expanding his exposition out of proportion, Barth errs on the side of brevity. The sub-section is hurried, but nonetheless bold and resolute in affirming that God's grace to us is also a perfection of the divine life itself. This affirmation represents something of a Pyrrhic victory, however, because the way in which Barth explains it verges unnecessarily on the nominalism he so decisively rejected in §29.

According to Barth, God's grace, like God's love (275–84), is free, self-grounded, unconditioned by its object. God 'is gracious in himself and therefore gives himself to be known as gracious and acts graciously' (353).[17] As attested in Scripture, 'Grace denotes, comprehensively, the manner in which God, in his essential being, turns towards us' (353–4). Grace, as the very being of God and as supremely enacted and exemplified in the incarnation, involves 'no third mediating element between God and man': God's grace is 'God himself...offering *himself* to fellowship with the other' (354).[18] All of this might have been said of God's love.

Beyond this, however, in further specification of the divine love, grace shows itself also in the fact that it overcomes opposition.

> Grace is the being and conduct of God, which, by his act of seeking and creating fellowship, is shown to be determined by his own free inclination, goodwill and favour, unconditioned by any merit or claim in its object, but also unhindered by any unworthiness or opposition in the latter – able, on the contrary, to overcome all unworthiness and opposition. (353 rev.; *KD* 396–7)

Grace is defined here as the *capacity* to overcome opposition. Insofar as grace includes merely the capacity to overcome opposition, and is not also the active overcoming of opposition, there can be no objection to understanding grace as a perfection of God's own life. Barth explains further that

---

[16] G. C. Berkouwer, *The Triumph of Grace in the Theology of Karl Barth: A Scriptural Examination and Assessment*, trans. Harry R. Boer (London: Paternoster, 1956); cf. Wilfried Härle, *Sein und Gnade: Die Ontologie in Karl Barths Kirchlicher Dogmatik* (Berlin: de Gruyter, 1975), 36.

[17] Härle, *Sein und Gnade*, 37.

[18] On Barth's rejection here of the Roman Catholic view of grace, see further *CD* IV/1, 84–8. Grell (*Der ewig reiche Gott*, 292) notes the parallel here to Barth's description of righteousness (e.g. *CD* II/1, 386, 390–1): It is Christ himself who is our righteousness, not some third thing between God and man.

grace is always also an act of condescension. 'The fact that God is gracious means that he condescends, he, the only One who is really in a position to condescend, because he alone is truly transcendent, and stands on an equality with nothing outside himself' (354). This obviously raises the question of how such grace could obtain in God's own life, since presumably there is neither opposition nor condescension nor inequality between Father, Son and Spirit.

A hint at an answer comes in Barth's comment that God's 'inmost essence in grace is that he wills not to remain' merely transcendent over his creatures (354 rev.; *KD* 398). This reference to God's creatures and then to God's 'gracious election' (355) may suggest that the opposition, condescension and inequality Barth has in mind are those between God and creatures, not anything obtaining in the divine life itself. But while it might be tempting to understand what Barth says here as applying to God 'not as he is in himself, but as he is toward us', this can hardly be his intention. Everything Barth has said so far about God's being-in-act and about God's self-revelation would appear to have ruled out any such separation between God *in se* and *pro nobis*.

This apparent tension between Barth's description of grace as manifest to us and as a perfection of the divine life is only heightened when Barth goes on to elaborate on capacity of grace to overcome opposition (355–6). Here it becomes apparent that the condescension inherent in grace is not merely an ontological, but also a moral condescension. 'The biblical conception of grace involves further that the counterpart which receives it from God is not only not worthy of it but utterly unworthy of it, that God is gracious to sinners' (355). Particularly when Barth adds that grace 'presupposes…opposition', it would appear once again that he is describing grace strictly as it is manifest in the economy. But this simply cannot be the case. 'No, God himself is gracious, and grace itself is properly and essentially divine' (356 rev.; *KD* 400). Barth could hardly be clearer in affirming that 'it is in this way, graciously, that God not only *acts* outwardly towards his creature, but *is* in himself from eternity to eternity' (357) – threatening indeed 'to collapse the orders of time and eternity rather than relating them positively'.[19]

It is only in the final paragraph of his exposition that Barth addresses this tension explicitly:

> One might object that in [God's] own being there cannot be a creature standing over against him, still less any opposition from this other, and therefore that there cannot take place any special turning, or condescension, or overcoming of the resistance of the other, and consequently that there cannot be any scope for grace. Our reply is that there is not in fact any scope for the form which grace takes in its

---

[19] Gunton, *Act and Being*, 98 n. 6.

manifestations to us. The form in which grace exists in God himself and is actual as God is in point of fact hidden from us and incomprehensible to us. (357)

Astounding. Grace involves both moral condescension as well as the overcoming of resistance, but neither of these has any place in God's immanent life (358). How then is grace a divine perfection? Barth explicitly affirms that grace marks the immanent life of God. Strictly speaking, therefore, he avoids nominalism. In order to secure this critical affirmation, however, Barth is forced to strip 'immanent' grace of everything that might correspond to God's gracious action in the economy. Yes, grace truly is a perfection of the divine essence. But it exists 'in a form which is concealed from us and incomprehensible to us' (357). This leaves the character of grace in the divine life, if not disconnected, then at least so incomprehensibly and mysteriously connected to God's grace to us, that a *de facto* nominalism inevitably follows. God's grace only acquires 'vividness' in relation to us (324), whereas his 'immanent' grace is left an entirely empty concept.

Barth offers no explanation of how God's immanent and economic grace correspond. How then can it be said that God's grace is revealed? How is the grace of God's being in the grace of his act? How is God the Lord of this particular glory? Once again: 'It is dangerous and ultimately fatal to faith in God if God is not the Lord of glory, if it is not guaranteed to us that in spite of the analogical nature of the language in which it all has to be expressed God is actually and unreservedly as we encounter in his revelation' (325). Without some concrete indication of the character of grace in God himself, it is precisely such a guarantee which Barth's account of grace does not supply.

One way in which Barth might have supplied such a guarantee is suggested by his opening definition of grace as the *capacity* to overcome opposition (353). Had Barth not gone on to insist that this capacity, this readiness to overcome opposition, is also somehow an active overcoming, he would have been able to identify an aspect of the divine life which corresponds to grace as revealed. The problem, of course, is the contingency of both creation and sin. And for divine perfections to be God's own, essential perfections, they 'cannot be resolved into a description of his relationship to his creation. All that God is in his relationship to his creation...is simply an outward manifestation and realisation of what he is previously in himself apart from this relationship' (462). Therefore, where a divine perfection is defined in terms of the created order or in terms of the creature's sin – as Barth has done with grace – one of two things would appear to follow. Either this perfection takes a form in the divine life which is sufficiently similar to the form it takes in revelation that creation and sin, or at the very least some reference to them, are drawn into the divine essence. Barth clearly wants to avoid this. He later objects to Schleiermacher's doctrine of sin and grace: 'Can a grace which lives by its opposition to sin, which is referred and related to it, be real grace?'[20] Or this perfection takes a form in the divine life which is so different from the form it takes in revelation as to bear no discernable relationship to it. With respect to grace, Barth opts for the latter.

His handling of other attributes, however, suggests that a third option (grace as the capacity or readiness to overcome opposition) was open to him. As an example of a perfection closely but not strictly related to the created order, take the divine eternity. Though 'there is nothing of what we call time' in the divine eternity, eternity constitutes the 'possibility, the potentiality of time' and 'absolute readiness for it' (615, 617–18). Presumably, if the temporality of God's self-revelation in Jesus Christ requires not the actuality of time in the divine life, but only the readiness for it, surely the graciousness of God's self-revelation in Jesus Christ requires as a sufficient basis not the active overcoming of resistance in the divine life but only the readiness to do so – a readiness from which it can 'become what in our experience we know it to be' (358).[21] As an example of a perfection closely but not strictly related to sin, take the divine holiness. While God's holiness is indeed 'the flame of his love' which is manifest in threats against sin and in wrath and punishment upon sin (367), it is also that by which God maintains his own will and the purity of the triune life (359, 368). Because holiness is not defined strictly with respect to sin, there can be holiness as holiness in the divine life, even though such immanent holiness does not include that active opposition to sin, which is so prevalent a feature of its manifestation towards us. Once again, grace could presumably be handled similarly.[22]

This 'third option' solution to the problem of grace, however, is not without problems of its own. If grace is merely an antecedent readiness to overcome opposition (should it arise), what is to distinguish such readiness from love itself? To affirm that God is gracious would not seem to add anything to the affirmation that God is loving. Without an active overcoming of opposition, but merely the potential for it, there is nothing – at least here in II/1 – to distinguish grace, 'in which God turns his inclination, goodwill and favour towards another' (360), from the love in which God seeks and creates fellowship with another.[23]

---

[20] *CD* IV/1, 377.

[21] Cf. *CD* II/1, 462–3, Barth's similar comments on the relation between the divine omnipresence and the created order.

[22] Another possible parallel may be found in §26.1, Barth's discussion of 'The Readiness of God' to be known by man (*CD* II/1, 63–128). Human knowledge of God (God's secondary objectivity) is not actual in God's knowledge of himself (his primary objectivity), but is grounded in it and made actual only by grace (*CD* II/1, 69).

[23] As will be briefly indicated in the final chapter, interesting things have happened to Barth's handling of the perfections by the time he sits down to write *CD* IV. In *CD* IV/1, for example, Barth develops his concept of grace further in light of the resurrection. The resurrection, according to Barth, shows Christ as 'a pure object and recipient of the

This tension in Barth's thought on grace finds some relief in his doctrine of election, where Barth associates grace not with the divine essence understood apart from election, as seems to be the case here in II/1, but with God as he has determined himself to be in Jesus Christ.[24] Thus, it is grace which is 'the beginning of all the ways and works of God' *ad extra*.[25] As 'a spontaneous *opus internum ad extra* of the trinitarian God', election always has 'the character of grace'.[26] It is this qualification of grace as contingent not upon human sin, but upon divine election, which is lacking in Barth's account of grace as a perfection of the divine life itself.[27] Had Barth identified grace as a consequence of election, he could have avoided drawing any reference to sin up into the divine life, while at the same time securing the inalienable graciousness of God's being. In light of Barth's doctrine of election in II/2 and of the prominence of the concept of covenant in the ensuing discussion of holiness here in II/1, this absence of recourse to the doctrine of election is indeed perplexing. Perhaps this is some indication that, though Barth had already in 1936 expressed the basic insights into the doctrine of election which he would develop in *CD* II/2, he was, in the course of preparing II/1, still very much in the process of 'unfolding the consequences of what he had known theoretically since long before'.[28]

God's grace, then, is that condescension in which he acts to overcome the sinful resistance of the creature. This grace, moreover, is the grace of the divine life itself – an affirmation which is perhaps Barth's primary goal in

---

grace of God', and this is 'not merely in human history but first and foremost in God himself' (*CD* IV/1, 304). Just as 'in the relationship of the Son to the Father ... there is a pure obedience, subordination and subjection, so too in the relationship of the Father to the Son ... there is a free and pure grace which as such can only be received, and the historical fulfilment of which is the resurrection of Jesus Christ' (*CD* IV/1, 304). Here grace is understood in terms of the Father's action toward the subordinate and receptive Son, both in eternity and as manifest in the resurrection. This is a concrete indication of the reality of grace in God himself well beyond what appears in II/1. On the role of the Spirit in God's eternal and historical grace, see *CD* IV/2, 338–53, esp. 346.

[24] Van der Kooi, *As in a Mirror*, 338.

[25] *CD* II/2, 3.

[26] *CD* II/2, 25.

[27] Härle, *Sein und Gnade*, 36–46, is right to appeal to Barth's doctrine of election to explain how Barth might ultimately speak appropriately of grace within the divine life itself; he is wrong to imply that the logic of election is sufficiently operative in Barth's account of grace to overcome its problematic disjunction between God's grace *ad intra* and *ad extra*.

[28] Christophe Chalamet, *Dialectical Theologians: Wilhelm Herrmann, Karl Barth and Rudolf Bultmann* (Zürich: Theologischer Verlag Zürich, 2005), 245. Cf. Bruce L. McCormack, *Karl Barth's Critically Realistic Dialectical Theology: Its Genesis and Development 1909–1936* (New York: Oxford University Press, 1995), 455–62; *idem*, 'Seek God where he may be found: a response to Edwin Chr. van Driel', *Scottish Journal of Theology* 60.1 (2007): 63–4.

this exposition. Barth affirms unequivocally that grace is not merely a way in which God behaves in the economy but a divine perfection, a reality in the divine life itself. Barth also insists, however, that this 'immanent' divine grace involves neither the condescension nor the encounter with opposition which characterise grace in the economy. God's 'immanent' grace remains an empty concept, or is dissolved into the concept of love, and so its relation to grace as revealed in the economy cannot be specified. Because Barth makes no appeal either to the doctrine of election or even to something like the idea of a readiness (potential) in God to be gracious, Barth's central affirmation of the reality of grace within the triune life is compromised. Grace, as Barth has defined it here, still stands under the threatening shadow of nominalism.

Holiness

With grace Barth pairs the divine holiness. While the sub-section on holiness receives roughly twice the space accorded to grace, a fair amount of this space is devoted to clarifying further both grace itself and its relation to holiness. Because what holds for the relation between grace and holiness holds *mutatis mutandis* for every subsequent pair of perfections, Barth explains in some detail here what later he will either briefly note or simply assume.[29] He begins his exposition of the divine holiness with something of a riddle:

> In grace, we have characterised God himself, the one God in all his fulness. We are not wrong, we do not overlook or neglect anything, if we affirm that his love and therefore his whole being, in all the heights and depths of the Godhead, is simply grace. (358)

If the fulness of the Godhead is wholly and simply grace, why set alongside an exposition of this divine grace an exposition of another perfection – an exposition, moreover, which is not intended 'either to qualify or to expand what is denoted by the concept of grace' (358)? The solution to this riddle hinges on the distinction between grace as itself the divine essence and grace as one of the concepts by which we attempt to understand the divine essence.

> In our heart and on our lips, in our mode of knowledge, this thing grace is in no sense so fully and unambiguously clear, or above all so rich and deep, as it is in the truth of God which by this concept we apprehend – yet apprehend as we men apprehend God by faith, i.e., in such a way that our knowledge must needs expand and grow and increase. For this reason the idea of grace, not in itself, not in God, but

[29] Cf. Cross, *Dialectic*, 186.

in our mode of knowledge, requires qualification and expansion. Our notion of grace is not able to grasp in its clarity and richness all that grace is in God himself. (358)

Therefore, Barth goes on to describe the divine holiness, not by way of adding anything to what grace itself is, that is, the divine essence, but adding much to the *concept* of grace just expounded. In Barth's usage, the term 'grace' can refer either to the divine essence or to our human concept of grace. The same applies to all of the terms by which Barth designates divine perfections, and this makes interpretative demands of a reader.[30] When Barth says of the divine unity, for example, 'All the perfections of God's freedom can be summed up by saying that God is One' (442), he could be easily misread as claiming that the concept of divine unity holds a privileged rank among the other divine perfections. But it is not the *concept* of the divine unity to which Barth refers in this instance, but the divine unity itself, and therefore the very essence of God. Only God's essence could in any way be said to sum up (our concepts of) the other perfections.

Not only, then, is the divine loving a gracious loving, but it is also a holy loving. As holy, it is characterised by the fact that God, as he seeks and creates fellowship, is always the Lord. He therefore distinguishes and maintains his own will as against every other will. He condemns, excludes and annihilates all contradiction and resistance to it. (359)

The first thing to note about this definition is its context. Holiness characterises God 'as he seeks and creates fellowship'. As a perfection of the divine loving, holiness is a 'relational' perfection.[31] It is not, as in Rudolf Otto's immensely popular conception,[32] primarily a matter of God's exaltation over and separation from his people (360), but of God as he 'is and acts for Israel' (361). Positively, God's holiness is that lordship by which he maintains his own will and 'gives it validity and actuality' (359). Negatively, it is that same lordship by which he annihilates whatever resists his will. In both aspects it is directed toward fellowship with the creature.[33] Barth then notes a selection of Protestant-orthodox definitions of God's holiness as that

---

[30] Meinrad Benz faults this as a lack of clarity in Barth's exposition: review of *Die kirchliche Dogmatik, Die Lehre von Gott*, by Karl Barth, *Divus Thomas: Jahrbuch für Philosophie und spekulative Theologie* 3.21 (1943): 220.

[31] John Webster, *Holiness* (Grand Rapids: Eerdmans, 2003), 43–8.

[32] Cf. CD I/1, 135.

[33] John Webster, 'Holiness and Love', in *idem, Confessing God: Essays in Christian Dogmatics II* (London: T&T Clark, 2005), 124–5.

purity or opposition to evil which is expressed in the hatred and punishment of human sin. Anticipating a point he will develop in his discussion of the divine righteousness, Barth faults these definitions – acceptable as far as they go – for not also indicating how the holiness of God is at the same time a *gracious* holiness, and thus how God's judgement upon sins is also attended by the forgiveness of these sins (360). 'From the outset…the problem is to show…that God as gracious is also holy, and again that as holy he is also gracious' (359). Without such an indication, the unity of the divine perfections is compromised.

It is Barth's own attempt to safeguard this unity which gives rise to an initially confusing feature of his exposition. He defines grace and holiness in ways that seem to overlap. While it is hardly responsible to claim that grace and holiness are 'simply identical' for Barth,[34] neither is it quite clear precisely where grace ends and holiness begins. Grace is said to be 'able…to overcome' resistance 'by opposing and breaking [it] down' (353, 361), while holiness 'condemns, excludes and annihilates' resistance (359). Exactly how these two differ is not obvious. Pokrifka-Joe offers the following helpful explanation:

> When Barth articulates various divine perfections, each perfection has a range of meaning marked by a clear centre that makes it distinct from other perfections, but with 'fuzzy' or permeable boundaries between it and the concepts of other divine perfections.…These perfections exhibit a conceptual inter-penetration made possible by a legitimate kind of conceptual vagueness. Precise and sharply differentiated concepts have the advantage of clarity, but they also lack the flexibility and conceptual inter-connectedness (a kind of coherence) that are made possible by more vague or ambiguous terms.[35]

The 'fuzzy' boundaries of the concepts with which Barth attempts to indicate the reality of the divine life are therefore at least partially deliberate.[36] Certainly Barth could have tightened his definitions and invested them with a higher degree of clarity without compromising their serviceability or mutual coherence. But it is only when Barth's concepts become objects

---

[34] Michael S. Horton, *Lord and Servant: A Covenant Christology* (Louisville: Westminster John Knox, 2005), 59; cf. 78.

[35] Todd Pokrifka-Joe, *Redescribing God: The Roles of Scripture, Tradition, and Reason in Karl Barth's Doctrines of Divine Unity, Constancy, and Eternity* (Ph.D. diss., University of St. Andrews, 2002), 159.

[36] As elsewhere, so here the English translation occasionally makes its own contribution to the fuzziness of Barth's concepts. Grace is said to be 'able…to overcome [*überwinden*]' resistance (*CD* II/1, 353; *KD* 397). Holiness, too, is said to be that which 'overcomes [*widerlegt*]' resistance, where 'refutes' might have preserved more of the distinction (*CD* II/1, 360; *KD* 404).

of independent interest, and when the divine reality recedes from view, that this fuzziness can be regarded as an outright fault of his exposition rather than a merit.

God's holiness, then, does indeed express itself in judgement upon sin. Yet Barth maintains that this judgement is always a gracious, and thus an electing and redeeming, judgement. Not only is this the case in God's dealings with Israel. 'The same applies precisely to the most important use of the notion [of holiness] in the New Testament', namely, the sanctification of the church and its members by the gift of the Holy Spirit (361).

> To be sure, in this case too, and especially, 'holy' means separate, that which confronts, arousing awe and the sense of obligation. But it clearly means primarily and fundamentally that which singles out, blesses, helps and restores, and only in this positive connexion does it have that other significance. (361)

It is of crucial importance to grasp that, between this 'primary' and 'other' significance of the divine holiness – or between God's exercise of grace and his exercise of holiness, or for that matter between any of the divine perfections whatsoever – no tension exists. On Barth's account, to admit to such a tension would be to fall back into the error of the Protestant scholastics (and others), compromising the unity of the divine perfections. Thus, it is not as if God, in his holiness, would destroy the sinful resistance of his creature but, because he is also gracious, decides to overlook this resistance. On the contrary, God's grace is manifest in his holy destruction of sinful resistance.

This aspect of Barth's conception of the unity of the divine perfections raises the question whether God's holy judgement could ever be ordered toward anything other than a gracious redemption. Could the gracious God ever punish sin non-redemptively, finally, eternally? While this question will be pursued in connection with Barth's discussion of the divine mercy, it can be stated here that Barth's answer seems to be yes. According to Barth, the unbeliever remains 'without repentance and without knowledge, and therefore without help and without hope', and so will 'fall an eternal victim to judgement' (362).

Within the covenant, however, God's wrath is never a 'sheer abstract opposition', as even Luther occasionally acknowledged, but is always an expression of his 'gracious, beneficent and saving will towards us' (362–3). It is therefore in God's very opposition to us that we find 'our ground of confidence and hope' (362). God's holiness, then, is 'the unity of his judgement with his grace': 'God is holy because his grace judges and his judgement is gracious' (363). Despite the 'too fashionable exegesis' of Ritschl on this matter, 'the unity of the Old and New Testament is at this point unmistakable and indisputable' (363–7): 'When we look at Jesus Christ we cannot fail to see how the apparently varied threads in the Old Testament witness of God all intertwine, his election and his wrath, his forgiveness of sins and his commandments, his graciousness and his holiness; and that according to the Old Testament witness the Lord who deals with Israel is the one God in all this diversity' (367).

This diversity of God's holy dealings with his people has, moreover, an eternal ground, which Barth addresses in a brief, final paragraph:

> For again we must add that God not only acts as the Holy One, but that as he acts he is, from everlasting to everlasting. In him, of course, there is no sin which he has first to resist. But in him there is more. There is the purity,...the purity of the life of the Father, Son and Holy Spirit, [which] eternally reacts against it, resisting and judging it in its encounter with it, but in so doing receiving and adopting it, and thus entering into the fellowship with it which redeems it. (368)

As in his account of grace, Barth defines holiness with respect to sin. Both God's grace and his holiness 'characterise and distinguish his love and therefore himself in his action in the covenant' (360). However, whereas Barth gives no indication what grace might look like within the divine life and thus apart from sin, with holiness Barth points explicitly to the 'purity' of Father, Son and Spirit. Barth also hints at one point that holiness in the divine life might also be a matter of the perfecting of fellowship, something akin to God's sanctification of his people: 'As we have already indicated, he is the Holy Spirit, who epitomises all perfected fellowship between God and man, and who according to 1 Cor 2:10 is also the epitome of the "deep things" of God' (364).[37] Barth's explanation of God's 'immanent' holiness is not an empty concept like his explanation of God's 'immanent' grace. While Barth is clear that there is no sin in God, he also describes God's holiness as eternally reacting against sin – and not just reacting against it, but also eternally receiving, adopting and entering into fellowship with the sinful creature. Since neither sin nor the creature have any place in the divine essence, if either of these is to have an 'eternal' aspect, Barth's reference must be to election, to God's being and action 'in the covenant' (360). God's eternal fellowship or covenant with the reconciled creature can only be consequent upon or 'implicated in the marvellous work of his election and favour' (362).

God's holiness, then, is that purity of God in which, as he seeks and creates fellowship, he also maintains his own will in itself and against anything that opposes it. In its encounter with opposition, God's holiness shows itself to

---

[37] Cf. CD I/1, 480: Barth clearly affirms the role of the Spirit in the fellowship between Father and Son as well as between God and man, but he does not explicitly connect this with holiness. Cf. CD IV/1, 647–8; CD IV/2, 322–3, 331, 513; ChrL, 256; Webster, Holiness, 41.

be also a gracious holiness, a holiness expressed in his covenant fellowship with his people, in his removing their opposition to him, and in his sanctifying them for himself.

§30.2 *Mercy and Righteousness*

To the divine grace and holiness Barth now adds a second pair of attributes, the divine mercy and righteousness. This turning to a second pair of perfections of the divine loving does not mean, Barth insists, that everything necessary has already been said about the first pair. Rather, mercy and righteousness together actually constitute 'a further analysis and elucidation' of grace and holiness (368). In saying this, Barth is playing once again on the distinction between a given perfection as itself the divine essence and as a concept by which we indicate the divine essence. Insofar as mercy and righteousness are identical with the divine essence, they merely repeat what was already said of the divine grace and holiness. Insofar as mercy and righteousness function as concepts in our understanding, they do, in fact, coherently develop what was said of grace and holiness and, in so doing, give us new insight into God's identity.

> In this one thing, in God himself, in the plenitude of his being, there is no division and therefore no mutual qualification and augmentation of his attributes. But this does apply to the concepts by which we are allowed to recognise God on the basis of his revelation and in the truth of his unity and plenitude. (375)

This accumulating 'plenitude' of concepts, moreover, is not without basis in the unity of the divine life. 'In God himself, and therefore also for us, there is a fulness of the divine perfections, not in poverty, but in richness, and therefore continually different, and to be viewed and conceived in its development' (368). This is the iterative and expanding nature of the knowledge of God which is bound to the biblical witness: it requires that 'we now learn and repeat that the one thing which God is, is also mercy and righteousness' (369). This repetition, moreover, must proceed 'in the order determined by the object, by the revelation of God in Jesus Christ', according to which 'the mercy of God must precede his righteousness' (376).

As with grace and holiness, Barth pairs mercy and righteousness because of their frequent association in Scripture and their respective implications for God's confrontation with the sinful creature. As in his mercy God shares 'the distress of another' and wills 'to engage himself for the removal of this distress' (369 rev.; *KD* 415), so in his righteousness God 'does that which is worthy of himself' and 'asserts his worth' even as he shows mercy (376–7). Mercy and righteousness are also similar in their indication of an affective dimension in God's response to sin: a merciful pity and compassion on the one hand (370–1), and a righteous wrath and anger on the other (394).

Mercy

Barth's discussion of the divine mercy is almost as short as that of grace, but like the latter spills over into that of its counterpart, righteousness. As with grace, the same vagueness plagues Barth's explanation of the form of mercy within the divine life itself.[38] His language here, however, is not as strict in pressing God's sharing in the distress of another up into the divine essence, thus allowing, and perhaps even suggesting, that the merciful encounter between the divine essence and creaturely distress is to be understood as the result of God's decree of election.

Barth begins by noting the development of *misericordia* and *Barmherzigkeit* from the respective words for 'heart'. This is not an argument from etymology, but (for the moment) merely a heuristic device for indicating that, in dealing with the concept of mercy, 'we are not merely in the proximity but in fact at the very centre of the concept of divine love and its specific determination as grace' (369). For while many a love may flourish even in the absence of grace and mercy, the uniqueness, the divinity of the love of God consists (in part) in the fact that it is also always a gracious and a merciful love. God's mercy in fact flows from his grace. 'The free inclination of God to his creature, denoted in the biblical witness by grace, takes place under the presupposition that the creature is in distress and that God's intention is to espouse his cause and to grant him assistance in his extremity' (369). This is Barth's opening definition of the divine mercy: it is that by which God relieves the distress of his creature.

> The mercy of God is his sharing the distress of another, a sharing which lies in his nature and constitutes his being and action. It is, therefore, his will, which again lies in his nature and constitutes his being and action, to engage himself for the removal of this distress. (369 rev.; *KD* 415)

The thrust of this opening definition is clearly to emphasise the reality of mercy in the divine life itself. God's mercy 'lies in his nature and constitutes his being and action'. In light of Barth's account of grace, what is remarkable about this definition is that it just as clearly locates the reality of mercy in the divine will, a move which, on its own, might suggest that mercy is not a matter of what God is in himself, but merely as he is toward us. Of course, this move does not stand on its own, and Barth's emphasis

---

[38] Bertrand de Margerie, *Les Perfections du Dieu de Jésus-Christ* (Paris: Cerf, 1981), 256.

is quite the contrary: mercy has reality in the divine life itself. Moreover, God's 'will...to engage himself for the removal of this distress' is itself the decree of election. Barth does not explicitly identify God's will with election in this instance, though he does clearly frame his discussion in terms of 'the Creator's will for fellowship with his creature' (369). Nor does Barth draw out the implication that the divine mercy, as characterising the divine life itself, should be conceived as consequent upon election.[39] However, by drawing in the logic of election, of God's self-determination in Jesus Christ, Barth gives warrant for his emphasis on the reality of mercy in the divine life. Election indicates the depth of God's 'will...to engage himself' and thus secures the contingent character of the divine mercy *ad intra* from drifting off into an empty nominalism.

There is, of course, a more substantive point underlying Barth's mention of the etymology of the Latin and German words for mercy. Mercy also expresses the fact that, when God acts to remove the distress of the creature, this is not merely the 'mathematical or mechanical' execution of a task but the genuine expression of 'the movement of the heart of God' (370). Mercy expresses that 'affective aspect of love' so prominent in Scripture, one of the terms which the AV on occasion memorably renders 'bowels' (371).

Barth briefly notes two implications of this affective character of the divine mercy. First, a merciful God cannot be impersonal (cf. 267–8, 271–2, 284–97). The concept of the personality of God is absolutely necessary if justice is to be done to Scripture's description of the relation between the *misericordia Dei* and 'the "miserable" creature' (370).[40] Second, neither is God impassible – not, at least, in the way the tradition has occasionally maintained. It is only to be expected that Schleiermacher, who held an impersonal view of God, also thought it 'impossible to ascribe to God a state of feeling specially awakened by the suffering of others' and so denied

---

[39] The English translation certainly does (*CD* II/1, 369; *KD* 415). God's 'sharing [*Beteiligung*]' the distress of another becomes merely a 'readiness to share in sympathy', making this sharing potential rather than actual. Likewise, God's mercy no longer 'lies in [*liegender*]' and 'constitutes [*konstituierende*]' the divine nature but merely 'springs from' and 'stamps' it. Later, the divine mercy as '*Gottes in seinem Wesen liegende aktive Beteiligung am Elend eines Anderen*' becomes 'God's effectual participation in the misery of another, a participation prompted by his inmost being' (*CD* II/1, 377; *KD* 423–4). Once again, this opens up a certain logical distance between God's essence and God's mercy, a conceptual space which the decree of election may be understood to occupy. While it will be argued that this is in fact how Barth's conception of mercy in the divine life must be understood, his language is not so unambiguous as the English translation would suggest.

[40] One of the central contentions of Raynal's thesis is that Barth's concept of divine personhood is actually incompatible with realistic predication of attributes to God. Reviewing Barth's present argument, Raynal stubbornly insists that 'Barth does not here say that God is a person'! See Charles Edward Raynal, III, *Karl Barth's Conception of the Perfections of God* (Ph.D. diss., Yale University, 1973), 135.

that God is merciful (370). Barth's own assertion of such a feeling in God constitutes a remarkable and tantalisingly compressed reformulation of the concept of divine impassibility.

> The source of the feeling of absolute dependence has no heart. But the personal God has a heart. He can feel, sense, be affected. He is not impassible. He cannot be moved from outside by an extraneous power. But this does not mean that he is not capable of moving and stirring himself. No, God is moved and stirred, yet not like ourselves in power-lessness, but in power, in his own free power, in his innermost being: moved and stirred by himself, i.e., open, ready, inclined (*propensus*) to compassion with another's suffering and therefore to assistance and to taking the initiative against this other's suffering. (370 rev.; *KD* 416)

As with his reformulation of the associated concept of constancy or immutability,[41] Barth preserves the core concern of the traditional affirmation of divine impassibility while avoiding what he considers its errors.[42] That God 'cannot be moved from outside' preserves the traditional concern for God's transcendence of the created order. That God is nevertheless 'capable of moving and stirring himself' avoids that static conception of the divine essence into which the tradition often lapsed.[43] Thus, there is 'no suffering' in God himself, and 'no cause outside God can cause him suffering if he does not in his freedom will it so' (cf. 410); but this 'cannot in any case mean that it is impossible for him really to feel compassion' (370–1 rev.; *KD* 416–17).[44]

Barth does not explain how it might be that God could freely will to join in the suffering of another without suffering in himself.[45] Nor does he make any direct reference to the cross at this point – though the cross is never

---

[41] Barth also argues here that God's *Unveränderlichkeit* (mistranslated 'impassibility') does not prevent him from taking pity on man (*CD* II/1, 371; *KD* 417).

[42] Cf. Gunton, *Act and Being*, 125–7.

[43] Note the very similar logic which informs Barth's description of the way in which the immutable God allows himself to be conditioned by prayer (*CD* II/1, 510–11).

[44] Cf. Paul S. Fiddes, *The Creative Suffering of God* (Oxford: Clarendon, 1988), 60–1. Fiddes objects that such self-imposed 'suffering' is 'masochistic' and at best 'a very weakened notion of suffering', since it does not involve the helplessness ingredient to human suffering. This presupposes that human suffering is the measure of divine suffering. Might it not be the case, as Barth argues, that 'as God is far greater than we his creatures, so much greater is his sorrow on our behalf than any sorrow which we can feel for ourselves' (*CD* II/1, 373)? There are presumably also instances of human suffering which involve neither masochism nor helplessness. Fiddes rightly acknowledges that, for Barth, there is in the being of God 'an area which is *always* impassible'; *ibid.*, 120; cf. 118–22.

[45] It has been plausibly suggested that, according to Barth, God does suffer in that he feels pain, but God does not suffer in that he is not acted upon from without. See John M.

farther from Barth's thoughts than Grünewald's depiction of it from his gaze (cf. 399, 400). But Barth could hardly ignore these issues for long, and his discussions later in the *Dogmatics*[46] have helped drive a broad and ongoing debate about the nature, extent and implications of divine suffering, particularly through their influence on Jürgen Moltmann.[47] It is not a little ironic that, to date, some of Barth's most lasting impact on subsequent thought on the divine perfections should come with respect to a perfection which receives no independent treatment here in II/1, but only passing comments.

There exists, then, an affective dimension to the divine mercy,[48] in light of which man's resistance and the distress it brings take on a different appearance. 'Arrogance is seen as pitiable folly, the usurpation of freedom as rigorous bondage, evil lust as bitter torment' (371). While these all bring down upon themselves God's righteous judgement, they also, as it were, bring down God's merciful compassion. 'In concrete the mercy of God means therefore his compassion at the sight of the suffering which man brings upon himself, his concern to remove it, his will to console man in this pain and to help him to overcome it' (371–2). While hating the sin, God yet loves the sinner, and does so with a pity which is 'no mere sentiment, but power and deed' (372).

This pity, moreover, is a pity 'from all eternity' (372). Citing the lyrics of Luther's *Nun freut euch*, 'God grieveth in eternity', Barth maintains that God's mercy is not first 'an attitude in the economy of salvation' but a matter of the freedom and power of his eternal Godhead:

> God the Father, Son and Holy Spirit is merciful in himself. In this *essential* freedom and power he speaks and acts mercifully in his revelation, reconciliation and sanctification, in his covenant with Israel, in the epiphany and parousia of Jesus Christ. (372 rev.; *KD* 418)

While Barth has already noted that mercy and compassion are essential to God, he has also very explicitly tied both mercy (369) and compassion (370) to the divine will. This may suggest that God's mercy and compassion may

---

Russell, 'Impassibility and Pathos in Barth's Idea of God', *Anglican Theological Review* 70.3 (1988): 226–7.

[46] For example, *CD* II/2, 163–5; IV/1, 244–56, 485; IV/2, 225–6, 357–8; IV/3.1, 396–7, 411–13.

[47] Fiddes, *The Creative Suffering of God*, 12–13 n. 36 (citing *CD* II/2, §33 and IV/1, §59): 'All modern thought along these lines is heavily indebted to Karl Barth'; cf. 15. Cf. Marc Steen, 'Jürgen Moltmann's Critical Reception of K. Barth's Theopaschitism', *Ephemerides Theologicae Lovanienses* 67.4 (1991): 278–311; Hans Urs von Balthasar, *Theo-Drama: Theological Dramatic Theory*, 5 vols., trans. Graham Harrison (San Francisco: Ignatius, 1988–1998), 5.212–46; Thomas G. Weinandy, *Does God Suffer?* (Notre Dame: University of Notre Dame Press, 2000), 11–13 n. 38.

[48] Van der Kooi, *As in a Mirror*, 328.

be understood as consequent upon election and yet 'essential' to who God has determined himself to be in electing.[49] In fact, in the subsequent discussion of the divine righteousness, Barth appears to explain the divine mercy in precisely this way:

> Let it be clearly understood that it did not have to happen in this way if we mean by that that God was under an obligation to clothe his righteousness in mercy and therefore in fulfilment of his righteousness to give his only Son to die for us. God could have been true to himself without giving his faithfulness the determination of faithfulness to us. It could easily have been God's good-pleasure to express his righteousness in quite another way, namely in the form of our destruction. God would not have been any the less God if this had happened. (401)

Here, God's mercy is not strictly an essential, but a willed determination of his faithfulness to himself. It is only as a result of 'the decision made in God's good-pleasure' (402) that his faithfulness to himself also has the determination of faithfulness and hence mercy towards us. On such an understanding, God can be described as 'essentially' merciful without making either the creature or its distress constitutive of the divine essence.

Here in his discussion of the divine mercy, however, Barth is in no hurry to drive the wedge of election between God in himself and God for us. Perhaps Barth feels that to have done so at this point might have been misread as a nominalistic qualification of mercy. His emphasis, particularly in the final pages of exposition (374–5), is thus almost entirely on the unqualified reality of mercy in God himself. Barth is not unaware of the tension this creates. How can God be essentially merciful without essential distress? As in his discussion of 'immanent' grace, Barth does not answer this question either directly or without a certain defensiveness. 'It is not even remotely possible', says Barth of the reality of God's mercy, 'to demonstrate this as a logically deducible truth' (373). Clearly, it is not irrefutable logical deduction which is required here, but merely some indication of what mercy might look like within the triune life. The confession that God himself is merciful is, of course, grounded in his self-revelation in Jesus Christ, 'the epitome of the reality of God's mercy'. 'What else can we produce as a proof of this confession except the fact that God has given himself to be known by us as merciful in the name of Jesus Christ?' (373). Appeal to Jesus Christ makes it abundantly clear that, as he is toward us, God is indeed merciful. But it offers no indication how God can also be merciful in himself – which must be the case if mercy is properly to be

[49] Cf. *CD* IV/1, 65: 'In the eternal decree of God revealed in Jesus Christ the being of God would have been seen as righteous mercy and merciful righteousness from the very first.'

understood as a divine perfection. Barth affirms 'that God is as merciful in himself as he is merciful in his action', and that God's mercy is 'not simply...an appearance, but...the disposition of the heart and being of God' (375). As with grace, however, the reality of mercy in the divine life is a matter of sheer assertion:

> We cannot get behind this name to learn why God is merciful. But we can infer from this name with unshakable certainty that he is. (373)

Against his typical procedure, Barth refuses to enquire into the divine ground of possibility which underlies the actuality of God's mercy in the economy.

However, while the emptiness of the resulting concept of God's 'immanent' mercy might, on its own, very well fuel a moderate-nominalist's doubts as to its actual existence even within the economy, Barth leaves his readers in no doubt that God is indeed full of mercy in his encounter with human suffering (373–4). There is an affective, pastoral, existential urgency to Barth's depiction of the divine mercy which is entirely befitting the compassion in which God comforts and revives his ruined creature.

> Before we are touched or can be touched by any pain which we have brought on ourselves by our sin and guilt, before we are sorry for or can be sorry for our sin, before death and hell can frighten us, and before we feel the greater terror that we are such sinners as have deserved death and hell, already in the One against whom we sin and are guilty and whose punishment threatens us we have to do with the God who himself suffers pain because of our sin and guilt, for whom it is not an alien thing but his own intimate concern. (373)

Because God has taken our place in his Son, himself sorrowing for our sins more deeply than ever we could sorrow for them, an inordinate grief over sin on our part, 'an, as it were, divine, eternal, irremovable weight of sorrow...is not only taken away from us, but forbidden us as something presumptuous – a tragic consciousness to which we may not pretend' (374). Because God has in mercy 'taken to himself and removed from us our sin and guilt', true faith in him, a faith willing 'to let God be God', is a matter of 'joy and gratitude, an assurance which can no longer look back, only forwards' (374–5).

God's mercy, then, is that perfection of the divine life whereby God feels in his heart the distress of his creature and acts effectively to assuage it. As with grace, Barth does not explain how this mercy obtains within the triune life itself. He does however hint that God's mercy *ad intra* is to be understood as following upon the decree of election – a hint which becomes explicit affirmation in the following discussion of the divine righteousness.

Righteousness

With the divine mercy Barth pairs the divine righteousness. Presumably because righteousness 'is specially significant in Scripture and has been so much disputed in the history of the Christian confession' (375), Barth slows the pace of his exposition, producing a much fuller account of the divine righteousness than of the divine grace, holiness or mercy, and anticipating the tone, structure and movement of the more leisurely accounts of the perfections which follow. With this account of righteousness, in other words, Barth has finally hit his stride. Yet, despite the historical and dogmatic significance of the concept of the righteousness of God, and despite also the quality and interest of Barth's exposition, it has attracted little more attention in the secondary literature than have the other perfections of the divine loving. Following his introductory comments (375–6), Barth's exposition is divided into three stages. The first stage defines the righteousness of God as that which is worthy of God and which must therefore be carefully described in terms that are coherent with both the mercy and the holiness of God (376–81). The second stage attempts such a description of the divine righteousness in unity first with the divine mercy and then with the divine holiness (381–93). The third flows directly out of the second and examines the righteousness of God as manifest in Christ's death (393–406).

Barth begins by posing again his riddle of the multiplicity of divine perfections. Righteousness is not 'a second thing side by side with' mercy but 'one and the same thing' (375). Both, in other words, are the divine essence. Yet, as concerns 'the concepts by which we are allowed to recognise God', righteousness is also 'a second thing' beside mercy and so requires its own exposition (375).[50] Such exposition cannot proceed arbitrarily, however, but only 'in the order determined by the object, by the revelation of God in Jesus Christ, and therefore by his being' (376). Thus 'the mercy of God must precede his righteousness, just as his grace had to precede his holiness' (376). With respect to mercy, therefore, righteousness is identical in referent, distinct in our concepts, and ordered according to divine revelation. The same could be said of any of Barth's pairings of perfections. The divine perfections stand in 'a relationship of mutual penetration and consummation' (376), but this no more obliterates the intrinsic order of these perfections than does the divine perichoresis the intrinsic order of Father, Son and Spirit.

The first stage of Barth's exposition develops the claim that the divine loving, as righteous, always involves the assertion and maintenance of what Barth calls the divine 'worth' (376–81). 'The characterisation and

---

[50] Cf. Claus-Dieter Osthövener, *Die Lehre von Gottes Eigenschaften bei Friedrich Schleiermacher und Karl Barth*, Theologische Bibliothek Töpelmann 76 (Berlin: de Gruyter, 1996), 197–8.

determination of this love as righteousness and therefore divine springs from the fact that when God wills and creates the possibility of fellowship with man he does that which is worthy of himself, and therefore in this fellowship asserts his worth in spite of all contradiction and resistance, and therefore in this fellowship he causes only his own worth to prevail and rule' (376–7). It is far from clear at this point what Barth means by the divine 'worth' and how righteousness so defined differs from that holiness in which God 'distinguishes and maintains his own will' in his fellowship others (359). This ambiguity in the opening definition is, however, deliberate. It is an invitation to read on and discover. Barth explains, 'The definition must be framed on these lines if there is not to take place here a cleavage in the being of God, if the righteousness of God is to be seen in its unity with his mercy and also with a backward reference in its unity with his holiness' (377). Thus, whatever is entailed by righteousness understood as the assertion of the divine worth, it cannot be in any conflict with either the divine mercy or the divine holiness. For God certainly does nothing unworthy of himself in being merciful and holy. The goal of defining righteousness in terms of the divine worth is to make it clear that righteousness, mercy and holiness 'can co-exist and equally denote the one being of God' (377).

In a first excursus (377–81), Barth supplies two definitions of God's righteousness, those of Quenstedt and Polanus, which commit opposite errors. Quenstedt's definition 'fits in only too well with [his] definition of the holiness of God', but does not obviously cohere with his definition of the divine mercy (377–8; cf. 370). Polanus's definition of righteousness, by contrast, is certainly not 'in conflict with that of [God's] mercy', yet it 'threatens to compromise the holiness of God' (379). Barth then suggests corrections to these definitions from passages in Luther and Anselm, respectively, as well as from passages of Scripture.[51] It is in his discussion of Anselm that Barth's puzzling references to God's worth become clearer. According to Anselm (*Proslogion* 10–11), God is merciful to the wicked not because they have deserved it but because to do so befits the divine goodness:

> 'Therefore you are righteous, not because you repay us as we deserve, but because you do what befits you as supremely good....Thus, your mercy if born of your righteousness. For it is righteous that you should be so good as also to be good in pardoning.' It is righteous because God wills it. And what God wills is righteous because he wills what is worthy of himself. (380 rev.; *KD* 427)

---

[51] In Scripture, according to Barth, 'the attestation of God's mercy frequently takes the form of an admonition'. Inexplicably, three of the passages which Barth quotes, given in full in the German, are elided in the English so that the reference either to God's mercy or to the admonition or to both are missing (*CD* II/1, 381; *KD* 428).

This is what underlies Barth's reference to God's worth. In saying that God, in his righteousness, does and establishes what is worthy of himself, Barth means in part that this righteousness is also a merciful righteousness. God's righteousness entails his having mercy on the wicked. But, again following Anselm, God's righteousness also entails his refusal to allow to persist either the moral 'disorder' in his kingdom caused by sin or the moral disorder of the sinner (380). This twofold aspect of the divine righteousness, or rather the unity of God's mercy and righteousness – Barth deliberately alternates between these two ways of speaking – this finds its confirmation in Scripture in the way in which God's people are called upon both to love him and to fear him. The relationship between love and fear on the one hand, and mercy and righteousness on the other, is not what we might expect. Rather, 'According to Scripture it is as the merciful God that God is to be feared, and as the righteous that he is to be loved' (381).

With that, Barth embarks upon his second stage of argument: his own attempt further to define the divine righteousness in explicit unity with the divine mercy (381–90) – this is Barth's chief concern – without in any way compromising its unity with the divine holiness (390–3). As is always the case in Barth's understanding of the perfections, this unity is not something achieved by the mutual limitation of conflicting concepts.[52] Such a procedure is implicit in the two definitions of the divine righteousness (those of Ritschl and Nitzsch) which Barth here criticises (382). For all Barth's concern to understand righteousness and mercy together, he wants to make clear right up front that God's righteousness is no less righteous for being merciful. Thus, the fact that 'there is no righteousness of God which is not also mercy and no mercy of God which is not also righteousness' (380) does not exclude the truths that God, in his righteousness, is 'wholly and utterly...the Judge', and that God's righteous revelation 'is wholly and utterly the law' (381). According to Scripture, in God's demonstration of his righteousness 'there is never any question of a regard for individual circumstances, or a limitation of his justice by his gentleness, or allowing grace to precede strict righteousness, but it is everywhere stated that he unconditionally maintains right as right and wrong as wrong, judging, rewarding and punishing according to this standard without deviating a hair's breadth either to the one side or the other' (382). God's righteousness 'must be understood strictly as *iustitia distributiva*' (382), according to which he either rewards or punishes strictly according to man's works.[53]

---

[52] It is no exception to this when Barth later appropriates scholastic talk of a *moderatio* of wrath by the divine patience (*CD* II/1, 410). First, wrath is not a divine perfection. Second, this moderation does not make God's wrath less wrathful, but, in a way, more so. This moderation makes God's wrath a divine wrath, that is, a wrath aimed at the creature's restoration, and not a demonic wrath which merely breaks out and destroys.

[53] Barth may appear to have gotten ahead of himself with this passage (*CD* II/1, 381–3), for in identifying God's righteousness as law and as *iustitia distributiva*, he more clearly

The older orthodoxy understood this aspect of the divine righteousness perfectly well. Its failure, according to Barth, came in not appreciating the unity of this very righteousness with the divine mercy. 'God cannot affirm himself more strongly as the righteous God, he cannot more effectively attest and implement the law as the most proper and characteristic revelation of himself,...than by his grace which pardons the sinner' (383).[54] There is a conceptual parallel here to Barth's claim that, in revelation, God is not 'partly revealed and partly concealed', but rather 'wholly revealed and wholly concealed at one and the same time' (341). It is similar with the divine mercy and righteousness: God is wholly both at one and the same time. For it is precisely as God in pure righteousness judges sin in Christ that he also in pure mercy justifies those who believe (382–3 on Rom 3:24–6).

> God does not need to yield his righteousness a single inch when he is merciful. As he is merciful, he is righteous. He is merciful as he really makes demands and correspondingly punishes and rewards. (383)

This is the 'relation of mutual penetration and consummation' between mercy and righteousness of which Barth initially spoke (376), and it finds expression also in the fact that the call to embrace God's gospel mercy is attended by the demand for repentance in light of his righteous law (384).[55]

God's righteousness is not merely law, however, but also gospel, the establishment of the covenant. 'For according to the Scriptures of the Old and New Testaments what constitutes the demonstration and exercise of God's righteousness...is precisely the fact that God enters in to a covenant with [man] and promises that his sins are to be forgiven and eternal life assured' (384). This is why faith in Christ, who is the righteousness of God, is a matter of 'seriousness, assurance and joy'. In establishing his covenant with man, God 'distinguishes his action from all caprice and contingency...[and] does what is in the highest sense the right: that in which he himself is righteous; that which befits him and is worthy of him as God' (384).

---

shows its unity with the divine holiness than with the divine mercy. In the second part of this second stage of argument, Barth does in fact return to righteousness as *iustitia distributiva* in order to make the connection with holiness explicit (*CD* II/1, 391). Here, however, the passage functions to secure righteousness against simply dissolving into mercy, as Barth feels was the case in Ritschl's dogmatics (*CD* II/1, 382).

[54] Cf. Hermann Cremer, *Die christliche Lehre von den Eigenschaften Gottes*, ed. Helmut Burkhardt (1897; Gießen: TVG/Brunnen, 2005), 59. On the close relationship of Barth's exposition of the righteousness of God to that of Cremer, see Grell, *Der ewig reiche Gott*, 280–7, 291–9.

[55] The English translation frequently renders *Buße* as 'penitence' (e.g. *CD* II/1, 384, 385, 391, 399, 406; *KD* 431, 432, 440, 449, 457). Thus, 'penitence and impenitence [*Bußfertigkeit und Unbußfertigkeit*]' (*CD* II/1, 416; *KD* 469). No distinction from the idea of 'repentance' is intended.

Because God, in establishing his covenant with us, does what is worthy of himself, because 'he is wholly himself and true to himself in the fact that he is true to us', the divine righteousness also involves 'God's most jealous demand upon man' (385).

> To this extent the revelation of God's righteousness means in fact judgement upon us, implying our condemnation and the death of the old man. To this extent faith means that we accept this condemnation...and that as condemned sinners, divested of our own righteousness, we flee from ourselves and take refuge in God who wills alone to be both our righteousness and our life, who, making us righteous by himself, wills that there should be no division between himself and us. (386)

This demand, the demand for faith in and obedience to God, also has direct implications for the relationship between human beings, not least in the political sphere.[56] The Old Testament in particular depicts the human righteousness demanded by God as having 'necessarily the character of a vindication of right in favour of the threatened innocent, the oppressed poor, widows, orphans and aliens' (386). The reason for this is that, in light of God's own righteousness, 'We are all widows and orphans who cannot procure right for themselves' (387). This is the connection between *Rechtfertigung und Recht*,[57] between personal justification and political justice (386; *KD* 434–5). The righteousness in which God establishes the right of 'the poor and wretched' requires a human righteousness which does likewise (387). The Christian life is 'allowed to become an analogy to the righteousness of God'.[58] This is yet another way in which God's righteousness is manifest as itself God's mercy. Finally, to the Old Testament witness to human righteousness before God (387–90) there corresponds the full-blown doctrine of justification in the New (390), which Barth summarises in very traditionally Protestant terms:[59]

> It is he [Christ] who is made righteousness for us (1 Cor 1:30). And it is faith in him...which is the condition on which the righteous God justifies the ungodly. It is faith in him which God reckons to the ungodly as righteousness, and in which he becomes and is truly righteous. (390)

---

[56] Grell, *Der ewig reiche Gott*, 295–7.
[57] Barth delivered a lecture with this title in June 1938; ET Karl Barth, *Church and State*, trans. G. Ronald Howe, with an introduction by David L. Mueller (Greenville: Smyth and helwys, 1991); cf. Eberhard Busch, *Karl Barth: His Life from Letters and Autobiographical Texts*, trans. John Bowden (Grand Rapids: Eerdmans, 1994), 287–9, 305.
[58] Grell, *Der ewig reiche Gott*, 297.
[59] Grell, *Der ewig reiche Gott*, 281, 291–2.

Thus far, the righteousness of God in its unity with the divine mercy. But righteousness is also a perfection of the holy God (390–3). It is therefore 'necessarily bound up with the concept of judgement,...a decision about good and evil, about reward and punishment' (391). This, once again, is righteousness as *iustitia distributiva*. As the definition of a divine perfection, this threatens to draw up into the divine life some reference to human sin.[60] Since Barth's focus is clearly on the reconciling work of Christ, however, he does not address this concern here.[61] He is content to note that the 'unequivocal' witness of Scripture to the divine righteousness includes the 'severity and relentlessness' of God's vengeance upon the wicked (392). Such vengeance, the condemning, punishing operation of the divine righteousness, is 'the judgement which we certainly will not escape without faith' (392).

> It is the abyss from which we are held back by faith alone. It is the damnation from which we are preserved only by faith. (392)

The damnation which God's righteousness threatens presents both a duty as well as a temptation. On the one hand, 'It is necessary that faith should remember the abyss from which it has been saved' in order that it may duly praise and honour God and 'be bound in total obedience to the God who owed it nothing and to whom it owes everything' (393). At the same time, we must neither 'fear that it might again threaten us' nor commit 'the unbelief of Lot's wife' by trying 'to look back and again reckon or even trifle with the reality or the possibility of damnation and death' (392–3).

But can this damnation ever do more than merely threaten? Those who have faith in Christ certainly need not reckon with the possibility of their own damnation, but Barth's reference to 'faith alone' clearly implies that those who do not have faith might do very well to engage in such a reckoning. The question then arises, as it did concerning Barth's discussion of the divine holiness (362) and as it commonly does in regard to Barth's doctrine of election,[62] whether actual damnation is even possible on Barth's account. Has Barth so construed the unity of God's mercy and righteousness that God

---

[60] Noted by Osthövener, *Gottes Eigenschaften*, 197.

[61] Curiously, Barth nowhere insists, as he has with the divine grace (*CD* II/1, 357–8), holiness (*CD* II/1, 369), and mercy (*CD* II/1, 375), and as he will with the divine patience (*CD* II/1, 416) and wisdom (*CD* II/1, 426–7), that God's righteousness is first and foremost a perfection of God's life *ad intra* before it is expressed in the economy. Clearly there is ample scope for such an insistence in Barth's talk of righteousness in terms of God doing what is worthy of himself. Presumably the reality of God's 'immanent' righteousness may be taken for granted.

[62] Emil Brunner, *Dogmatics*, vol. 1, *The Christian Doctrine of God*, trans. Olive Wyon (London: Lutterworth, 1949), 348–52; Berkouwer, *The Triumph of Grace*, 290–5; cf. Matthias Gockel, *Barth and Schleiermacher on the Doctrine of Election: A Systematic-Theological Comparison* (Oxford: Oxford University Press, 2006), 207–11.

could never exercise an unmerciful righteousness? Could God pronounce a purely condemning judgement which does not aim at purifying, healing and restoring the sinner? It would appear that any affirmation of God's capacity righteously to damn a sinner would compromise the unity of God's righteousness with his mercy – the very error of the older orthodoxy which Barth has so carefully attempted to avoid. Those less sanguine than Barth about the prospects for universal redemption may suspect that he has construed the unity of the divine perfections in such a way as to require it.

But he has not. As noted, the clear implication of this passage is that damnation is a possibility. Even in light of his doctrine of election, Barth will continue to maintain that God is in no way obligated to show mercy to all.[63] How God might damn while remaining merciful (and gracious and patient, for that matter) Barth does not explain here. A possible explanation can be found, however, in Barth's concept of the divine personhood, particularly as he develops it in his account of the divine omnipotence. Barth has already identified the divine personhood as indicating that God is utterly free and consciously self-moved (267–72). Much later he writes:

> Because God's power is the power of his personality, the power of his knowing and willing, we can say that it also belongs to God's will not to will many things....It is also his power not to do what he knows to be impracticable and therefore will not do....[H]e is the master of his omnipotence and not its slave. (544)

God, as a person, a knowing and willing agent, is 'possessor of his power and the Lord of its use' (564). By implication, God is equally the Lord of the use of all of his perfections, including his mercy. Because Barth maintains that damnation remains a possibility, he must presumably also maintain that God is free finally to withdraw his mercy (and grace and patience) from sinners and righteously damn them, yet without thereby compromising the unity of his mercy and righteousness.[64] What Barth would presumably *not* maintain is that God's mercy (and grace and patience) would remain

---

[63] CD II/2, 417; IV/3.1, 477–8; Joseph D. Bettis, 'Is Karl Barth a Universalist?' *Scottish Journal of Theology* 20.4 (1967): 423–36; Wolf Krötke, *Sin and Nothingness in the Theology of Karl Barth*, trans. and ed. Philip G. Ziegler and Christina-Maria Bammel, *Studies in Reformed Theology and History* ns. 10 (Princeton: Princeton Theological Seminary, 2005), 94; John Colwell, 'The Contemporaneity of the Divine Decision: Reflections on Barth's Denial of "Universalism,"' in *Universalism and the Doctrine of hell: Papers Presented at the Fourth Edinburgh Conference on Christian Dogmatics, 1991*, ed. Nigel M. de S. Cameron (Carlisle: Paternoster, 1992), 139–60; Michael O'Neil, 'Karl Barth's Doctrine of Election', *Evangelical Quarterly* 76.4 (2004): 318–20, 323; Chalamet, *Dialectical Theologians*, 246.

[64] Cf. CD III/4, 441–3, where Barth denies that capital punishment can reflect God's retributive justice.

operative even in the actual damnation of a sinner, for this would empty mercy (and grace and patience) of any content, completely nominalising them. Thus, Barth's 'hopeful' universalism does not arise from his conception of the unity of the divine perfections, as if by some 'purely human idea of righteousness' (391) God were unable to withhold his mercy.[65] As should be expected with Barth, it is not out of loyalty to abstract concepts – and certainly not under the supposed influence of the universal aspirations of the Enlightenment[66] – but rather as he feels 'plainly compelled by the testimony of Scripture and in particular by the testimony of Scripture to Christ', that he gives his exposition the shape that it has (391 rev.; KD 440).[67] It is 'only as we look at what God has in fact done in Jesus Christ' that we can say of God's mercy that 'it had to be so' (401).

The specific implications of Jesus Christ himself and the gospel events for the divine righteousness have never been far from Barth's mind, but it is only in his third stage of argument that they receive extended, urgent, worshipful attention (393–406). The question so far has been to what extent the mercy and righteousness (and holiness) of God cohere. Now Barth can announce that 'God's revelation in Jesus Christ supplies to this question the answer that the condemning and punishing righteousness of God is in itself and as such the depth and power and might of his mercy' (393). For 'it is where the divine love and therefore the divine grace and mercy are attested with ... supreme clarity' that the righteousness of God appears unequivocally in both of its aspects: in the crucifixion as an act of 'wrath, judgement and punishment', and in the resurrection as an act of 'pleasure, acquittal and reward' (394).

In a deeply provocative excursus (394–6), Barth draws out some of the implications of the crucifixion for human suffering generally, while also setting up what he will later say about the nature of human sin (398–9). The cross itself stands 'as the judgement whose frightfulness causes even the most dreadful judgements of Old Testament Scripture to fade; or conversely, as the judgement whose continual fire is the light in which is first revealed the true terror of those Old Testament threats and executions of judgement'

---

[65] At one point, in view of the possibility that man might 'cast himself headlong and be swallowed up in the abyss', Barth asks, 'What then becomes of God's faithfulness to man, his mercy?' (CD II/1, 401). While this might suggest that the divine mercy might somehow prevent God from damning, in context it seems that Barth is not considering the damnation of certain human beings, but of the entire human race. It is Anselm's concern which lies before him, and so Barth affirms that the damnation of the entire race would not befit the divine goodness and its 'requirement' that, in such a scenario, God do 'what is worthy of himself' by showing mercy.

[66] Van der Kooi, As in a Mirror, 341–2, 346. Van der Kooi here follows Trutz Rendtorff's thesis; see John Macken, The Autonomy Theme in the Church Dogmatics: Karl Barth and his Critics (Cambridge: Cambridge University Press, 1990), 112–13, 125–8.

[67] Grell, Der ewig reiche Gott, 280; cf. CD II/2, 171.

(394). While this applies to all human suffering throughout history, including our own, the suffering of the Jews in particular has exemplary force (cf. 367). It is both relativised and given its true value as a token or indicator of the crucifixion of Christ.

> What Israel undergoes up to the present time is undergone as an echo and aftermath of what the heathen long ago did to the Messiah of Israel and had to do as instruments of God, as an echo and aftermath of the one real outbreak, smiting and slaying of the divine wrath on Golgotha. This is the reason for the ceaseless futility and inevitable ineffectiveness of all that human beings at any time have perpetrated against the Jews or can perpetrate even today. They can only set up again the token of the crucifixion of Christ and therefore of the real judgement of God. (396)[68]

Barth's intention in saying this, in subordinating all human suffering to that of Christ, is to make it clear that 'the real judgement of God is alone the crucifixion of Christ' (396), that 'there and there alone' 'the sins of Israel and of all men' were borne (395).[69]

Though hardly crucial to his argument, one problematic point which Barth adduces in support of this claim, and to which he returns several times in the ensuing discussion, is that no mere creature could bear 'the real judgement of God' without being 'annihilated' or 'destroyed'.[70] Whether Barth means that the creature would cease to exist if faced with the divine wrath, or merely be ruined beyond repair, this claim is problematic in that it seems to assume that there can be but one single form of wrath: the full

---

[68] Barth completed this volume of the *Dogmatics* in the summer of 1939, before the war began (1 September). See Busch, *Karl Barth*, 292. Cf. *CD* III/3, 210–26, where, curiously, Barth makes no reference to the Book of Esther – neither here nor, if the index volume is to be trusted, anywhere else in the entire *Church Dogmatics*. Barth's silence is the more puzzling given the passionate defence of the Christian significance of Esther by Wilhelm Vischer, 'Esther', *Theologische Existenz heute* 48 (1937): 1–29 (the volume immediately following the published version of Barth's Debrecen lecture on election).

[69] The more explicitly universalist leanings of this passage are clearly attributable to Barth's reading of the 'testimony of Scripture to Christ' rather than to any abstract and independent idea of the divine mercy or righteousness.

[70] Barth makes a bizarre appeal to the *Heidelberg Catechism* for support (*CD* II/1, 396). According to the response to question 14, 'no mere creature can bear the burden of the eternal wrath of God against sin'. Barth takes this to mean that, were the creature to encounter the wrath of God, 'the creature would be annihilated'. The point at issue in question 14, however, is not whether the creature can endure the wrath of God, but whether one creature can endure the wrath of God so as to redeem another creature from it. Barth conveniently omits the continuation of the response he quotes: '...and redeem others therefrom'. Barth appeals to subsequent articles of the *Heidelberg* to the same effect (*CD* II/1, 400).

expression of it. Otherwise what is expressed is not 'real' wrath but merely a 'symbol' of it (396, 399, 420). But if God is the Lord of his perfections, he should presumably be acknowledged the Lord of his wrath as well, able to wield it in any variety of degrees should he choose to do so. Barth appears to acknowledge this in his discussion of God's patience, in which 'he does not pour out the whole of his wrath in a single moment' (Quenstedt). 'The wrath of God...is guided and shaped...by God himself who is Lord of his wrath in virtue of what he knows and wills' (410). In the same way, Barth will later explain that the divine omnipresence, according to which God is always wholly and undividedly present, does not exclude a rich variety of particular presences to his creation (472–3, 476–86), including both a presence 'in wrath' and a different presence 'in grace' (476). Whether or not God ever chooses to do so, he should on Barth's account be acknowledged as capable of pouring out his wrath on the creature in such a way as *not* to annihilate or destroy it. Conversely, the supposition that the annihilation or destruction of the creature necessarily follows from the outpouring of the divine wrath should not be used to suggest that God does not in fact pour out his wrath on the creature.

What happened on the cross, then, is that 'God's condemning and punishing righteousness broke out, really smiting and piercing human sin', both 'for Israel and for us', so that 'the wrath of God which we had merited...was now in our place borne and suffered as though it had smitten us' (396–7). This is the good news of the suffering of God's own Son, the central concern of 'the whole of the New Testament' (397). 'In his love', says Barth, 'God has been hard on himself' and has stepped into the conflict between himself and man.

> He took this conflict into his own being. He bore it in himself to the bitter end. He took part in it from both sides. (397)

He was both the offended God and the offending man, 'the object of his own anger, the victim of his own condemnation' (398). In the midst of one of the most magnificent passages in all the *Dogmatics*, Barth unfolds this mystery in terms of Christ as 'The Judge Judged in Our Place'.[71]

Because of this, 'Because it was the Son of God, i.e., God himself, who took our place on Good Friday', four things follow (398–405). First, sin is manifest. By uniquely showing the severity of God's wrath against sin, Christ's death also uniquely shows 'the full implication of sin, what it means to resist God, to be God's enemy' (398–9). Neither Scripture's commands and threats against sin, nor history's frightful record of examples of God's judgement upon sin, nor even personal experiences of grief over sin can really indicate sin's seriousness. The cross alone can teach this. 'What symbol can be plain

---

[71] CD IV/1, §59.2 (211–83); cf. CD II/1, 401–2.

and strong enough to indicate the enormity of our opposition to God when it has been indicated in this way by God himself through what he has done in order to remove it?' (399).[72]

Second, from the human side, sin is fully dealt with (399–400). Because it was God the Son who suffered on the cross, 'the righteousness of God in condemnation and punishment could take its course in relation to human sin', and this without the destruction of the creature. The cross thus supplies a 'double proof of the omnipotence in which God did not abate the demands of his righteousness but showed himself equal to his own wrath; on the one hand by submitting to it and on the other by not being consumed by it' (400).

Third, from divine side, God's own righteousness is legitimately fulfilled (400–3). Thus, recalling Anselm, 'the faithfulness of God himself was maintained, and therefore his honour was not violated' (400). Both aspects of God's righteousness are satisfied: the condemnation and punishment of sin as well as merciful faithfulness to the sinful creature.

> For in him who took our place God's own heart beat on our side, in our flesh and blood, in complete solidarity with our nature and constitution, at the very point where we ourselves confront him, guilty before God. Because it was the eternal God who entered in in Jesus Christ, he could be more than the Representative and Guarantor of God to us. He could also be our Representative and Guarantor towards God. He could be the fully accredited Representative not only of the divine Judge, but also of the judged: of fallen Adam in his sin; of the whole of sinful humanity; of each individual sinner in all his being and sinning. (402)

Fourth, reconciliation between God and humanity is effectively achieved (403–5). Christ's passion brings about 'the victory of God's righteousness, and therefore our own righteousness in his sight' (403). From 'his own Word made flesh, God hears that satisfaction has been done to his righteousness, that the consequences of human sin have been borne and expiated, and therefore that they have been taken away from man' (403). This is what Barth calls the 'divine colloquy' between Father and Son, which the resurrection reveals may be joined by man in faith (403–4).

In a concluding meditation (405–6) which forms an *inclusio* with the opening paragraphs (393–6) of this final stage of argument, Barth reflects once again on the significance (literally) of human suffering. There exists

---

[72] Thus in *Church Dogmatics* IV, Barth expounds the human sins of pride, sloth, and falsehood (§§60, 65, 70) only after and in light of his exposition of the obedient humiliation, the lordly exaltation, and the glorious truthfulness of Jesus Christ (§§59, 64, 69).

'an inner, essential connection between the one passion of the Son of God and the many sufferings which we see afflicting Israel, the church, the world and ourselves' (405). These latter are 'no more than signs and shadows', 'announcements and echoes', 'traces and tokens' of the cross (405–6). The 'necessary exercise of faith' is to see them as such, as reminders that the suffering we really deserved has been 'vanquished and ended' (406). To fear them is an act of unbelief (406). This, says Barth, is the church's 'theodicy': to view suffering as merely the shadow of Golgotha – a shadow which 'would not fall if the cross of Christ did not stand in the light of the resurrection' (406).[73]

Barth thus defines the divine righteousness as *iustitia distributiva*, a righteousness by which God rewards good and punishes evil, thereby maintaining the cosmic moral order envisioned by Anselm. As definitively revealed in the cross, this righteousness must be seen not merely in its unity with the divine holiness but also in its unity with the divine mercy. It is thus also a saving righteousness – a righteousness that saves man precisely in condemning and punishing man's sin. In expounding this, Barth has also touched upon the major themes of the Protestant doctrine of justification and its implications for the life of faith.

§30.3 Patience and Wisdom

The third and final pair of perfections of the divine loving consists of patience and wisdom. Barth began his exposition of the perfections of the divine loving by refusing any claim to direct scriptural warrant for his particular selection of perfections (352). He now speaks not of a 'clear' but of a 'certain [*gewisse*]' (i.e. unspecified) necessity, in light of a series of passages of Scripture (Ex. 34:6, etc.), of expounding the divine patience (407 rev.; *KD* 458). While on Barth's account no necessary reason can be given for the pairing of patience and wisdom, Barth does give practical reasons for doing so, and others may be surmised. Barth explicitly relates these two perfections to divine providence and so to creatures' response to God. God in his patience expects creaturely response (408), and in his wisdom God is recognisable, rational and meaningful to the creature, thereby showing himself to be one to whom the creature may respond (423–4). Thus, God's wisdom evokes what his patience awaits. One could just as well say that God's powerful, effective patience attains the response it seeks by means of the divine wisdom, 'the proper instrument of the divine providence'

---

[73] Barth preached on these themes on 23 June 1940, the Sunday following his brother Peter's tragic death: 'Psalm 46,2–4.8', in *idem*, *Predigten 1935–1952*, Karl Barth Gesamtausgabe 26, ed. Harmut Spieker and Hinrich Stoevesandt (Zürich: Theologischer Verlag Zürich, 1996), 202–9.

(427). Large-scale structural considerations may also have led Barth to pair patience and wisdom. The temporal dimension of the divine patience (408, 409–10) and the truth and clarity which characterise the divine wisdom (426) clearly anticipate what Barth will say of the divine eternity and glory. The final pair of perfections of the divine loving thus mirrors the final pair of perfections of the divine freedom.[74]

As Barth affirmed concerning God's mercy and righteousness, exposition of a third pair of perfections does not mean that the richness of the foregoing perfections has been 'exhausted and abandoned' (407). Rather, this same richness is reaffirmed in a new way, for 'all further consideration of the divine attributes can but move in a circle around the one but infinitely rich being of God whose simplicity is abundance itself and whose abundance is simplicity itself' (406).[75] Such reaffirmation is a necessary pursuit of 'the movement demanded by the object', according to which 'We have again to magnify the plenitude of the divine being by not lingering unduly over any one proposition or letting it become the final word or the guiding principle, but by proceeding from one to another' (407). This development of a 'final' pair of perfections of the divine loving thus represents merely 'a provisional halt'. It 'does not mean that we have spoken the last word' (407).

> What end can there be to this development? We are drawing upon the ocean. We are therefore faced by a task to which there is no end. (406)

Nevertheless, with the exposition of the divine patience and wisdom enough will have been said to give 'at least the authorised and commanded view of this inexhaustible ocean' in its determination as the divine loving (406).

Patience

Barth's account of the divine patience stands as one of the most lovely subsections in this chapter of the *Dogmatics*. It is an exquisite portrait of the interplay of divine and human action in the history of salvation. According to Barth, God in his patience is so effectively in control of creaturely reality that he can grant it its measure of freedom and independence, allowing it to go its own way even as he keeps it on the way to himself.[76] The discussion

---

[74] Cf. *CD* IV/3, 360–2, where Barth connects the divine patience with the 'specific glory' of the middle form of Christ's *parousia*.

[75] Cf. Augustine's description of the divine simplicity (*CD* II/1, 323, 329).

[76] See also Barth's appeal to the divine patience (and to nearly every other divine perfection treated here in *CD* II/1) in his sermon of 11 June 1939, 'Der Grund unseres Bauens, 1. Korinther 3,11', in *idem*, *Predigten 1935–1952*, 162–72. Barth clearly had the divine perfections on his mind, ending the service with allusion, in prayer, to Prov. 1:7 (the motto of the University of Aberdeen, to which *CD* II/1 is partly dedicated) and

is 'remarkably rich' in exegetical detail,[77] appropriately tranquil in tone, obediently direct in summoning the reader to the very response of faith at which God's patience aims.

Barth's exposition of the divine patience falls into three short stages. First, Barth defines patience and gives his reasons for affirming it as a divine perfection (407–9). Second, Barth shows that God's exercise of patience is an exercise of power, thus distinguishing it from both impotence and impatience (409–16). Finally, Barth expounds the divine patience as the patience of God's Word (416–22).

Why affirm, then, that patience is a divine perfection? Just as there is no dogmatic necessity of including patience among the divine perfections, so Barth insists that neither is there any logical necessity of doing so. That God is patient is not a logical entailment of grace and mercy – even of the divine grace and the divine mercy (407–8). It is a confession in response to revelation (407). It is only of the God who spoke to Moses, of 'the God revealed in Jesus Christ', that it may be said, 'his love bears essentially the character of patience' (408).

> Patience exists where one grants space and time to another with a definite intention, where one expectantly allows another to do as it pleases. That God does this, that he makes this purposeful concession of space and time, that he expectantly gives opportunity to another – this lies in his being. Indeed, this is entirely his being. (408 rev.; KD 459)[78]

The reference to space and time may suggest that Barth speaks merely of God's action in the economy. But, in fact, this is not the case. As he makes quite clear later on, patience is just as much, indeed, primarily a perfection of God's eternal being *ad intra* (416). Barth does not explain here what this 'space' and 'time' might look like in the divine life. Instead, he leaves it to the reader's curiosity and imagination – Barth is not one to blur the Creator-creature distinction – and perhaps also to the reader's own patience. It is not until the expositions of the divine omnipresence (461–90) and eternity (608–40) that the reader learns how it is that God, in his own way, has both space and time in himself. Jumping ahead for the moment to those expositions, Barth explains that God's 'space' is that union in the divine life of both remoteness and proximity – a union which is itself grounded in God's triunity, in 'the togetherness of Father, Son and Holy Spirit at the distance posited by the distinction that exists in the

---

with the final verse of Rinkart's *Nun danket alle Gott* (*ibid.*, 172 and 173 n. 13; cf. CD II/1, 322).

[77] De Margerie, *Les Perfections*, 272.

[78] Cf. Barth, 'Der Grund unseres Bauens', 165.

one essence of God' (468). God's eternity is not the negation of time, but 'pure duration', the simultaneity of 'beginning, succession and end,' which, again, is grounded in God's triunity (610, 615). God's eternity includes 'the time of his patience' (612). Returning to the present passage, one might imagine that the granting of space and time to another within God's own life is an allusion to filiation and spiration. God's 'immanent' patience is the Father 'allowing' the Son and Spirit to be, or perhaps the Father's loving and effective expectation of the Son's free response in the Holy Spirit. Barth hints in this direction when he says of God's gift of space and time, 'Strictly speaking, he grants them to his Word and therefore to himself' (417 rev.; *KD* 469). Yet this would represent a more trinitarianly specific identification of the immanent aspect of a given perfection than Barth is willing to venture here in II/1.

The economic aspect of Barth's opening definition is a simpler matter – or so it might appear. God gives to the creature not just space and time *per se*, but also its own existence in distinction from God as well as scope and opportunity (408) for repentance (415) and faith (418–19).[79] God continues to give these as he waits for the creature make appropriate use of them. But God need not have done so and could just as well have done otherwise. Even granted that God has done so, in light of 'all the assaults and torments which are obviously unavoidably bound up with space and time and with our existence as such', the likelihood of the creature making 'appropriate use' of the divine patience may seem an impossible fantasy (408). From 'the logic of abstract ideas', as in the case of 'ostensibly Christian' mysticism, or from observation of the human situation itself, 'we might equally well infer that God is impatient' (409). The reality of God's patience towards the creature is, once again, a matter of revelation. 'Here then we can actually speak of the necessary patience of God only if we take as the pure source and necessary determination of our knowledge the factual and concrete revelation of God in Jesus Christ in its factual and concrete attestation in Holy Scripture' (409). In light of the 'demonic' impatience of the god projected by mysticism, Barth insists again that revelation constitutes the 'pure source' of human knowledge of God. Perhaps also in light of the stunning intricacy and conceptual allure of his own unfolding exposition of the divine perfections, Barth feels it necessary to point out that theology is not a matter of logically profound or aesthetically pleasing ideas, but of Jesus Christ, obediently followed and humbly confessed.

It is with such confession that Barth turns to a second stage of argument (409–16). In words which recall his definition of the divine mercy (369),

---

[79] Cf. Emil Brunner and Karl Barth, *Natural Theology: Comprising 'Nature and Grace' by Professor Dr. Emil Brunner and the reply 'No!' by Dr. Karl Barth*, trans. Peter Fraenkel, with an introduction by John Baillie (1946; reprint Eugene: Wipf and Stock, 2002), 83; CD I/2, 68.

Barth states:

> We define God's patience as his will, which lies in his nature and con-
> stitutes his being and action, to allow to another...space and time for
> its own existence, thus conceding to this existence a reality side by side
> with his own, and thus fulfilling his will towards this other in such a
> way that he does not suspend and destroy it as this other, but rather
> accompanies it, sustains it and allows it to do as it pleases. (409–10
> rev.; KD 461)

Compared to their definitions of the divine righteousness, the Protestant
orthodox did a better job of indicating that it is 'for the sake of his own
grace and mercy and in the affirmation of his holiness and righteousness'
that God exercises his patience (409–10 rev.; KD 461). Thus, God's mercy,
as a patient mercy, does not 'override, overpower or cancel out' the life of the
creature but includes, transforms and renews it (411 rev.; KD 462–3). Barth
is even willing to concede that this is the kernel of truth behind Thomas's
maxim that grace does not destroy but rather perfects nature (411). God's
patience, moreover, is not inactive. It does not simply confer existence on the
creature and then withdraw. 'The exercise of patience is not to be confused
with the mere creation of time.'[80] Rather, God's patience actively accompanies and sustains and gives opportunity to the creature:

> God is not more powerful in his action than in his forbearance from
> action. Indeed there is no antithesis here: God's forbearance is only a
> specific form of his always powerful doing and being. (410)

As will become clearer in his account of the divine omnipotence, Barth does
not see divine and human action in competitive terms. God's patience is by
no means the 'sole effective reality' in this relationship (408).[81] Rather, it is
God's powerful action which enables and sustains human co-action. The
'long-suffering' of which Scripture speaks stands in 'no antithesis' to this
powerful action. It suggests no hesitation or weakness in the divine will, but
rather the fact that it is 'relentless and victorious' (410), as Barth illustrates
from God's dealings with Cain, Noah, Jonah and others (412–15).

    While these dealings represent notable episodes of the exercise of the divine
patience, Barth raises the question whether they can really be considered
victorious.[82] Was the creaturely response which was empowered and evoked

---

[80] Gotthard Oblau, *Gotteszeit und Menschenzeit: Eschatologie in der Kirchlichen
Dogmatik von Karl Barth* (Neukirchen-Vluyn: Neukirchener Verlag, 1988), 56.

[81] Cf. *CD* IV/3.1, 331–3.

[82] Cf. de Margerie, *Les Perfections*, 270: Barth does not explain how God's patience might
be related to the possibility of 'damnation and hell' (*CD* II/1, 648).

by the divine patience really and fully as it ought to have been? 'Indeed, is there anywhere or at any time a real act of human repentance for the sake of which it is worth while to God to spare men and to give them time and life?' (415 rev.; *KD* 467). If not, 'Why has God allowed history to go on so long?'[83] For that matter, are these scattered episodes sufficient even to justify the claim that God is patient rather than impatient?

> How often do we read that God 'repented' not only of his anger but also of his kindness and mercy? How often, to how many people, and how destructively his impatience also seems to take effect! (415; cf. 497–8)

And does not Scripture also testify that God will end this present world in a 'final catastrophe', 'a night that is without end' (415–16)? *Solvet saeclum in favilla*. According to Barth, even when the divine patience is clearly understood as a matter of revelation as attested in Scripture, it might well appear that God is neither victorious in his patience nor ultimately patient at all.

That even Scripture might be read in such a way as to call in question the reality of God's patience throws into sharp relief the importance of a christological hermeneutic, which Barth makes explicit in the third and final stage of his argument (416–22). 'The decisive moment of the biblical testimony to God's patience is that according to Heb 1:3 God upholds all things by the Word of his power' (416). God's patience is powerful and effective in his Word, regardless of 'what becomes manifest and actual from our side as repentance and conversion' (416 rev.; *KD* 469).

> The Word of God has not been spoken to man in vain, and God's Son has not himself become incarnate in vain. ... Because this happened for God's sake and therefore for man's sake, in spite of all its sinfulness human existence is justified before God by God himself, and therefore the patience of God, which leaves man his existence and space and time for it, is both well grounded and effective. (417)

In light of God's patience in his Word, the entire course of God's relation with humanity can be seen as 'an exercise in patience' (417 rev.; *KD* 469). That is, because 'God always, and continually, has time for Israel', Israel for its part 'has time to hear God's Word, and therefore time to live for the sake of God's Word and by its power' (417; cf. 62). The perpetual 'alternation between penitence and impenitence' in the history of Israel, with its 'predominating measure of impenitence', is therefore no discredit to the divine patience, but rather a clear sign of the fact that God is not merely patient,

---

[83] Van der Kooi, *As in a Mirror*, 345, in reference to 'Albert Schweitzer's discussion of the failure of the imminent expectation of the Second Coming'.

but effectively patient (417–18; cf. 420). For while no mere human has ever so truly repented as to justify God's patience, Jesus Christ did bring forth 'genuine fruits' of repentance (418). He did so 'genuinely and finally and in sufficient measure for us all in the perfect obedience which he, the one and only direct and true hearer of God's Word, has rendered in human flesh' (418). This is indeed 'a vision of history which is completely theological',[84] in which all human being and activity, whether by way of anticipation or recollection, finds it origin, justification, and goal in Jesus Christ.

God is not the 'sole effective reality' in this history, it will be recalled. In this history, God calls for a specific human response. Christ's vicarious repentance – he 'stands in place of them all and for them all has accomplished the genuine repentance which was expected from all' – this was not accomplished in order that human beings might 'continue in their impenitence', but in order that they might repent and 'appropriate the life which has been secured for them' (418 rev.; KD 471).

> To go the way of faith is what God's patience leaves to them and concedes to them. Therefore, the meaning of the divine patience is a summons to have faith. (419)

Faith is the human action, the human response, at which God's patience aims. The summons to faith is a summons to hear Jesus Christ 'as God's eternal Word spoken to us,…the decisive Word, the central truth of the biblical testimony to God's patience' (420). 'We must accept the fact that God can be patient to us because he is patient in his Word' (421). Yet even this summons to faith, while remaining a summons, has itself been fulfilled. In Christ 'the obedience which [God] demands from his creature has been rendered', and so 'there can be no question of disappointment or self-deception on the part of God', for Christ has made it possible 'for God in faithfulness to himself to be faithful to us too' (419).

> The only way open to us now is the way of gratitude for our life which has been undeservedly left to us; the way which will become and be of itself the way of the patience that we now have to show in suffering the judgements and punishments which strike us. The fact that, in spite of our infinite guilt, we are permitted to suffer them in the fellowship and shadow of the innocent suffering of Christ, by which we have been spared the suffering of the eternal wrath and judgement of God, is sufficient reason for us to suffer them patiently and to allow them to serve the purpose which they have for us: turning us away from every illusion of our own worthiness and turning us to the One who has made us worthy of God and so turning us to faith, in which we can

---

[84] Van der Kooi, As in a Mirror, 347.

give ourselves to the God who in his Son has taken our cause into his own hands. (421 rev.; *KD* 474)

Along this way of faith, 'answering his patience with our patience' and awaiting our redemption, we confess the patience of God (422).

God's patience, then, captures something of the teleology of providence. It is God's continual granting of space and time to the creature in the expectation that the creature will respond in repentance and in faith and in its own patient bearing of suffering. This divine expectation is not a matter of either weakness or passivity, but the powerful and active upholding of the creature which God accomplishes through his Word. It is thus strictly by faith in God's Word, incarnate as Jesus Christ, that God's patience can be confessed. But by faith in Jesus Christ, who alone has responded perfectly to God's patience, and who has done so for us all – in him this patience must be confessed as an effective and indeed a victorious patience.

Wisdom

Undoubtedly by design, the final perfection of the divine loving – like glory, the final perfection of the divine freedom – has particular reference to the outward movement of God and to the human perception which this movement effects. Talk of light, illumination, recognition and liberation recurs in both sub-sections. There is naturally nothing 'final' about wisdom; it serves as merely 'a provisional conclusion' to Barth's account of the perfections of the divine loving (422). Fittingly, the conclusion to Barth's account of wisdom is less than conclusive, the argument trailing off at the end of a long excursus, as if Barth were bowing before 'a task to which there is no end' (406). In traditional accounts of the divine perfections, wisdom is often clustered along with the divine knowledge and will. But while Barth does make mention of God's knowledge and will (and power) in the course of his exposition (423), he reserves fuller treatment of these for the second stage of his account of the divine omnipotence (§31.2, 543–99). Barth's exposition of the divine wisdom occurs in three stages. In the first, Barth identifies the divine wisdom as that by which God is rational, recognisable, intelligible, and purposeful (422–4). Second, Barth traces the connections between God's wisdom and his other perfections, from which wisdom emerges as that which both orders the other perfections and also liberates the creature to live before God (424–7). The third stage (427–39) addresses the biblical testimony to wisdom, first in the wisdom literature of the Old Testament (427–32) and then as this is given unique expression in Solomon and taken up in the New Testament witness to Christ (432–9).

Whereas Barth gives two succinct, explicit definitions of the divine patience (408, 409–10), which are elaborated like section theses in subsequent exposition, it is more by way of extended description that he arrives at the meaning of the divine wisdom. Following his introductory comments, Barth begins his first stage of argument (422–4) by noting that the divine patience is 'thankfully and obediently to be accepted because it is [God's] will' (423). This raises the question how God's will, as expressed in his patience, can be accepted by the creature. Barth's answer is a first hint at the meaning of the divine wisdom: 'God does not reveal himself and is not God in such a way that his expressed will is not in itself and as such light and recognisable as light' (423). Thus God's wisdom, 'recognisable as light', is accepted by the creature in recognition, in acknowledgment (423).

> That is to say, it is meaningful in itself, and it shows itself to be meaningful to us who hear it. The wisdom of God is that God not only wills but knows what he wills...[and] why and wherefore he wills it. (423)

God's wisdom is the 'why and wherefore' of his will, that is, its reason and purpose, its 'meaning, plan and intention' (423). Worldly wisdom, by contrast, is simply 'random and capricious' (424 rev.; KD 477).

> The Word of God, however, as the foundation of his patience is neither random nor capricious. The Word of God shines as light in the darkness. When we hear it, we hear the reason, meaning, purpose and intention of God. When we hear it, we are instructed, enlightened, knowing and wise. When we hear it, the darkness of chance and caprice is lightened. (424 rev.; KD 477)

To recognise and adore such wisdom, to respond to the divine patience, is no less than 'the acceptance of reason, of the sense and purpose for our life'; to reject it is to 'repel all reason' (424). Barth then makes the startling claim that 'On *rational* grounds...we really cannot *not* believe!' (424 rev.; KD 478). By 'rational' Barth does not mean 'what the creature, apart from God and his revelation, considers to be wise', but faithful reason, reason which stands 'on the basis of the revealed Word' (424). The claim is nonetheless a bold one, and it sets up the contrast Barth will draw in his third stage of argument between a strictly human 'art of living' and the obedience which constitutes true human wisdom before God.

The second stage of Barth's argument takes up the relation between wisdom and the other perfections of the divine loving (424–7). Insofar as wisdom is itself the divine essence, Barth can affirm of God both that 'he is gracious and merciful just because and as he is wise' and that 'he is holy and righteous just because and as he is wise' (425). We have heard Barth say as much of other perfections. Once again, such claims must not be misread as implying that wisdom is somehow more basic to Barth's conception of the divine essence than any of the other perfections. Wisdom is a divine perfection. *Eo ipso* it can play no more central a role than any of the other perfections. It is against precisely such a misunderstanding that Barth warns when he says that 'due humility' before God's self-revelation will not allow any single concept 'to usurp authority' (375; cf. 213–14, 338). Likewise, there can be no 'lingering unduly over any one proposition or letting it become the final word or the guiding principle' (407). Barth speaks as he does of the divine wisdom because (as he will explain concerning the divine constancy and omnipotence) 'The whole essence of God must be seen and understood from this standpoint too, as if it were the one and only standpoint' (491).

In all of the perfections of God's loving, then, God is wise. Thus, 'God is not guilty of impulsiveness or irrationality when he is gracious and merciful'. Rather, 'in this as in every other respect he is the God of order' (425). God's grace and holiness, mercy and righteousness are neither capricious nor paradoxical but wise, that is, purposeful and reasonable. This constitutes the possibility not merely of our recognition of God's will but also our confidence in him. For such 'confidence is based on the appreciation of reason, meaning and order' (425), and it is this appreciation which gives us freedom before him. 'God is wise in so far as his whole activity, as willed by him, is also thought out by him, and thought out by him from the very outset with correctness and completeness, so that it is a meaningful and to that extent a reliable and a liberating activity' (425–6 rev.; *KD* 479).

If the reader brings to Barth's text a modern understanding of freedom as the capacity to choose between alternatives, 'a power of acting or not acting, according to the determinations of the will',[85] it will not be at all clear how God's order and correctness could serve to enable rather than suppress human freedom. For Barth, however, following the Augustinian tradition, human freedom is not a matter of choice but of goodness. Barth hints at this at the beginning of *CD* II/1 as he explains how faith and the knowledge of God are themselves obedience:

> This obedience is not that of a slave but of a child. It is not blind but seeing. It is not coerced but free. (36)

Faith must be understood as obedience (37), says Barth, and this obedience is itself the creature's freedom. 'The command of God sets man free.'[86] Much later in the *Dogmatics*, Barth explains in detail:

> Freedom is not an empty and formal concept. It is one which is filled out with a positive meaning. It does not speak only of a capacity. It

---

[85] David Hume, *An Enquiry Concerning Human Understanding*, ed. Tom L. Beauchamp, The Clarendon Edition of the Works of David Hume 3 (Oxford: Oxford University Press, 2000), §8.1 (72).
[86] *CD* II/2, 586.

speaks concretely of the fact that man can be genuinely man as God, who has given him this capacity, can in his freedom be genuinely God. The free man is the man who can be genuinely man in fellowship with God. He exercises and has this freedom, therefore, not in an indefinite but in a definite choice in which he demonstrates this capacity. But since this capacity is grounded in his fellowship with God, this means in the choice in which he confirms and practises his fellowship with God; in the election ... of faith and obedience and gratitude and loyalty to God.[87]

Here Barth points out the correspondence between divine and human freedom. Just as God's freedom is not an abstract freedom from the creature, but a freedom for it (cf. 313–14), so creaturely freedom is not an abstract (and dubious) capacity to act either for or against God, but a freedom for God – the God whose service is perfect freedom. The wisdom and order of the divine being and action thus provide the grounds for a correspondingly wise and ordered and therefore free human life.

At the close of this second stage of argument, Barth turns again to the wisdom of the divine life itself. God's wisdom characterises not only 'his activity in his works' but also 'his inner activity, ... the essential actuality of his divine being' (426).

The wisdom of God is the inner correctness and clarity with which the divine life, in its self-fulfilment as such and in its works, justifies and confirms itself and in which it is the source and sum and criterion of all that is correct and clear. It is in this inner correctness and clarity that God loves, and this is the source of the dignity with which he is free in his love. (426 rev.; KD 480)

This means that wisdom marks everything that God is and does, both in his 'self-fulfilment' (i.e. ad intra) and in his works (i.e. ad extra), both in his loving and also in his freedom. God is wise in the fact 'that God apprehends himself and is therefore eternal reason, that he lives and is active in himself in correctness and clarity'; and wisdom also 'characterises his whole activity as reliable and liberating, as something in which we can have confidence' (427 rev.; KD 481). As with the divine righteousness, it is the scope of the divine wisdom, its marking everything God is and does, including every other divine perfection, which was not grasped on Barth's account by various earlier attempts to define it (426).

The final stage of argument (427–39) takes up Scripture's testimony to God's wisdom as the 'instrument of the divine providence' and as the 'meaning of his patience and forbearance' (427). Barth's chief aim is to show that

[87] CD IV/2, 494; cf. III/4, 647–8.

God's wisdom is God himself, ultimately manifest as Jesus Christ crucified and risen. God's wisdom, therefore, cannot be separated from Jesus Christ and reduced, for example, to the establishment and maintenance of some kind of universal moral order. Neither can the human wisdom which corresponds to the divine wisdom have anything to do with what might be called common-sense good living, with an achievable adherence to a naturally discernable moral order. Wisdom is not, for example, primarily a matter of 'trying to integrate knowledge, understanding, critical questioning and good judgement with a view to the flourishing of human life and the whole of creation'; nor is wisdom 'in principle…available' to 'Jews, Christians, Muslims, Hindus and others', to 'those of various religions and none', so that one may just as well be 'wisely religious' as 'wisely secular'.[88] Barth does indeed claim that the divine wisdom is at some level the recognisable, intellectually graspable order and reason of the divine being. True human wisdom, however, and therefore true human recognition of and correspondence to the divine wisdom manifest in Christ, must be strictly a matter of repentance, faith and obedience.

Barth turns first to the wisdom literature of the Old Testament (427–32). Here, particularly in the Book of Proverbs, 'wisdom is equated with God himself'. Thus there can be no 'independent principle of world interpretation, but only the self-explanation of God' (429). According to Barth, while the divine identity of the wisdom figure in Proverbs has long attracted attention, the particular message of this figure has not. In fact, it is 'clearly nothing other than the well-known preaching of repentance, judgement and salvation' (428). It is true enough to say that '[t]he whole art of living and understanding life consists in heeding and accepting divine wisdom and in this way becoming wise' (430). But such heeding and accepting must be clearly understood as 'the fear of the Lord' and as living 'in covenant with him'. God's wisdom, therefore, cannot be construed as 'an imminent divine wisdom accessible to and recognisable by man of himself' (430). Rather, the divine wisdom is to be found only 'in his holy and righteous, gracious and merciful dealings with Israel' (432).

This Old Testament witness to the divine wisdom becomes even clearer, according to Barth, as it is summed up in the figure of Solomon and then taken up in the New Testament (432–9):

> What moves [God] to exercise patience is his holy and righteous, gracious and merciful meaning, his will to reveal to us this meaning, to

---

[88] David F. Ford and Graham Stanton, 'Introduction', in *idem*, eds., *Reading Texts, Seeking Wisdom: Scripture and Theology* (London: SCM, 2003), 2; David F. Ford, 'Jesus Christ the Wisdom of God (1)', in *ibid.*, 4, 20; David F. Ford, 'Knowledge, meaning, and the world's great challenges', *Scottish Journal of Theology* 57.2 (2004): 201 and 201 n. 31.

lead us to repentance, and therefore to make our own lives meaningful. The meaning of his patience is his wisdom. (432 rev.; *KD* 487)

It is God's 'meaning' which constitutes the true 'worldly wisdom' – a wisdom Barth describes provocatively as 'the philosophy of the created universe and the philosophy of human existence' (432 rev.; *KD* 487). As in his earlier assertion of the rationality of faith (424), Barth is perfectly happy using such terminology, provided is it 'properly understood'.

This 'philosophy' is certainly not to be derived from reflection upon the universe or upon the being of man. It can be appreciated only by the hearing of God's own Word which as such gives us the right philosophy of the universe and of our own human existence. (432 rev.; *KD* 487)

If, as Scripture says, 'Jesus Christ is made not only our justification, sanctification and redemption, but with a special emphasis our wisdom', then this 'right philosophy' can only be a matter of faith (432). This emerges with particular clarity from the accounts of Solomon, whose wisdom is explicitly 'a gift of God which has to be sought' (433). As becomes explicit in the New Testament, particularly in 1 Cor. 1–2, this wisdom, the gospel of the crucifixion of the 'greater than Solomon', is utter 'foolishness' to those who are perishing (435).

To this divine wisdom in which 'we ourselves may now be wise in faith' (437), there corresponds a life lived 'at the disposal of God's wisdom' and testifying faithfully to it (437). Such true, Christian wisdom, says Barth, is 'a wisdom apart, alien to all the human wisdom of this world as such, and to that extent, where there is no faith, alien to all who live within it' (437). In polemic such as this against any so-called wisdom that does not proceed from faith, Barth can give the impression that there is no moral component to living at God's disposal and testifying to him.[89] Actually Barth takes this moral component for granted. 'How can God be understood as the Lord if that does not involve the problem of human obedience?'[90] Barth does not explain how a uniquely Christian obedience is related, if at all, to what might appear to be a very similar morality based on the 'wisdom of this world'. But if Barth does not explain this relationship, he does at one point describe such Christian obedience in terms which appear suitable to a non-Christian morality. According to Barth, the very wisdom which is Jesus Christ himself is the same described in James 3:17 as 'first pure, then peaceable, gentle, and easy to be intreated, full of mercy and good fruits, without partiality, and without hypocrisy' (439). Jesus Christ is therefore the divine

[89] Cf. Webster, *Barth's Ethics of Reconciliation*, 57–8.
[90] CD II/2, 512.

wisdom itself, God 'turning to man in grace and mercy,...in his love but also in his freedom' (439), and he also constitutes and brings about 'man's attainment of wisdom,...his winning through to faith' (438).

The divine wisdom, then, is the reason, meaning, and order of the divine life which is manifest, recognisable and to be adored in Jesus Christ. Jesus Christ himself also constitutes the human wisdom which corresponds to the divine, and he enables us to participate in this wisdom through the gift of faith and obedience. While Barth gives few examples of the particular ethical shape which this faith and obedience will take, he clearly maintains (as he will later express it) that despite 'all its human questionableness and frailty the life of the elect should become...[the] image and repetition and attestation and acknowledgment' of God's electing love in Jesus Christ.[91] With this final indication of the centrality of Jesus Christ both for our understanding of the divine life as well as for our living of the Christian life, Barth concludes his exposition of the perfections of the divine loving.

[91] *CD* II/2, 512.

4

THE PERFECTIONS OF THE DIVINE FREEDOM (§31)

One might have thought that Barth would have less to say about the kinds of divine attributes beloved of the more philosophically inclined thinkers in the tradition. In fact, Barth has more to say about them – much more. And precisely because he is dealing with concepts to which even theologically inclined thinkers have often given highly abstract formulation, his critiques of these aspects of tradition are the more incisive. Correspondingly, his positive formulations of these perfections, his drawing them into healthier proximity to the gospel, are – at least for those who share some of Barth's basic convictions – the more rewarding. It is with the perfections of the divine freedom that Barth makes the more decisive contribution to theology.

The perfections of the divine freedom, according to Barth, must come after those of the divine loving. The logic of this sequence is straightforward. Barth argues in §28 that God reveals himself as the one who loves in freedom. In the event of revelation, God's loving is logically prior to his freedom. Moreover, because God's being is in his act of revelation, Barth concludes that there is an analogous priority of love over freedom in God's own life. It is in following this 'order of the divine life' (440) that Barth treats first the perfections of the divine loving (§30) and now turns to the perfections of the divine freedom (§31). This sequence does not, however, imply any subordination or inferiority of the divine freedom, either in God's revelation or in his own life: 'God's freedom is no less divine than his love' (440).

Mirroring the perfections of the divine loving, but now moving 'in some sense in the opposite direction' (440), Barth selects three further pairs of perfections. Both members of each pair are 'directed to God's freedom, but the second in such a way that it reminds us of the cohesion and unity of God's freedom with his love' (440). In other words, all six perfections of §31 indicate primarily the divine freedom, but the second of each pair also secondarily indicates the divine loving.[1] Driving this love-freedom dialectic in part is Barth's desire to capture what he often describes as the 'divinity' of a given perfection (e.g. in the theses of both §30 and §31). What Barth calls the 'divinity' of any given perfection is its co-inherence with all other divine perfections and consequent transcendence of human concepts. 'The divinity of his freedom consists and confirms itself in the fact that even in his unity he is omnipresent, in his constancy omnipotent, and in his eternity glorious' (441). As Barth says later of the 'divinity' of God's omnipotence:

> This raises his grace and holiness, mercy and righteousness, patience and wisdom absolutely above the perfections which, under these or similar names, could be ascribed to the creature or any of its fictitious creations. They possess the strength and truth to be perfections of the true God, and each of them individually the true God himself, because they are all of them omnipotent: omnipotent grace, omnipotent holiness, etc. (523 rev.; *KD* 588)

This constant shifting of attention from one perfection to another represents in part Barth's deliberate attempt to mark the provisionality of his exposition. No single concept, nor even any collection of concepts, is ultimately adequate to describe the divine identity. Barth therefore sets his account into a perpetual motion of dialectic in order to keep before his readers the God whom human concepts can never more than partially indicate.

Why these six particular attributes? First, as with the attributes of the divine loving, the selection is fairly complete. With Barth's incorporation of various subordinate concepts under these six, little is missing from what one might find in more comprehensive lists of attributes. What Barth does omit – infinity, for example, or the divine incomprehensibility or invisibility[2] – may reflect either his denial that God's relation to the world is to be understood in oppositional terms (God as opposed to all that is finite) or his insistence on the positive validity of human knowledge of God in faith. Barth claims neither direct scriptural warrant nor even hallowed dogmatic precedent for this selection. 'We have to admit that basically this selection and juxtaposition can possess and claim only the character of an attempt or suggestion' (441; cf. 352). Looking back from the end of his exposition, Barth says again, 'We have not made any presumptuous claim that these are

---

[1] Colin E. Gunton, *Act and Being: Towards a Theology of the Divine Attributes* (London: SCM, 2002), 100, wrongly describes the six attributes of §31 as 'three perfections of the divine freedom ... balanced and controlled by their "love" counterparts'. Likewise Charles Edward Raynal, III, *Karl Barth's Conception of the Perfections of God* (Ph.D. diss., Yale University, 1973), 102, 138–9.

[2] As part of §27.1, 'The Hiddenness of God', Barth does briefly discuss God's incomprehensibility or invisibility (*CD* II/1, 184–6).

the only right ways or that our ways are God's ways' (658). By implication, no exposition of the divine attributes can achieve more than this for the simple reason that God cannot be comprehensively or exhaustively described. Those who would object to the form of Barth's exposition cannot do so, he protests, merely by pointing out its 'inevitable defects and deficiencies', but only by giving a better exposition of their own (442).

Barth also issues an occasionally unheeded warning:

> It must not be forgotten that the unavoidable schematic form here in evidence is only a means to an end. On no account should it attract independent attention, for example on account of the symbolic numbers 2, 3 and 12. (442; cf. 352–3)

At the very least, what Barth must mean by this warning is that he could just as well have treated more or (perhaps) fewer attributes (cf. 406–7), and that he could have done so either singly or in different sub-groups than pairs. This need not invalidate William Stacy Johnson's claim that Barth's successive pairs of perfections move 'from primordial ground, to gracious encounter, to consummate effect'.[3] There undoubtedly exists some such movement in both series of attributes, a resonance of the respective pairs with past creation, present reconciliation, and future redemption.[4] This resonance, however, cannot be pressed into service of Johnson's further claim that 'Although Barth does not make this explicit, the three pairings correspond to the trinitarian pattern of God's relationship with the world'.[5] While Barth, following the creedal pattern, does loosely appropriate creation, reconciliation and redemption to Father, Son and Spirit, to appropriate the paired attributes to Father, Son and Spirit as Johnson suggests is both to move Barth's 'selection and juxtaposition' well beyond the realm of the provisional and simply to claim more than the exposition itself will bear. Eternity and glory, for example, constitute the third pair of freedom attributes and should, therefore, be appropriated, on Johnson's reading, to the Spirit. Barth insists, however, that the divine eternity is just as much the eternity of Father and Son as it is the eternity of the Holy Spirit (615). Likewise, Barth says of the divine glory, 'It is as well to realise at this point that the glory of God is not only the glory of the Father and the Son but the glory of the whole divine Trinity, and therefore the glory of the Holy Spirit as well' (669). In both cases Barth explicitly denies that this third pair of perfections corresponds to the third person of the Holy

---

[3] William Stacy Johnson, *The Mystery of God: Karl Barth and the Postmodern Foundations of Theology* (Louisville: Westminster John Knox, 1997), 52.

[4] Johnson, *The Mystery of God*, 52–7.

[5] Johnson, *The Mystery of God*, 52.

Trinity. In *CD* I/1 Barth identifies some of the dogmatic logic behind his warning:

> All the perfections...are as much the perfections of the Father as of the Son and the Spirit. *Per appropriationem* this act or this attribute must now be given prominence in relation to this or that mode of being....But only *per appropriationem* may this happen, and in no case, therefore, to the forgetting or denying of God's presence in all his modes of being.[6]

Nowhere in *CD* II/1 does Barth appropriate any perfection to Father, Son or Spirit. This would appear to have changed significantly come *CD* IV. For the present, however, Barth maintains that God's being 'is whole and undivided, and therefore all his perfections are equally the being of all three modes of the divine being' (660). Johnson's suggestion ascribes to respective persons what Barth insists belongs to all. As Barth clearly states, the selection and arrangement of attributes, including their sequence, cannot be read as more than suggestive.

Given the highly symmetrical plan of Barth's treatment of the perfections of the divine loving and those of the divine freedom, the question arises why the latter runs to nearly three times the length of the former. A number of possibilities suggest themselves. While nearly all of the perfections of the divine freedom receive further and occasionally even extended treatment elsewhere in the *Church Dogmatics*,[7] they are nevertheless not so constantly

---

[6] *CD* I/1, 375. In *CD* I/1 (361–4, 380–2), Barth does appropriate holiness, mercy and love to Father, Son and Spirit, respectively. However, while Barth goes on to discuss eternal love in relation to the Spirit (§12.2, 480–4), he does not develop holiness or mercy in the corresponding sections on the Father (§10.2) and the Son (§11.2). Moreover, on at least one occasion, Barth substitutes goodness for love in reference to the Spirit (*CD* I/1, 372). The appropriation, in other words, is very loose. Cf. John Webster, *Barth*, Outstanding Christian Thinkers (London: Continuum, 2000), 57. On the various other 'appropriations' in *CD* I/1, see Dennis W. Jowers, 'The Reproach of Modalism: A Difficulty for Karl Barth's Doctrine of the Trinity', *Scottish Journal of Theology* 56.2 (2003): 233, 236.

[7] For example, God's unity is discussed in *CD* I/1, §9; omnipresence would presumably have occupied Barth again had he been able to include a discussion of the Lord's Supper in *CD* IV/4. Constancy comes up again, for example, in discussions of the incarnation, *CD* IV/1, 179–83, and of the divine and human in Christ, *CD* IV/2, 84–7; omnipotence appears as part of providence in *CD* III/3, §49. Eternity and its relation to time appear in *CD* I/2, §14, *CD* III/2, §47, and *CD* III/4, §56.1; glory would likely have resurfaced in the projected fifth volume of the *Dogmatics*. Some precedent for further discussion of omnipresence and glory can be found in §36 ('*Die Gegenwart Jesu Christi*') and §38 ('*Die Ehre Gottes*') of Karl Barth, *Unterricht in der christlichen Religion*, vol. 3, *Die Lehre von der Versöhnung, Die Lehre von der Erlösung, 1925/1926*, ed. Hinrich Stoevesandt, Karl Barth Gesamtausgabe 38 (Zürich: Theologischer Verlag Zürich, 2003), esp. 438–48, 489.

before Barth's gaze as are the perfections of the divine loving. As a result, Barth may have felt that the perfections of the divine freedom required fuller treatment here. With the perfections of the divine loving, on the other hand, Barth may have felt at liberty to be more brief. It is probably for this reason that, of all the attributes, the briefest exposition (a mere five pages in the English) is devoted to the very attribute with which Berkouwer attempted to sum up the entirety of Barth's theology: grace. There are also in §31 many more subordinate concepts which Barth finds necessary to elaborate, for example, simplicity and uniqueness as part of unity, knowledge and will as part of omnipotence, and pre-temporality, supra-temporality and post-temporality as part of eternity. Furthermore, since Barth finds that he has more to correct in the tradition's handling of the attributes of the divine freedom, he engages the tradition at greater length.[8] With regard to the attributes of the divine loving, particularly grace and righteousness, the Reformation had already done much of Barth's work for him. Even the absence of a developed pre-Reformation tradition on certain of these attributes may have eased Barth's way. Colin Gunton claims, for example, of Stephen Charnock's 1682 discourse on holiness, 'The power of the account derives largely from the fact that there is no tradition ... for the doctrine other than scripture, so that what we read is an account of God's holiness entirely derived from the shape God's action takes in the witness of the Old and New Testaments.'[9] While Gunton's assessment of the tradition is certainly hyperbolic, it makes the point that Scripture played a more controlling role in traditional expositions of several of what Barth classifies as perfections of the divine loving. Consequently, Barth's consideration of these perfections requires less polemic. Other reasons for the disproportionate brevity of §30 or length of §31, perhaps including Barth's lecturing schedule, could undoubtedly be added to those offered here.

§31.1. Unity and Omnipresence

'I believe in one God.' Following the Nicene Creed, and acknowledging the prominence of the concept both in Scripture and in patristic thought, Barth begins his treatment of the perfections of the divine freedom with an account of the divine unity.[10] Barth also gains a rhetorical advantage in placing unity first. This enables him to emphasise, as he embarks on his exposition of a

---

[8] Jan Štefan, 'Gottes Vollkommenheiten nach KD II/1', in Karl Barth im europäischen Zeitgeschehen (1935–1950): Widerstand – Bewährung – Orientierung, ed. Michael Beintker, Christian Link, and Michael Trowitzsch (Zürich: Theologischer Verlag Zürich, 2010), 97–8.

[9] Gunton, Act and Being, 90; cf. 88 for a more careful statement.

[10] As with grace among the perfections of the divine loving, Cross imagines 'a primacy of ... unity' among the perfections of the divine freedom. See Terry L. Cross, Dialectic

whole new series of perfections, that all of these are yet one, a unity, with those that went before. It is the one God who is the goal toward which these many concepts strain. The divine unity also bears a strategically significant, if merely apparent, relationship to one of the most assured results of natural theology, 'monotheism'. This enables Barth, as he begins his exposition of those attributes traditionally more susceptible to the influence of natural theology, to draw once again the sharpest of contrasts between a theology derived strictly from revelation and one derived with the assistance of anything else.

With unity, which expresses in part God's free distinction from creation (442), Barth pairs omnipresence, which counterbalances unity by expressing God's loving nearness to creation (462). Charles Raynal, however, sees a different counterbalancing at work here – one which he claims to be operative to some degree in the other pairs of attributes. According to Raynal, 'The restriction of unity by the perfection of omnipresence affirms that the unity in question is not a simple projection of oneness [via eminentiae] onto a cosmic screen.'[11] To begin with, this assumes that the relation between paired perfections is one of mutual limitation rather than mutual expansion. Moreover, a little reflection on the content of Barth's exposition of unity, constancy and eternity shows that none can be claimed – even without the 'restriction' of their counterpart – as the mere projection of ordinary concepts. God's unity includes both his triunity as well as the multiplicity of his perfections. God's constancy includes the eternal liveliness of Father, Son and Spirit. And God's eternity, as pure duration, includes an ordered simultaneity of past, present and future in the divine life. None of these attributes needs its counterpart to exonerate it of the charge of being merely a projection of a human concept.[12] If such exoneration were needed, Barth's explicit claim, as already noted, is that what distinguishes a given perfection from ordinary concepts, what marks a given perfection as divine, is not its pairing with a single other perfection but its unity with all of the other perfections. There is a deeper problem, however, in Raynal's proposal. Not only does it fail on examination of the specific content of Barth's exposition. It also reflects a tendency to see method, as opposed to dogmatic content, as the driving consideration 'below the surface'[13] of Barth's exposition. Against this, it must be insisted that Barth's intent with the entire love-freedom dialectic, including the pairing of the attributes, is to give a faithful account of God's self-revelation as the one who loves in freedom. While this positive, dogmatic goal clearly

---

in *Karl Barth's Doctrine of God* (New York: Peter Lang, 2001), 192. Neither claim has any basis in Barth's exposition.

[11] Raynal, *Perfections*, 110.

[12] Raynal appears to acknowledge this in the case of eternity (*Perfections*, 115–16), but this does not lead him to qualify his claims for the logic of the pairing of perfections.

[13] Raynal, *Perfections*, 105.

involves methodological commitments, it is not primarily method which accounts for the structural features of Barth's account.

Unity

'If we understand it rightly, we can express all that God is by saying that God is One' (442). Thus, Barth's provocative entrée, for how, the reader asks, can 'one' be an adequate indication of God? Barth's qualification, 'if we understand it rightly', highlights the inadequacy of the concept 'one' which motivates such a question. God's unity is fundamentally different.

> By this he differentiates himself from everything that is distinct from himself. By this he rules and determines it, and by this he is also in himself what he is. He is One. (442)

These are hardly the implications a reader could be expected to discern in the claim, 'God is One'. The divine unity, Barth will go on to explain, is a matter of both trinitarian and christological confession, a far richer concept than any mathematical or logical definition of oneness. To begin with, God's oneness consists of both uniqueness and simplicity (442). Following this opening definition, Barth's argument proceeds in two stages, beginning with parallel, introductory discussions of uniqueness (442–5) and simplicity (445–57). These initial discussions both emphasise the way in which uniqueness and simplicity manifest the divine freedom. Barth then repeats this structure in a second stage of argument, which consists of a clarification of concepts (447–50) and more detailed discussions of uniqueness (450–7) and simplicity (457–61). These concluding discussions bring uniqueness and simplicity to their christological resolution and emphasise the way in which they also manifest the divine love.

God's uniqueness, then, as an indication of his freedom, consists in the fact that 'he is the only one of his kind' (442):

> It is he alone who lives. It is he alone who loves. He alone is gracious, merciful and wise. He alone is holy, righteous and patient. And he alone is also free, with all that this involves. To be one and unique is true only of him in the sense proper to him. For it is only in him that everything (including uniqueness) is essential, original, proper, and for this reason also creative, so that now it can all belong to other forms of being also in a created, dependent, derived and improper way. (442–3)

God's uniqueness is thus what Barth elsewhere designates the 'divinity' of individual perfections. While creatures may exhibit aspects of the these perfections, they do so only derivatively and improperly and therefore 'not in a way that competes with God' (443). If creaturely freedom, for example,

105

were to compete with God's freedom, the creature would in effect 'stand beside him as a second of his kind', and so God's freedom would no longer be unique, no longer 'incomparable' (443).

From this aspect of God's uniqueness, Barth draws two forceful conclusions. First, in the human sphere, God's uniqueness presents 'a claim that is total and unlimited', an 'exclusive demand' that God alone be recognised as God, and that humans recognise themselves as loved and elected by him (443). Second, and grounding the first conclusion, God's occupancy of the divine sphere is exclusive and total. 'Beside God there are only his creatures or false gods' (444). Barth then turns a prophetic eye to contemporary events and declares the dramatic implications of God's sole and unique deity:

> There is a real basis for the feeling, current to this day, that every genuine proclamation of the Christian faith is a force disturbing to, even destructive of, the advance of religion, its life and rightness and peace. It is bound to be so. Olympus and Valhalla evacuate when the message of the God who is the one and only God is really known and believed. The figures of every religious culture are necessarily secularised and recede. They can keep themselves alive only as ideas, symbols, and ghosts, and finally as comic figures....It is on the truth of this sentence, that God is One, that the Third Reich of Adolf Hitler will make shipwreck. Let this sentence be uttered in such a way that it is heard and grasped, and at once 450 prophets of Baal are always in fear of their lives. (444 rev.; *KD* 500)[14]

---

[14] Citing letters written by Barth on 7 and 18 September 1939, Eberhard Busch reports that, at the outbreak of war, 'Barth thought "with sadness" of all the sorrow that this war would bring to "many dear people in Germany" and to "countless others in every land". But he also believed that now, at any rate, "the beginning of the end of Hitlerism...has surely dawned. In that respect one could breathe a sigh of relief."' See Eberhard Busch, *Karl Barth: His Life from Letters and Autobiographical Texts*, trans. John Bowden (Grand Rapids: Eerdmans, 1994), 298. See Barth's similar comments on the war in his sermon of 24 September in *idem, Predigten 1935–1952, Karl Barth Gesamtausgabe* 26, ed. Harmut Spieker and Hinrich Stoevesandt (Zürich: Theologischer Verlag Zürich, 1996), 173–82, esp. 175–6. As astonishing as his prophecy is in retrospect, Barth was not alone at this time in thinking that the 'beginning of the end' of Hitler was at hand. At Germany's reoccupation of the Rhineland (7 March 1936) and in the months preceding the Munich Agreement (29 September 1938), the German populace was in a state of mass depression or 'war psychosis' for fear of the certain destruction of Germany should war break out. In stark contrast to the widespread optimism of 1914, 'apprehension and anxiety were the commonest emotions' when Hitler finally swept into Poland and war began. See Richard J. Evans, *The Third Reich in Power: 1933–1939* (New York: Penguin, 2005), 150, 635, 674–7, 704. Even a year and a half into the war (April 1941), Barth's confidence was unshaken; see his *Ein Brief aus der Schweiz nach Grossbritannien*, in *idem, Offene Briefe 1935–1942, Karl Barth Gesamtausgabe* 36, ed. Diether Koch (Zürich: Theologischer Verlag Zürich,

In other words, because God is uniquely God, 'the fear, trust, honour and service' due to him are due exclusively to him and must be jealously safe-guarded as his alone (445). Barth's quotation here of the opening line of the *Scots Confession*, the subject of his 1937–1938 Gifford Lectures at the University of Aberdeen, is significant.[15] 'We confesse and acknawledge ane onlie God, to whom only we must cleave, whom onelie we must serve, whom onelie we must worship and in whom onelie we must put our trust' (445). Barth has not yet spoken explicitly of natural theology in his discussion of divine unity. This quotation, however, like the first article of the Barmen Declaration,[16] which in context it may be intended to recall, implies that the totalitarian aspirations of Hitler cannot be decisively opposed by the merely human and therefore quite relative uniqueness which natural theology might ascribe to deity.

Simplicity, the sister component to uniqueness, is also formulated in this first stage of exposition as an indicator of the divine freedom. God's simplicity means that he is not 'composed out of what is distinct from himself' and that 'in all that he is and does, he is wholly and undividedly himself' (445). Behind these strong and very traditional affirmations of non-composition and indivisible action lies Barth's even stronger rejection of the apparent importance accorded the concept of simplicity in scholastic formulations of the doctrine. As Barth argued earlier, certain scholastic formulations of divine simplicity as an absolute sameness and uniformity were often (though inadvertently) stated so categorically as both to nominalise the multiplicity of divine perfections as well as to call into question even the personal distinctions between Father, Son, and Spirit (327–30). Such formulations set a concept of simplicity in tension with the revealed distinctions between God's multiple perfections and between Father, Son and Spirit. Barth, on the other hand, argues that no such tension exists between God's simplicity and either his triunity or the multiplicity of his perfections (cf. 330–5):[17]

> He is One even in the distinctions of the divine persons of the Father, the Son and the Holy Spirit. He is One even in the real wealth of his distinguishable perfections. (445)

2001), 302–3; ET *A Letter to Great Britain from Switzerland*, trans. E. H. Gordon and George Hill (London: Sheldon, 1941), 28–9.

[15] Karl Barth, *The Knowledge of God and the Service of God According to the Teaching of the Reformation: Recalling the Scottish Confession of 1560*, trans. J. L. M. Haire and Ian Henderson (London: Hodder and Stoughton, 1938).

[16] *CD* II/1, 172–8; cf. Busch, *Karl Barth*, 245–8.

[17] The tradition would, of course, agree. It is overly abstract definitions of simplicity which Barth opposes, not the tradition's general approach to simplicity. See Stephen R. Holmes, '"Something Much Too Plain to Say": Towards a Defence of the Doctrine of Divine Simplicity', *Neue Zeitschrift für systematische Theologie und Religionsphilosophie* 43.1 (2001): 137–54.

God's simplicity, in other words, is such that, though 'God is One in him-self...he is not alone.'[18]

Barth goes on to explain the puzzling claim of his opening definition, that it is by God's unity that he 'rules and determines' created reality (442). The reason God's unity function like this is because God, as also simple, never exists except in full possession, that is, in full control, of 'all the other attributes' (445):

> Nothing can affect him, or be far from him, or contradict or withstand
> him, because in himself there is no separation, distance[19] contradiction
> or opposition. He is Lord in every relationship, because he is the Lord
> of himself, unconditionally One as Father, Son and Holy Spirit, and in
> the whole real wealth of his being. (445)[20]

Barth is not saying that God somehow acquires lordship by means of his simplicity. God's simplicity God means that he is never without his lordship (or any other attribute) when he confronts creation. Conversely, one of the decisive implications of God's simplicity is he remains categorically distinct from creation:

> We must not understand or interpret creation, or even the incarnation
> of the Son of God in Jesus Christ, either as a commixture of God with
> the world, or his becoming identical with it, or as a kind of outgoing
> of God from himself. (446 rev.; *KD* 502)

Barth alludes here to one of the standard Reformed objections to the Lutheran *genus maiestaticum* (cf. 487–90). If omnipresence were 'commixed' with Christ's human nature, so would all the other divine attributes 'on account of the perfect simplicity of the [divine] essence'.[21] Barth is aware that such

---

[18] *CD* III/2, 218.

[19] Barth here denies that there is in God any 'distance' (*Ferne*; *KD* 501; repeated on *CD* II/1, 608; *KD* 685). He must presumably intend a stronger, more divisive sense of 'dis-tance' than in his subsequent affirmations of both 'remoteness [*Ferne*] and proximity' in God (*CD* II/1, 461; *KD* 518) as well as 'togetherness at a distance [*Distanz*]' (*CD* II/1, 468; *KD* 527).

[20] The quotation continues, 'For every distinction of his being and working is simply a repetition and corroboration [*Wiederholung und Bestätigung*] of the one being.' In light of Barth's well-known description of Father, Son and Spirit as a 'threefold repe-tition [*Wiederholung*]' of the Godhead (*CD* I/1, 350; *KD* 369), this could easily be misread as implying that the distinctions between Father, Son and Spirit are of the same order as the distinctions between his attributes.

[21] Francis Turretin, *Institutes of Elenctic Theology*, trans. George Musgrave Giger, ed. James T. Dennison, Jr. (Phillipsburg: Presbyterian and Reformed, 1992–1927), 13.8.9 (2.324); cited by S. Holmes, 'Something Much Too Plain to Say', 145–6.

reasoning – that simplicity precludes ubiquity – suggests a subordination of Christology to a prior concept of simplicity. In self-defence, Barth insists that historically, and by implication in his own though, the logic flows in the opposite direction:

> The early battle for a recognition of the simplicity of God was the same as for the recognition of the Trinity and of the relation between the divine and human natures in Jesus Christ. We can put it equally well both ways. The church clarified its mind about the simplicity of God by means of the essential unity of the Son and the Holy Spirit with the Father, and the undivided but unconfused unity of the divine with the human nature in Jesus Christ. But it also clarified its mind about the *homoousia* of the Son and the Holy Spirit in the one divine being, and the unity of the two natures in Jesus Christ, by means of the simplicity of God. Properly considered, the two things are one. The unity of the triune God and of the Son of God with man in Jesus Christ is itself the simplicity of God. (446)

Whether or not this is an historically accurate account of the development of the doctrine of simplicity,[22] Barth's point is that, dogmatically, simplicity ought both to derive from and subsequently to inform the doctrines of the Trinity and of Christology.[23] Barth makes the brilliant and crucial observation that simplicity does much the same work as the *homoousia* of Son and Spirit with the Father. This central claim of Nicaea was manifestly intended as a conclusion drawn from revelation. So also is Barth's reading of simplicity. To consider the *homoousion* an *a priori* concept of metaphysics, as subsequent tradition came to consider simplicity, is thus a 'flat contradiction' of both the historical reality as well as what Barth regards as dogmatic necessity (447).

Having completed his initial account of the divine unity as indicating God's freedom, Barth now turns to the second stage of his argument: the exposition of the divine unity as indicating God's love.[24] Barth begins with

---

[22] S. Holmes, 'Something Much Too Plain to Say', 147–9, suggests that it is. Cf. Gunton, *Act and Being*, 82.

[23] Christopher A. Franks, 'The Simplicity of the Living God: Aquinas, Barth, and Some Philosophers', *Modern Theology* 21.2 (2005), 293.

[24] Van der Kooi makes the bewildering and unsupported claim that Barth's reinterpretation of the divine unity consists in his tying it exclusively to the divine love, as though the first stage of Barth's argument, in which unity indicates the divine freedom, were overruled by the second stage, in which unity indicates the divine love. He concludes by saying, 'The unity of God therefore does not mean' – as Barth clearly argues in the first stage – 'that God is a [*sic*] unique or single'. See Cornelis van der Kooi, *As in a Mirror: John Calvin and Karl Barth on Knowing God: A Diptych*, trans. Donald Mader (Leiden: Brill, 2005), 348–9.

a clarification of the three central concepts of unity, simplicity and uniqueness (447–50). What Barth wants to make clear about these concepts is,
first, their singularity. 'When we say that God is one, unique and simple, we
mean something different from when we ascribe unity to any other quantity'
(447). God's uniqueness is 'his own, a divine, a unique uniqueness, unique in
comparison with all human uniquenesses' (453).[25] The same could be said
of unity and simplicity. Second, Barth also wants to make perfectly clear
yet again that these concepts, indeed, all concepts used to describe God, are
entirely subordinate to the reality of God:

> We have to accept, then, that these concepts are determined and also
> circumscribed wholly and completely by his deity. We cannot accept
> the converse that his deity is circumscribed by the concepts of unity,
> uniqueness and simplicity – concepts which are at our disposal. The
> relation between subject and predicate is an irreversible one when it is
> a matter of God's perfections. (448)

One cannot, therefore, absolutise the human concept of the unique (448–9),
nor seek the supreme antithesis to human complexity (449–50), and arrive
at true description of God. To do so is to exchange revelation for the *viae
eminentiae* and *negationis* of a natural theology and so to remain entirely
embroiled in merely creaturely realities. On the contrary:

> Knowledge of the unity of God is not in any sense the result of human
> divining or construction. It is the result of the encounter between man
> and God, brought about by God....Recognition of the unity of God is
> the human response to the summons and the action of this incompar-
> able and undivided being. (450)

The knowledge of God, as Barth so often says, is always the gift of God, one
which evokes human witness and confession.

The confession of the divine uniqueness, as it derives from this encounter
and manifests God's love, is the theme of the following section (450–7).
Barth traces this theme, as he often does, through the Old and New
Testaments, the latter culminating in what he calls the 'direct' witness to the
divine uniqueness, Jesus Christ. All along, however, the contest is against
natural theology and its conception of the divine uniqueness in the form of
an abstract monotheism.[26] Barth's critique of this monotheism ranges widely
from the nature of human religion (448–9) to the semantics of a Greek conjunction (455) and culminates in an appeal to the Reformation *sola* and to

---

[25] Cf. John Webster, *Barth's Ethics of Reconciliation* (Cambridge: Cambridge University
Press, 1995), 41–2.
[26] Cf. *CD* I/1, 353–4.

one of Luther's most famous hymns (457). The censure of the (supposedly) Jewish instantiation of such monotheism in the first century, 'at the height of its religious development' (453), recalls Barth's denunciation of religion in *Romans*.[27] Further allusions to his Gifford Lectures[28] set the discussion – if this were not already apparent – squarely in the light of Barth's broader critique of natural theology. Clearly the stakes are high, and Barth plays every card in his hand.

According to Barth, while the Old Testament bears witness to God's *intrinsic* uniqueness, it was precisely in the uncompromising monotheism of first-century Judaism that this testimony was displaced by an abstract *principle* of uniqueness (451–3).[29] It was 'this very Judaism with its mono-theism' which rejected Christ (453), himself the 'direct conception' of the divine uniqueness and 'the final establishing of the monotheism of Moses and the prophets' (455). Barth's abrasive tactics are clear: he wants to dis-credit natural theology by holding it responsible for the crucifixion. But while the monotheism of first-century Judaism was in fact quite exclusive,[30] it is far from clear that this exclusivity had more to do with natural theology than with reflection on 'Moses and the prophets'.[31] Historical claims aside, Barth's point is that a natural-theological account of the divine attributes can never be more than a caricature of God and a warrant for rejection of Christ:

> In face of the cross of Christ it is monstrous to describe the uniqueness of God as an object of 'natural' knowledge. In face of the cross of Christ we are bound to say that knowledge of the one and only God is gained only by the begetting of men anew by the Holy Spirit, an act which is always unmerited and incomprehensible, and consists in man's no longer living unto himself, but in the Word of God and in the knowledge of God which comes by faith in that Word. (453)

[27] For example, Karl Barth, *The Epistle to the Romans*, trans. Edwyn C. Hoskyns (Oxford: Oxford University Press, 1968), 185.

[28] For example, Barth's several references to the 'knowledge of God and service of God' (*CD* II/1, 453). Compare Barth's statement, 'It is, therefore, unthinking to set Islam and Christianity side by side, as if in monotheism at least they have something in common' (*CD* II/1, 449), with the following comment from his second Gifford Lecture: 'The God of Mohammed is an idol like all other idols, and it is an optical illusion to characterize Christianity along with Islam as a "monotheistic" religion'; see Barth, *The Knowledge of God and the Service of God*, 21.

[29] Cf. Schleiermacher's talk of unity as 'the principle of monotheism' in *The Christian Faith*, ed. H. R. Mackintosh and J. S. Stewart (London: Continuum, 1999), §56 (230).

[30] Larry W. Hurtado, *Lord Jesus Christ: Devotion to Jesus in Earliest Christianity* (Grand Rapids: Eerdmans, 2003), 32–7.

[31] Cf. Bertrand de Margerie, *Les Perfections du Dieu de Jésus-Christ* (Paris: Cerf, 1981), 126–7.

Natural-theological conceptions of uniqueness (or any other attribute) are thus separated from the true, divine uniqueness by nothing short of the miracle of revelation and faith (cf. 455).

The concluding section of Barth's argument is a parallel development of God's simplicity as it, too, appears now as the 'simplicity of his love' in Jesus Christ (457–61). Like the preceding section, these concluding pages are immensely instructive in their critique of conceptual abstraction in theology. As before, so here, the underlying logic is that God, because he is simple, is always everything that he is:

> He is in himself indivisible, indissoluble, and unwavering. This is God's simplicity according to the testimony of the Bible, which refers us to his revelation as to him himself: the trustworthiness, truthfulness, and fidelity...in which he is what he is, and does what he does. If he were divisible, dissoluble, or wavering, he would not be trustworthy. (458–9 rev.; *KD* 516)

Presumably, Barth means that, because God is simple, he is never divided against himself.[32] For example, the God who comes to fulfil a promise is always the same God who once made that promise. The conceptual link between simplicity and trustworthiness is loose, to be sure, more a matter of illustration than of strict definition. Barth's aim here is to show how simplicity indicates the divine loving. He no more intends to equate simplicity narrowly with trustworthiness, truthfulness and fidelity than previously with lordship (445).[33]

Barth concludes by emphasising that God's trustworthiness and faithfulness and, hence, his simplicity are definitively revealed in Jesus Christ (460). 'God's simplicity reveals itself and consists in his continual self-confirmation in his speech and action; his continual self-confession and self-attestation in his identity' (460). Though Barth does not develop here his earlier observation about the connection between simplicity and the *homoousion*, appeal to the trinitarian dimensions of the divine simplicity is not lacking. 'The God

---

[32] Cf. de Margerie, *Les Perfections*, 251: 'When God is faithful to the promises he has made to his creatures, he is also faithful to himself. Understood in this sense, faithfulness coincides with the divine unity.'

[33] Todd Pokrifka-Joe reads Barth as equating simplicity with trustworthiness and faithfulness, and he questions whether the conceptual distance between simplicity and these other concepts can be bridged. The several suggestions he offers for doing so remain, as he himself implies, unconvincing. While it must be conceded that Pokrifka-Joe's is a more natural reading of Barth's language here, the difficulties he uncovers suggest that Barth did not intend as tight a connection between these concepts as he seems to claim. See Todd Pokrifka-Joe, *Redescribing God: The Roles of Scripture, Tradition, and Reason in Karl Barth's Doctrines of Divine Unity, Constancy, and Eternity* (Ph.D. diss., University of St. Andrews, 2002), 174–8.

who is trustworthy is the Father who is one with the Son and the Son who is one with the Father in the Holy Spirit' (460). Barth then draws a fitting, final parallel between the divine simplicity of faithfulness and trustworthiness and the corresponding human simplicity of faith, 'in which man for his part ascribes to God's faithfulness and truth the glory due to it, acknowledging its legitimate right, and to that extent himself... becoming faithful and true and himself simple' (460).

In this section, then, at the very outset of his exposition of the perfections of the divine freedom, Barth once again sets a theology derived strictly from revelation in clear antithesis to one which accommodates any degree of natural theology. The divine unity, as uniqueness, is a 'unique uniqueness' and thus cannot be confused with the 'monotheism' under which Christianity, along with Judaism and Islam, is often thought to be subsumed. As simplicity, it is the integrity and self-confirmation in which God always exists and acts as everything that he is; it is therefore strictly subordinate to God's triunity and to the real multiplicity of his perfections. With both uniqueness and simplicity, Barth has attempted to indicate both the divine freedom as well as the divine love. Barth has also drawn out the ethical implications of each: the total claim on human life and the summons to faith.

Omnipresence

Traditionally, God's omnipresence (his relation to space) has most commonly been associated with his eternity (his relation to time). Barth concedes that there exists 'an undeniable relationship' between them (465), yet he pairs omnipresence with unity, nonetheless. Barth's intention, as noted, is to balance God's free distinction from creation as indicated by the divine unity with God's loving nearness to creation as indicated by the divine omnipresence (462). The traditional association of omnipresence and eternity, Barth explains, while not inherently impossible, carries certain concomitant assumptions which he is eager to avoid.[34] First, Barth feels that to coordinate omnipresence and eternity would be to give to the created realities of space and time an inappropriately prominent and, thus, potentially distorting role in the description of God (464–5; cf. 344–6).[35] Second, Barth is wary of the master-concept traditionally thought to embrace omnipresence and eternity, the concept of infinity (465–8). Infinity is itself merely a creaturely concept, a concept which often enough arises from the 'demonic self-will' of sinful

---

[34] Gotthard Oblau, *Gotteszeit und Menschenzeit: Eschatologie in der Kirchlichen Dogmatik von Karl Barth* (Neukirchen-Vluyn: Neukirchener Verlag, 1988), 121–3.

[35] As subordinate concepts, however, Barth is perfectly happy to pair space and time in his description of the divine patience, which, it will be recalled, is that by which God grants space and time and hence opportunity to another in expectation of its development and free response (*CD* II/1, 408, 409–10).

creatures in their 'pride and revolt against the finite' (467).[36] As such, it is inherently bounded by and dependent upon the concept of the finite.[37] If God is nevertheless to be described as infinite, it must be remembered that 'God is infinite *in his own divine way*' (467 rev.; *KD* 525). Contrary, for example, to Newton's concepts of absolute space and time,[38] the divine infinitude does not exclude perfect finitude. Therefore, 'the concept of infinity as such is not adapted to serve as a description of God's essence' (468). By implication, the tempting combination of omnipresence and eternity which implies such a concept is also to be avoided.

Barth's exposition proceeds in three stages. The first stage gives an opening definition of the divine omnipresence both within the divine life itself and as manifest in the created order (461–8). The second stage expounds the divine omnipresence in terms of spatiality or the place which God occupies (468–73). The third enumerates the various forms which the divine omnipresence can take within the created order which (473–90).

Barth begins with a simple definition. God's omnipresence is that perfection of his freedom by which 'he is present to everything else' (461). God's presence includes his sovereignty because it confers and sustains creaturely presence. 'It is the sovereignty on the basis of which everything that exists cannot exist without him, but only with him, possessing its own presence only on the presupposition of his presence' (461). Moreover, in this sustaining of the creature in 'intimate relationship' there appears in omnipresence also an aspect of the divine love (462). Thus, as its place in the sequence of Barth's exposition suggests, omnipresence is an attribute of God's freedom which also indicates God's love.

God's presence also has an immanent dimension:

> We are not saying that God is omnipresent only in so far as there is this universe. God's omnipresence, like his other perfections, cannot be resolved into a description of his relationship to his creation. All that God is in his relationship to his creation, and therefore his omnipresence too, is simply an outward manifestation and realisation of what

---

[36] Cf. de Margerie, *Les Perfections*, 407–8; F. W. Camfield, 'Development and Present Stage of the Theology of Karl Barth', in *idem*, ed., *Reformation Old and New: A Tribute to Karl Barth* (London: Lutterworth, 1947), 60–1.

[37] Cf. Schleiermacher, *The Christian Faith*, §56 (230–1).

[38] T. F. Torrance, *Space, Time and Incarnation* (Oxford: Oxford University Press, 1969), 37–40, 63; Michael J. Buckley, *At the Origins of Modern Atheism* (New Haven: Yale University Press, 1987), 117–18, 135–9; cf. Louis Dupré, *The Enlightenment and the Intellectual Foundations of Modern Culture* (New Haven: Yale University Press, 2004), 22–4. Newton is followed by much 'perfect being theology' today; see references in John Webster, 'The Immensity and Ubiquity of God', in *idem*, *Confessing God: Essays in Christian Dogmatics II* (London: T&T Clark, 2005), 88.

he is previously in himself apart from this relationship and therefore apart from his creation. (462)

God's omnipresence in himself is traditionally designated God's 'immensity', as distinct from his 'omnipresence' with respect to creation.[39] According to Barth, God's omnipresence *ad intra* is the very reason why his presence to the creature is an expression of his love. 'It is in the fact that there is in God proximity and remoteness in indissoluble unity, no proximity without remoteness and no remoteness without proximity – it is in this fact (we recall anew his triune essence) that God is love' (462 rev.; *KD* 520). By proximity and remoteness, Barth means 'the togetherness of Father, Son and Holy Spirit at the distance posited by the distinction that exists in the one essence of God' (468).[40] This triune unity, as Barth has explained before, is the basis of the unity of God's multiple attributes:

> There does exist in him the wealth of his attributes. But above all there exists in the very unity of this wealth of his the triunity of his essence. Thus, there exists a divine proximity and remoteness, real in him from all eternity, as the basis and presupposition of the essence and exist-ence of creation, and therefore of created proximity and remoteness. God can be present to another. This is his freedom. For he is present to himself. This is his love in its internal and external range. God in him-self is not only existent. He is co-existent. And so he can co-exist with another also. To grant co-existence with himself to another is no contradiction of his essence. On the contrary, it corresponds to it. (463)

In saying this, Barth not only anticipates how he will affirm God's immut-ability in the act of creation, namely, because God is already co-existent before he creates (cf. 499–500). He also reiterates one of the leitmotifs of the entire exposition: 'God does not do anything which in his own way he does not have and is not in himself' (467). In other words, God's proximity to creation and his remoteness from it are not to be nominalised away into mere appearances. They tell us something real about God himself.

What they tell us is the astonishing fact that God himself, in his own way, is spatial. This second stage of argument (468–73) explains what it means to say that God 'possesses a place, his own place, which is distinct from all

[39] Webster, 'Immensity and Ubiquity', 93.
[40] Barth does not go so far as to identify remoteness with the distinction between Father and Son and proximity with their unity in the Holy Spirit. Cf. Paul D. Molnar, *Karl Barth and the Theology of the Lord's Supper: A Systematic Investigation* (New York: Peter Lang, 1996), 260–1.

other places and also pre-eminent over them all' (468).[41] God's 'space' is that which is implied by the distinctions within his own being as well as by his distinction from the world (468). The absence of space in God would mean 'existence without distance, which means identity' (468). Like simplicity, God's essential omnipresence secures the same distinctions between Father, Son and Spirit and between the multitude of divine perfections. But in ascribing some form of space to God, has Barth blurred the distinction between Creator and creature? Bertrand de Margerie, generally a very appreciative reader of Barth, objects strongly at this point:

> If one takes the word 'space' in the normal sense, implying mutually extrinsic parts, one can hardly see how it could be used analogically of an infinitely simple and immaterial Being. Barth, moreover, does not appear to have considered this difficulty. He falls victim here to a certain univocity of language...and also to his conception of presence itself, lacking as it does an ontological background.[42]

This is a poor reading of Barth at many points, and it may stem from Barth's employment of what T. F. Torrance identifies as a more 'relational' notion of space, rather than the 'receptacle' notion of space typical of de Margerie's Latin tradition.[43] To begin with, Barth makes quite clear that he is not using the word 'space' in its usual sense when he applies it to God. He says repeatedly that God has his space 'in his own way', and he says explicitly that he intends to capture by it an aspect of the distinction between trinitarian persons. A trinitarian elaboration of this concept of divine 'space' cannot be said to lack an ontology, nor should we expect univocity between it and a concept of created space.[44] Moreover, de Margerie misreads Barth's talk of 'difference' and 'distinction' in the divine space as implying mutually extrinsic parts and so charges him with being – 'inadvertently, no doubt' – materialistic.[45] Such a materialistic (and implicitly non-perichoretic) conception would indeed be ill-suited to describe the simple divine essence, but it is by no means the conception which Barth expounds. The differences and distinctions which Barth

---

[41] Cf. Eberhard Jüngel, *God's Being Is in Becoming: The Trinitarian Being of God in the Theology of Karl Barth*, trans. John Webster (Grand Rapids: Eerdmans, 2001), 113 n. 148, where Jüngel speculates on the possibility of affirming a divine corporeality.

[42] De Margerie, *Les Perfections*, 211. Cf. Iain MacKenzie's similar criticism of Barth's ascription of 'remoteness and proximity' to God: It is either 'simplistic application of an *analogia entis*' or a 'covert *via negativa*'. See *The Dynamism of Space: A Theological Study into the Nature of Space* (Norwich: Canterbury, 1995), 84–7.

[43] Torrance, *Space, Time and Incarnation*, 56–9; cf. Webster, 'Immensity and Ubiquity', 94–6, 100–1.

[44] Cf. Torrance, *Space, Time and Incarnation*, 18–20, 55–6.

[45] De Margerie, *Les Perfections*, 211 n. 55.

intends are those inherent in the 'togetherness' of the triune persons and in the unity of the many divine perfections.

Barth's ascription of 'space' to God has implications for the charge, frequently levelled against Barth, of holding a monistic or modalistic view of the divine nature. William Hill, for example, says of Barth, 'his theology is a modal trinitarianism in that it prefers not to conceive of three really distinct subjectivities constituting the one Godhead'.[46] According to Hill, Barth cannot acknowledge any distinct modes of operation within God's activity towards the world; instead, 'all such modes exist only in our thinking and, as said of God, collapse into the simplicity of the divine nature'.[47] Moltmann wields the name of Sabellius in his attack on Barth's supposedly 'non-trinitarian concept of the unity of the one God'.[48] Likewise, Alasdair Heron discerns a 'leaning toward modalism',[49] Robert Jenson senses a modalist 'temptation',[50] and Alan Torrance, following Hill, Heron and Meijering, sees 'modalist tinges',[51] even though he grants that charges of modalism against Barth cannot finally be made to stick.[52] Eternal distinctions between Father, Son and Spirit are some of what the modalist view of God lacks. But these are the very distinctions presupposed in Barth's talk of the 'divine proximity and remoteness' by which God is eternally 'present to himself' and 'co-existent' 'in three modes being at one and the same time' (475). Such distinctions are also inherent in Barth's earlier description of Father, Son and Spirit as the eternal 'threefold repetition' of God's being: '[T]his threeness

---

[46] William J. Hill, *The Three-Personed God: The Trinity as a Mystery of Salvation* (Washington, D.C.: Catholic University of America Press, 1982), 121; likewise Catherine Mowry LaCugna, *God for Us: The Trinity and Christian Life* (New York: Harper Collins, 1993), 252–4. Is the assertion of a single centre of consciousness in the Trinity, or the denial of 'distinct subjectivities', anything other than orthodoxy? Barth labels the idea of three centres of consciousness in the Trinity 'rationalistic mythology'. See Karl Barth, *Karl Barth's Table Talk*, ed. John D. Godfrey, Scottish Journal of Theology Occasional Papers 10 (Edinburgh: Oliver and Boyd, 1963), 58; cf. CD II/1, 296–7.

[47] Hill, *Three-Personed God*, 122. Hill goes on to make the bizarre claim that 'Barth...emphatically denies the possibility of distinctions within the divine essence'.

[48] Jürgen Moltmann, *The Trinity and the Kingdom of God: The Doctrine of God*, trans. Margaret Kohl (London: SCM, 1981), 143–4.

[49] Alasdair I. C. Heron, *The Holy Spirit in the Bible, the History of Christian Thought, and Recent Theology* (Philadelphia: Westminster, 1983), 164, 167–70.

[50] Robert W. Jenson, 'You Wonder Where the Spirit Went', *Pro Ecclesia* 2.3 (1993): 299.

[51] Alan J. Torrance, *Persons in Communion: An Essay on Trinitarian Description and Human Participation with Special Reference to Volume One of Karl Barth's Church Dogmatics* (Edinburgh: T&T Clark, 1996), 102–3. Torrance cites E. P. Meijering's *Von den Kirchenvätern zu Karl Barth: Das altkirchliche Dogma in der 'Kirchlichen Dogmatik'* (Amsterdam: Gieben, 1993).

[52] Alan J. Torrance, 'The Trinity', in *The Cambridge Companion to Karl Barth*, ed. John Webster (Cambridge: Cambridge University Press, 2000), 81–2.

must be regarded as irremovable and the distinctiveness of the three modes of being must be regarded as ineffaceable'.[53] It is these which prevent God's supposed 'collapse into simplicity' and, as Paul Metzger notes, provide that 'space for relational otherness' which is excluded in monistic views of God.[54] George Hunsinger's conclusion cannot be gainsaid: 'modalism can be charged against Barth only out of ignorance, incompetence or (willful) misunderstanding'.[55]

Following his initial ascription of 'space' to God, Barth attempts a closer definition of the divine spatiality in terms of two of its particular qualities. God's spatiality, Barth says, is that by which 'God possesses space in himself and in all other spaces' (470). This means, first, that God's relation to space cannot be described negatively or antithetically, for God is 'absolutely free and superior' in his relation to it (471). God is not nowhere, but somewhere, 'here, there and everywhere' (471). Second, in his spatiality, God is everywhere present 'undividedly and completely', for God is simple (472–3). That God is everywhere wholly present does not mean, however, that God is uniformly present. Just as God's unity includes his triunity and his simplicity includes a wealth of perfections, so God's undivided presence includes many unique, particular presences. God can be present 'in all the fulness of his being…in an individual way in individual cases' (472). 'God's true omnipresence, according to the testimony of Scripture, includes the possibility and actuality of his differentiated presence with himself and with everything else, without any curtailment or weakening or diminution of himself' (473).

In the course of this initial explanation of the divine spatiality, Barth's tone occasionally suggests that he expects some of his readers to be rather more alarmed than intrigued. It might appear that, despite his initial assurances to the contrary (462), Barth is compromising God's distinction from the created order. So Barth continues to reiterate his insistence on the uniqueness of God's space, its difference from created space. Further, as Barth explains these two particular qualities of the divine spatiality (God's positive relation to created space and the wholeness of his presence to it), in both cases he justifies his conclusions by rhetorically charged appeal to revelation. 'We have no right', says Barth, to limit God's possession of space to the created order and claim that he is non-spatial in himself. If God is non-spatial, then

---

[53] CD I/1, 350, 361. See also Barth's explicit rejection of modalism, CD I/1, 382, and CD II/1, 326–7, as well as the thorough treatment of Jowers, 'The Reproach of Modalism', 231–46.

[54] Paul Louis Metzger, 'The Migration of Monism and the Matrix of Trinitarian Mediation', *Scottish Journal of Theology* 58.3 (2005): 308–9.

[55] George Hunsinger, '*Mysterium Trinitatis*: Karl Barth's Conception of Eternity', in *idem*, *Disruptive Grace: Studies in the Theology of Karl Barth* (Grand Rapids: Eerdmans, 2000), 191 n. 7.

in all his dynamic relations to space 'God deceives us as to his true being' (472). Non-spatiality in God would be disastrous:

> In that case, the distinction of the persons in the unity of his essence, the manifold wealth of this one divine essence, and above all his speaking and acting as the Subject and Lord of his own dealings with his creation, is necessarily shown again to be an impossibility, a mere illusion which will be dispelled at some height or depth....We will again have to distrust his revelation. (473)

A non-spatial God could only be 'lifeless and loveless and, therefore, fundamentally unfree' (473). 'It is an ill "perfection" of God which means this, and has these consequences' (473).

With this, Barth turns to his third stage of argument (473–90), addressing the different ways in which God is present: first to himself (473–6) and then to the created order generally (476–7), specially (477–83) and in Jesus Christ (483–6), who is the basis of God's presence both to creation and also to himself (487). Barth then concludes his treatment of omnipresence with a foray into the debate over the ubiquity of Christ's body (487–90).

Beginning, then, with God's presence to himself, and as if anticipating readers' incredulity, Barth takes up again his insistence that God's omnipresence includes 'first and above all' God's own spatiality, that 'space which is exclusively his own space' (474). God's space is the presupposition of creaturely space: 'The space everything else possesses is the space which is given it out of the fulness of God' (474). It is to this fulness that Scripture points when it speaks of God's throne in heaven, 'the real place of God, and as such the one which is superior to all other places' (475).

> If a still more definite question is asked about this basic form of the divine omnipresence, and therefore about the throne of God itself, we can refer only to the triunity as such of the one being of God. This settles the fact that although God is certainly the One who alone is God, he is not therefore solitary, but is in himself both unity and fellowship, the One in three modes of being at one and the same time. This decisively rebuts the view that God is spaceless and therefore lifeless and loveless. (475)

Once again, God's spatiality is understood as an implication of his triunity.

Next, Barth addresses God's general presence to creation, his presence 'as a whole in relation to all creation as such' (476). Here is omnipresence, not in its various, specific forms, but as the tradition has been primarily concerned to depict it, that is, as *omni*-presence. 'Thus there are certainly different forms, very different forms, of God's presence in his creation, but there is no absence of God in his creation' (476). Everything that exists, exists both

119

in its own created space as well as in God's space. 'Indeed, we are far more in God's space than in our created space' (476). Though Barth does not make the point explicitly, his very traditional understanding of the relation between divine and creaturely space, like his understanding of the relation between divine and creaturely freedom, is entirely non-competitive. God's presence does not exclude creaturely presence, but rather grounds and sustains it. This is the unavoidable implication of his affirmations that created spaces 'are as little identical with his space as the world in general can be identical with God' (476) and that God and creatures share the same space. In his concluding survey of relevant biblical passages, Barth also notes that, though the very different forms of God's presence include both a presence 'in wrath and a presence in grace' (476), both a fearful and a comforting presence, it is the latter which is decisive, for it is 'in his love and for his love's sake' that God is 'present to everything and everywhere' (477).

God's general presence to creation is, however, merely the presupposition of his special presence. 'It is as we look back and forwards from God's special presence that his general presence in the world is recognised and attested' (478). God's general presence, in fact, is 'ontologically...and not merely noetically' dependent on his special presence (478). This means that there can be no natural theology of God's omnipresence. 'The general omnipresence of God in his creation is not in any sense a kind of general truth which is seen in a distinctive form in his particular presence' (478). Against this, Barth argues that in the Old and New Testaments it is from God's presence at particular places and to particular people that his general presence is deduced (478–83). Barth sees this confirmed in the fact that Jesus, as the fulfilment of Old Testament attestation to the divine dwelling place, replaces God's particular presence in Jerusalem not with a general omnipresence but with his own most particular presence:

> The opposite of Jerusalem and Gerizim and all temples made with hands – and we can apply it and say the opposite of Rome, Wittenberg, Geneva and Canterbury – is not the universe at large, which is the superficial interpretation of Liberalism, but Jesus. (481)

Contrary to what we might expect from the universal scope of gospel, the fulfilment of God's presence is not merely a different location than Jerusalem, nor even the sum of all locations, but Jesus. Like its Lord, the church is not to be found in no place, a single place, or all places. Rather, as the body of Christ, it has its own particular space, a primary, spiritual, invisible space in Christ, as well as a secondary, physical, visible space here on earth (482–3).

Christ 'is therefore the place to which every examination of the Old and New Testament witness to God's special presence must necessarily and unequivocally point in the last instance' (483–4). As the fulfilment of God's general and special presences, Christ must be 'radically distinguished' from them (484). The reason for this is that, in Jesus Christ:

> the Creator has given the creature not only space but his own most proper space. God has raised man to his throne. God's most proper space is itself the space which this man occupies in the cradle and on the cross, and which he cannot therefore leave or lose again, for, as his resurrection and ascension reveal, it is now his permanent space....Thus the human nature of Christ (and especially in this connexion his corporeality and therefore his spatiality), in its unity with the deity of the Son (unconfused with it, but also undivided from it, in real indirect identity), is the revelation, but as the revelation it is also the reality, of the divine space, by which all other spaces are created, preserved and surrounded. (486)

Christ reveals the special presence of God because he himself is and will remain God's presence to creation. In saying this, however, Barth comes full circle to where he began, for it is also in Christ that 'God is present to himself as the Triune' (487). It is in the incarnation that 'God is, and reveals himself to be, the One he is, omnipresent in himself and as such outside himself' (487). This is perhaps as near as Barth gets anywhere in his exposition of the divine perfections to the use of appropriation. Barth *almost* says that God's presence can be further specified as the Father's presence, both to himself and to the created order, in the Son and by the Spirit. Understandably, this comes in the christologically focused resolution to his exposition.

With this, Barth finally comes to the Lutheran-Reformed debate over the nature of Christ's bodily presence. In light of the long history and immense complexity of this debate, Barth is under no illusions of being able to say the definitive word or lay out a grand ecumenical formula of concord. What he offers is a modest suggestion – that Christ's bodily presence can be understood in two, distinct ways – in an effort to renew long-stalled discussion.

Barth begins with what he regards as their respective misunderstandings of Scripture's references to 'the right hand of God'. The Lutheran error was to interpret 'the right hand of God' as indicating not God's own, particular, divine space, but his general presence to all creation, in accordance with a conception of God as the non-spatial infinite:

> The correct statement about the omnipresence of Christ even in his human nature should have been interpreted in such a way that the particularity of the divine place, which is also the place of Jesus Christ in his human nature, is safeguarded. It should also have been interpreted in such a way that the creatureliness and therefore the true and limited spatiality of his humanity occupying that divine place is safeguarded,

and with it his whole position as very God and very man, Mediator, Revealer and Reconciler. (488)

The Reformed error was to interpret 'the right hand of God' as indicating (once again) not God's own, particular, divine space, but this time a purely creaturely space:

> [The] true statement concerning the indissolubly definite nature of the spatiality of Christ's human nature should have been interpreted in such a way that the divinity of its place is safeguarded, and with it Christ's omnipresence even in his human nature, and therefore the full reality of the unity of his person and work as Mediator. (489)

So, somehow, Barth wants to affirm 'the true and limited spatiality of [Christ's] humanity' as well as 'Christ's omnipresence even in his human nature'. How can both hold? Back in the opening section of *CD* II/1, Barth described Christ's human nature as the 'substance of the sacramental reality' of revelation (53). Christ's humanity is 'the first sacrament', the foundation of a sacramental continuity extending throughout God's dealings with his people (54).[56] In light of this, Barth here suggests that Christ's human, corporeal presence be conceived, with the Reformed, as definite and distinct from other spaces ('true and limited'), so as to safeguard the integrity of Christ's humanity (489–90), and yet also, with the Lutherans, as a real and entire omnipresence in the world ('even in his human nature'), so as to safeguard the unity of Christ's person (490). This dual conception is possible, Barth believes, because these two presences, though both definite and both of the whole Christ, are nevertheless not identical.

> Therefore we say: The whole Jesus Christ is there at the right hand of God in one way, and the same whole Jesus Christ is here in Israel and the church, but also in the world, in another way. We make a distinction (with the Reformed) and say: 'he is there properly and originally and here symbolically, sacramentally, spiritually'. But (with the Lutherans) we draw the two together and say: 'he is here no less than there, but really present both there and here, in both places the whole Christ after his divine and also after his human nature.' (490)

Alas, this cryptic confession hardly clarifies matters. Barth makes no further explicit reference to it in the *Church Dogmatics*, which trails off right at the point where he would presumably have returned to the doctrine of the Lord's Supper. Even in contexts where he takes up again the differences between

---

[56] Cf. John Yocum, *Ecclesial Mediation in Karl Barth*, Barth Studies (Aldershot: Ashgate, 2004), 42–4.

Lutheran and Reformed Christology or the nature of Christ's presence, this suggestion as it concerns Christ's eucharistic presence is passed over in silence.[57] The reason for this silence, and possibly for the corresponding silence in the secondary literature as well, may lie in the increasing suspicion with which Barth viewed sacramental mediation – a suspicion already evident from the time of the Basel lectures on the divine attributes.[58] Whatever the sacramental theology informing this proposal concerning Christ's twofold human presence, it does at least clearly resonate with Barth's claim here that God is present entirely, everywhere, and yet not identically. It may also represent Barth feeling his way toward his formulation of the simultaneity of Christ's twofold state of humiliation and exaltation that forms so intriguing a component of *Church Dogmatics* IV.[59]

One perplexing feature of Barth's treatment of the divine presence as a whole is the general absence of reference to the Spirit. It is an absence often noted elsewhere in the *Dogmatics* and criticised both for the specifically pneumatological deficiencies which it implies as well as for its systematic implications for Barth's Christology, ecclesiology and anthropology.[60] Philip Rosato argues that, had Barth given more consideration to pneumatology in the *Dogmatics*, 'he would have allotted the man Jesus a more substantial role in the unique salvific encounter which took place in him between God and man'.[61] Jenson claims that, in Barth's theology, because of its pervasively trinitarian character, 'Western trinitarianism's common difficulty in conceiving the Spirit's specific immanent initiative in God must become a difficulty in conceiving the Spirit's entire salvation-historical initiative.'[62] Gunton explains:

> Crucial to any understanding of salvation is the relation of the Holy Spirit first to Jesus and then, *and consequently*, to those who are incorporate in Christ by the act of that same Spirit. If the relation of the Spirit to Jesus is underplayed, if, that is to say, his humanity is made too much a function of his direct relation to the Father rather

---

[57] For example, CD IV/1, 180–3, 186–8; IV/2, 54–5, 66–9, 80–3, 652–4 (perhaps the nearest parallel).

[58] Cf. Webster, *Barth's Ethics of Reconciliation*, 116–23. Busch, *Karl Barth*, 286, reports that it was in the summer semester of 1938 that Barth first 'came to completely negative conclusions over Calvin's arguments for infant baptism'.

[59] Piotr J. Malysz, 'Storming Heaven with Karl Barth? Barth's Unwitting Appropriation of the *Genus Maiestaticum* and What Lutherans Can Learn from It', *International Journal of Systematic Theology* 9.1 (2007): 83–4.

[60] Webster, *Barth*, 138–9.

[61] Philip J. Rosato, *The Spirit as Lord: The Pneumatology of Karl Barth* (Edinburgh: T&T Clark, 1981), 159.

[62] Jenson, 'Where the Spirit Went', 300.

than of that mediated by the Spirit, thus far is the link between his humanity and ours weakened.[63]

Rosato, Jenson and Gunton all acknowledge both the many pages which Barth does devote to the Spirit in the *Dogmatics* as well as the fact that Barth would have had much more to say about the Spirit in the projected fifth volume of the *Dogmatics*, which he did not live to complete. Nevertheless, their concerns stand. To what degree, if any, does Barth's silence concerning the Spirit in the present passage fall under their general censure? In Barth's account of the divine omnipresence, is it perhaps the case, as Jenson suggests, that Barth's 'final reason for the whole web of Spirit-avoidance in the *Kirchliche Dogmatik* is avoidance of the church'?[64]

First, to substantiate what these interpreters freely acknowledge, it is not by any means that Barth denies the role of the Spirit in Christ's presence, either in connection with the Lord's Supper or otherwise. In the previous volume of the *Dogmatics*, Barth speaks directly of the Holy Spirit both as 'God himself in his freedom exercised in revelation to be present to his creature, even to dwell in him personally'[65] and as effecting 'the revelatory character of the sacraments'.[66] Elsewhere in *CD* II/1, 'Barth's most extensive experiment in conceiving of revelation as sacrament',[67] and despite his shifting sacramental theology, Barth speaks of the Spirit's presence as effecting 'our participation in the person and work of Jesus Christ' (157), as sanctifying humanity in faith (158–9; cf. 15–16), and as the 'temporal presence of the Jesus Christ who intercedes for us eternally' (158). In his account of the divine glory, Barth says explicitly that the Holy Spirit is 'the divine reality by which the creature has its heart opened to God and is made able and willing to receive him' (669; cf. 670).

Second, Barth hints at one of his positive reasons for silence in one of his few references to the Spirit in this section:

> The presence ... of the whole Christ as the occupant of the divine throne must not be restricted to his divinity, his Spirit, his grace, etc. Where his Spirit and his grace are, he himself is wholly present, very God and very man. (490)

Barth's dogmatic concern here is in part to preserve the wholeness and entirety of Christ's person particularly in his human nature. Therefore to

---

[63] Colin Gunton, 'Salvation', in *The Cambridge Companion to Karl Barth*, ed. John Webster (Cambridge: Cambridge University Press, 2000), 152.

[64] Jenson, 'Where the Spirit Went', 302.

[65] *CD* I/2, 198; cf. *CD* I/1, 468; *CD* I/2, 537.

[66] Rosato, *The Spirit as Lord*, 76. See esp. *CD* I/2, 228–32.

[67] James J. Buckley, 'Christian community, baptism, and Lord's Supper', in *The Cambridge Companion to Karl Barth*, ed. John Webster (Cambridge: Cambridge University Press, 2000), 201.

speak of God's presence with us in Christ as the presence of the Spirit could be seen as implying that Christ is not humanly, and therefore not wholly, present. Of course, Barth's dogmatic concern for 'the whole Christ' may also be motivated by tactical considerations. That is, in the context of a proposal for Lutheran-Reformed rapprochement over the Lord's Supper, too much emphasis on 'the miracle of the Spirit'[68] might have been read as too one-sidedly Reformed. At the very least, however, this reference to the Spirit does make clear that, when Barth speaks of the presence of Christ, he intends this to be understood as including the presence of the Spirit.

For Barth, however, perhaps the most compelling cause for silence at this point is the figure of Schleiermacher.[69] On Barth's account, Schleiermacher was ultimately unable, despite his better intentions, to safeguard the distinction between the Holy Spirit and 'a mode of human cognition'.[70] Barth saw the theology of the entire nineteenth century as dominated by Schleiermacher,[71] and he felt the need to begin his 1929 lecture, *The Holy Spirit and the Christian Life*, with an outright rejection of the idea that the Holy Spirit is 'identical with what we recognize as our own created life of the spirit'.[72] The greater part of the twentieth century had passed when Barth protested the fact that it was 'still too difficult to distinguish between God's Spirit and man's spirit!'[73] Barth's talk of Jesus where we might expect to hear talk of the Spirit is thus a function, not of any lack of concern for the full reality of the Spirit, but precisely to secure the Spirit's full reality in a theologically hostile context. As Barth saw matters, liberal Protestantism's preoccupation with the religious self-consciousness of the human spirit threatened to devour not only a right understanding of the Holy Spirit, but of Christ as well. Barth's occasionally rather exclusive talk of Jesus thus also reflects his intense concern to prevent that 'dissolution…of the objective moment in the subjective' which he lamented in Schleiermacher:[74]

I wanted to place a strong emphasis on the objective side of revelation: Jesus Christ. If I had made much of the Holy Spirit, I am afraid it

---

[68] Karl Barth, *The Theology of John Calvin*, trans. Geoffrey W. Bromiley (Grand Rapids: Eerdmans, 1995), 339.

[69] Rosato, *The Spirit as Lord*, 3–16.

[70] Karl Barth, *Protestant Theology in the Nineteenth Century: Its Background and history*, new ed., trans. Brian Cozens and John Bowden (Grand Rapids: Eerdmans, 2002), 448; see esp. 443–50 and 457–8.

[71] Colin E. Gunton, *Introduction*, in Barth, *Protestant Theology*, xv–xvi.

[72] Karl Barth, *The Holy Spirit and the Christian Life: The Theological Basis of Ethics*, trans. R. Birch Hoyle, forward by Robin W. Lovin (Louisville: Westminster John Knox, 1993), 3; cf. *CD* I/1, 467–8.

[73] Barth, *Table Talk*, 28.

[74] Barth, *Protestant Theology*, 457.

would have led back to subjectivism, which is what I wanted to overcome.[75]

Against what Barth saw as the overly subjective tendencies of the Protestant tradition from Schleiermacher and Hegel right up to Bultmann (and of other traditions as well), in which mystical religious experience was identified with an abstract, general presence of the Holy Spirit, Barth also sought to make clear that, just as the presence of Christ is inseparable from that of the Spirit, so also the presence of the Spirit is inseparable from that of Christ.[76] In other words, when Barth speaks of Jesus where talk of the Spirit might be expected, his concern is often not only to emphasise the objective side of revelation while presupposing the presence and activity of the Spirit. He also intends at the same time to make the point that there is no presence or activity of the Spirit, even eschatologically,[77] which does not have Jesus as its sole referent.[78] As so often in Barth, it is positive christological and, in this case, pneumatological concerns which guide his thought and exposition.

This is not to say, however, that these concerns, and the silence concerning the Spirit which often accompanies them, may not have harmful side-effects for Barth's teaching about Christ's humanity and, thus, about the church. Although Barth was keenly aware of the likelihood of being misunderstood on this point, he goes on (in the quotation above) to say, 'Today I would speak more of the Holy Spirit', and then, revealingly, 'Perhaps I was too cautious.'[79] Valid dogmatic, tactical and contextual concerns notwithstanding, Barth concedes that his reserve (at least in the early volumes of the *Dogmatics*[80]) was not entirely justified. By implication,

---

[75] Barth, *Table Talk*, 27.

[76] Rosato, *The Spirit as Lord*, 6–7; Molnar, *Lord's Supper*, 117.

[77] Cf. Jenson, 'Where the Spirit Went', 301–2.

[78] Cf. *CD* IV/1, 647–8.

[79] Barth, *Table Talk*, 27.

[80] As for Barth's treatment of the divine presence in *CD* IV, he can still speak of God's 'particular and highly particularised, presence' in Christ as 'itself the demonstration and exercise of his omnipresence' (IV/1, 187). But he also explains that it is the Spirit who is the 'form' of Christ's action 'in which it is made present to the man to whom [Christ] gives himself' (IV/1, 648). It is the Holy Spirit who 'is the power in which Jesus Christ attests himself, attests himself effectively, creating in man response and obedience' (IV/1, 648). It is the Spirit who, in the successive part-volumes of *CD* IV, is the 'awakening', 'quickening' and 'enlightening' power of Jesus Christ (e.g. in the theses of the central paragraphs on the Spirit's work in the community, §§62, 67 and 72). Barth may appear at points to maintain something like a human ubiquity of Christ. He can say, for example, 'Where the man Jesus attests himself in the power of the Spirit of God, he makes himself present;...he imparts himself' (IV/2, 654). However, Barth's typical designation of the church as the 'earthly-historical form' of Christ's existence (once again, in the theses of §§62, 67 and 72) leaves the emphasis to fall on a more

Barth concedes a measure of justification to the charges of his critics. A proper defence of the Spirit should have taken the form, not of silence or of counter-emphasis on the objective reality of Christ, but of positive dogmatic description. Only positive exposition of the particular role of the Spirit in the divine omnipresence can ultimately safeguard the distinction between the Holy Spirit and the human spirit. With respect to Barth's doctrine of the divine perfections, the same might also be said, for example, of the distinctions between God's own, proper space and time, the space and time granted to the creature in the divine patience, and the merely natural-theological realities of everyday experience. Only the explicit formulation of the Spirit's role can safeguard these distinctions. In the context of the Lord's Supper, what is required is an account of the way in which the Holy Spirit enables believers both to participate in and to bear witness to Christ in the Supper,[81] stirring in them 'the thanksgiving which responds to the presence of Jesus Christ in his self-sacrifice and which looks forward to his future'.[82]

More clearly than in his treatments of most of the other attributes, Jesus Christ occupies the centre of Barth's conception of the divine omnipresence. In Christ God is both present to himself and, in a multitude of ways, to creation, for in Christ God has inseparably united creaturely space to his own most proper space. Barth's conception of the divine space is explicitly trinitarian: it is that which is implied in the distinctions between the three persons and, subordinately, between God's wealth of perfections. This 'togetherness at a distance' within the divine life is manifest in God's presence to creation generally, specially, and uniquely in Christ, each in a multitude of distinct and individual ways. This manifestation includes – though one must draw this conclusion from what Barth says elsewhere – God's particular, manifold presence in the Spirit.

---

strictly 'heavenly-historical' locus of Christ's resurrected body (IV/2, 653). 'Risen from the dead, ascended into heaven, seated at the right hand of God the Father, Jesus is remote from earthly history and the community which exists in it. He is unattainably superior to it.... But this is only the one aspect...' (IV/2, 652). In IV/3, Barth develops the concept of the threefold form of Christ's *parousia*. Between his resurrection and return, Christ, in his prophetic office, gives 'the promise of the Spirit' (§69.4), the 'middle form' of his *parousia*. Here Barth says that 'The work of the Holy Spirit...is the form in which [Christ] comes to us and is present with us here and now after the first form of his coming again...and before its final form' (IV/3, 420). Thus, in this 'time between the times' (IV/3, 358), as in *CD* IV generally, Barth has little to say about a human ubiquity of Christ.

[81] Cf. George Hunsinger, 'The Mediator of Communion: Karl Barth's Doctrine of the Holy Spirit', in *The Cambridge Companion to Karl Barth*, ed. John Webster (Cambridge: Cambridge University Press, 2000), 181, 188; Molnar, *Lord's Supper*, 136.

[82] *CD* IV/4, ix.

§31.2. Constancy and Omnipotence

In taking up a second pair of 'freedom' attributes, Barth explains that he is not saying 'anything different' than what he said regarding God's unity and omnipresence (490). Rather, he is saying the same thing 'differently'. That is, he is describing the same divine essence but now from the standpoint of these two further divine perfections:

> The whole essence of God must be seen and understood from this standpoint, too, as if it were the one and only standpoint. For each of God's qualities and perfections declared and knowable in his revelation is at the same time his one, complete essence. (491)

In a typical move, Barth argues that the whole divine essence must be seen first from the standpoint of its constancy alone and then from the standpoint of its omnipotence alone. By now, agile readers should no longer stumble over the following thicket of claims:

> Because he is constant, and as the One who is constant, he is also omnipotent. And because he is omnipotent, and as the One who is omnipotent, he is also constant. (491)

What Barth means is that he will describe God's essence first *as if* constancy were its sole basis and then *as if* omnipotence were its sole basis. By expressing himself in an apparent self-contradiction, Barth offers his readers a simple exercise in interpreting him correctly. What he says about the divine perfections must be understood as said from the standpoint of the particular perfection being described, not absolutely as though no more needed to be said.[83]

Barth does not explain exactly why he has chosen to pair constancy with omnipotence. Just as eternity and omnipresence have traditionally formed something of a physical association, so eternity and constancy (or immutability) have traditionally formed something of a logical association (609). The divine eternity, in other words, as including God's 'time for us' (612), could reasonably have served as the counterpart to constancy. On Barth's categorization of these attributes, however, since both constancy and eternity are formally perfections of the divine freedom which show particularly this same freedom (i.e. each is the first in its respective pair), such a pairing is ruled out. This same dialectic criterion would not, on the other hand, have disqualified unity, for example, as a complement to omnipotence. Barth has already made clear, of course, that his selection and arrangement of the attributes is

---

[83] Taking Barth's statements absolutely, Anna Case-Winters puzzles over how Barth can classify omnipotence as a perfection of the divine freedom, and yet at times speak of freedom as a result of omnipotence. See her *God's Power: Traditional Understandings and Contemporary Challenges* (Louisville: Westminster John Knox, 1990), 100. Note Barth's warning to his readers, *CD* IV/1, x (cf. IV/1, 159).

provisional (441–2), so there is no necessary reason why constancy (immutability) and omnipotence must be paired. That said, the concept of God as a person provides a certain conceptual resonance between the two expositions. As we will see, God as a person, as a knowing and willing agent, simultaneously stirs immutability from sleep and restrains omnipotence from tyranny. Barth has already made it quite clear that God cannot be understood as other than a person (267–8, 271–2, 284–97, 370). In the exposition of these two attributes, however, God's being a person plays a more significant role than elsewhere, and it may be this which led Barth to treat them as a pair.

Constancy

As we have already seen Barth do in his passing comments on divine impassibility (370–1), so here, with the related concept of divine immutability or constancy, Barth aims to preserve a substantial core of the traditional doctrine while paring off implications which in his view have wrongly been drawn from it. Again, as with impassibility, the result is a remarkably rich and provocative reformulation of the tradition. Barth affirms in the most pointed terms the absolute changelessness of God. Yet, precisely because this absolutely changeless God is so eternally and irrepressibly alive in the free and creative love of Father, Son and Spirit, he can in perfectly changeless self-consistency bring about new things, change his mind, respond to the creature and even die forsaken on a cross. There are three stages in Barth's exposition: an initial definition and clarification of constancy in light of Scripture and tradition (491–9), an argument for God's constancy first in creating and then in reconciling the world (499–512), and a more focussed assessment of God's constancy as manifest in Jesus Christ (512–22).

Like the theses which open the numbered sections of the *Dogmatics*, the initial descriptive paragraph of Barth's account of constancy (491–2) is thesis-dense and lays out in the space of a single page much of the substance of what follows. Barth begins with so strong an affirmation of God's changelessness as to set at ease even the most stringent of Protestant orthodox theologians:

> There neither is nor can be, nor is to be expected or even thought possible in him...any deviation, diminution or addition, nor any degeneration or rejuvenation [*Veralten oder Neuwerden*], any alteration or non-identity or discontinuity. The one, omnipresent God remains the One he is. This is his constancy. (491; *KD* 552)

Even Richard Muller is prepared to concede that Barth's position is 'quite close to that of orthodoxy'.[84] But Barth immediately proceeds to remind his

---

[84] Richard A. Muller, *Post-Reformation Reformed Dogmatics: The Rise and Development of Reformed Orthodoxy, ca. 1520 to ca. 1725*, vol. 3, *The Divine Essence and Attributes* (Grand Rapids: Baker Academic, 2003), 309.

readers that the God whose constancy he has thus described is the *living* God. It is here that, according to Barth, the break from Protestant orthodox expositions becomes necessary. '[God's] life is not only the origin of all created change, but is in itself the fulness of difference, movement, will, decision, action, degeneration and rejuvenation [*Alt- und Neuwerden*]' (492; KD 553).[85] Nevertheless, the 'alteration and movement' of both God's being and his ways never make God other than he eternally is. For such alteration and movement are those of the 'eternal self-repetition and self-affirmation' of the divine life (492).

This is a crucial move in Barth's exposition, and he makes it so casually that it is easy to miss what he is affirming. The reference to God's self-repetition is the clue, recalling as it does Barth's famous explanation of the unity of the triune God back in *CD* I/1:

> The name of Father, Son and Spirit means that God is the one God in threefold repetition, and this in such a way that the repetition itself is grounded in his Godhead, so that it implies no alteration in his Godhead, and yet in such a way also that he is the one God only in this repetition.[86]

By 'threefold repetition', Barth means that the Father constitutes one 'repetition' or mode of the divine essence, the Son a second and the Spirit a third.[87] These self-repetitions of essence are themselves grounded in and inseparable from the essence. As strict repetitions, however, each is identical in essence; hence, there is 'no alteration' from one to the next. Thus, when Barth says that the divine constancy is grounded in the 'self-repetition' of the divine life, he means that constancy is a perfection of the divine essence in, and not abstracted from, the eternal triune relations between Father, Son and Spirit.[88]

---

[85] Barth thus affirms in God both the absence of *Veralten oder Neuwerden* and the 'fulness' of *Alt- und Neuwerden*. Perhaps by *Altwerden* Barth means something like 'maturation'. Or perhaps Barth alludes to Augustine's talk of God as both 'so ancient and so new' (*Confessions* 10.27.38; quoted on 651).

[86] *CD* I/1, 350.

[87] The active sense of 'repetition' might suggest the eternal processions, in which case Barth would mean that the Father eternally repeats himself in (i.e. generates) the Son, and Father and Son eternally repeat themselves in (i.e. spirate) the Spirit. In context (§9.1, 'Unity in Trinity'), however, it is clear that the processions, and thus the distinctions between persons, are not what Barth has in mind.

[88] Hendrikus Berkhof wrongly claims that Barth speaks of God's liveliness here as merely the 'transcendental possibility' of God's changes *ad extra* and that Barth only comes to locate this liveliness in the triune relations in *CD* IV/1. See his *Christian Faith: An Introduction to the Study of the Faith*, rev. ed., trans. Sierd Woudstra (Grand Rapids: Eerdmans, 1986), 153. Elsewhere Berkhof does affirm, with reference to the whole of Barth's thought (whatever its ambiguities), that 'God's nature is not subject to change,

This explicitly trinitarian location of the divine constancy also helps to clarify what Barth means by affirming both that there is 'alteration and movement' in God and that God nevertheless remains who he is. The alteration and movement are those of the triune relations, the liveliness of the communion between Father, Son and Spirit. Yet, this liveliness does not make God other than he is, because it is an inherently and eternally self-affirming liveliness.

> In all its forms and operations it will be *his* life. In every alteration and movement it will go out from the peace, return to the peace, and be accompanied, upheld and filled by the peace, which he has in himself as the only really living One. (492; cf. 503, 521–2)[89]

The communion of 'peace' between Father, Son, and Spirit can never turn against itself to threaten its identity. This is why God remains who he is.[90]

A final point that emerges from this opening paragraph is, once again, the relative weight Barth places on the doctrines of the Trinity and the divine attributes. For Barth, the trinitarian relations both ground and limit what he is willing to say about the divine constancy. In other words, God's triunity can clearly be seen here as more basic to Barth's understanding of God than the divine perfections. From the very first descriptive paragraph of his account of constancy, Barth is not merely presupposing a doctrine of the Trinity, but actively employing it as a primary dogma in shaping secondary dogmatic concepts.

Having given an opening statement of his position, Barth then turns to consider Protestant orthodox teaching (492–5). Whatever the older theology may elsewhere have said about God's triune life, when it came to speak of God's immutability, it tended to speak – by what Barth might have

---

but this unchanging nature implies the possibility of change, of condescendence, and of humiliation'. See Hendrikus Berkhof, 'The (Un)Changeability of God', in *Grace Upon Grace: Essays in Honor of Lester J. Kuyper*, ed. James I. Cook (Grand Rapids: Eerdmans, 1986), 26.

[89] Cf. Isaak August Dorner, *Divine Immutability: A Critical Reconsideration*, trans. Robert R. Williams and Claude Welch, Fortress Texts in Modern Theology (1856–1958; Minneapolis: Fortress, 1994), 137: Dorner speaks of 'an eternal going out from itself and eternal return to itself as...moments of the one divine life.'

[90] Rather unexpectedly, Mitchell Grell entirely misses the trinitarian basis of Barth's exposition of immutability, equating it instead with the primarily 'ethical' immutability he finds in Dorner. See his *Der ewig reiche Gott: Die Erkenntnis, Gewinnung und Bestimmung der Eigenschaften Gottes nach Isaak August Dorner, August Hermann Cremer und Karl Barth mit besonderer Berücksichtigung des Einflusses der Theologie Dorners und Cremers auf die Gotteslehre Barths* (Ph.D. diss., University of Tübingen, 1992), 299–310. Pokrifka-Joe, *Redescribing God*, 183–99, also misses Barth's point and falls back on an appeal to God's personal and ethical immutability as recast, following a suggestion of Trevor Hart, in Ricoeur's categories of idem- and ipse-identity.

called an 'unhappy inconsistency' – not of immutable life but of immutable motionlessness.[91] Such immanent divine stasis, abstracted from the triune relations, cannot account for the liveliness of God in the economy.

At this point, before launching into the development of the ideas set forth in his opening definition of immutability, Barth makes a very suggestive acknowledgement of his indebtedness to 'Dorner's great essay'.[92] This must not be taken as evidence of a slavish imitation of Dorner on Barth's part. Barth might indeed be indebted to Dorner for, among other things, his exposition of divine immutability in terms of the triune relations.[93] Barth's indebtedness to Dorner, however, is far from total.[94] Dorner, for example, is happy to concede that, while God is immutably Father, Son and Spirit, nevertheless:

> God is not immutable in his relation to space and time, nor immutable in his knowing and willing of the world and in his decree. On the contrary, in all these respects there takes place also on his side change, alteration, a permitting of himself to be determined.[95]

For Dorner, God's activity *ad extra* in some way causes a certain mutability *ad intra*.[96] For Barth, the changes or alterations in God's relations *ad extra* are strictly revelatory of his eternal and ontologically immutable liveliness.

---

[91] Richard Muller has argued that, in his critique of the Protestant orthodox, Barth has 'confused the notion of an ultimate, necessary, and, therefore, "unmoved" Being with ideas of inaction, physical stasis, and immobility'. See Muller, *Reformed Dogmatics*, 3.308. Barth is not confused. He has simply taken some particularly extreme statements, statements which he knows very well do not represent the whole of Protestant orthodox theology, and used them to point out a weakness in this doctrine – a tactic Muller acknowledges Barth to have favoured (*idem*, 3.25).

[92] It was Barth's glowing commendation of Dorner's work, in fact, which inspired its translation into English and now serves as a back-cover blurb. See Robert R. Williams, 'Introduction', in Dorner, *Immutability*, 38.

[93] Dorner, *Immutability*, 171–4; cf. Piotr J. Malysz, 'Hegel's Conception of God and its Application by Isaak Dorner to the Problem of Divine Immutability', *Pro Ecclesia* 15.4 (2006): 468–9.

[94] On Barth's relation to Dorner, see Matthias Gockel, 'On the Way from Schleiermacher to Barth: A Critical Reappraisal of Isaak August Dorner's Essay on Divine Immutability', *Scottish Journal of Theology* 53.4 (2000): 490–510, esp. 503–7; and Robert Sherman, 'Isaak August Dorner on Divine Immutability: A Missing Link between Schleiermacher and Barth', *Journal of Religion* 77.3 (1997): 380–402, esp. 393–9.

[95] Dorner, *Immutability*, 165; cf. Jonathan Norgate, *Isaak A. Dorner: The Triune God and the Gospel of Salvation* (London: T&T Clark, 2009), 45–6.

[96] Robert R. Williams, 'I. A. Dorner: The Ethical Immutability of God', *Journal of the American Academy of Religion* 54.4 (1986): 721: According to Dorner, 'God must be conceived as immutable in some respects and as mutable in other respects'; so Malysz, 'Hegel's Conception of God', 464–7.

It is certainly not the case, as Thomas Weinandy argues, that Barth follows Dorner in 'making God merely ethically immutable' by 'denying the onto-logical unchangeable perfection of God'.[97] It may actually be Barth's desire to avoid being misunderstood as advocating a merely ethical immutability in God which leads him to say almost nothing in this context of immut-ability as including God's faithfulness – through Barth certainly affirms 'the unchangeableness and therefore the reliability' of God elsewhere (609; cf. 425–6, 665). Barth's equivocal use of 'change' language in this section – both affirming and denying it in God – makes for an admittedly challenging read. By 'change' in God, however, Barth has made it sufficiently clear that he means the vitality, the ontologically prior and immutable vitality, of the triune relations.[98]

Interestingly, that Barth affirms an ontological constancy of God receives indirect confirmation from his treatment of divine eternity. There, Barth quotes Ritschl's definition of God's eternity. It is 'the unchanging continuity and identity of the divine will in relation to its goal', so that 'in all the changes in things which denote the alteration in his working, he is himself the same, as he also maintains the final goal and plan in which he creates and gov-erns the world' (618). While this sounds remarkably like Barth's claim here that God 'is always the same in every change' (496), Barth actually rejects Ritschl's definition. What is wrong with it? Barth concedes that Ritschl's def-inition of eternity (and by implication his own parallel description of divine constancy) is acceptable as far as it goes. Barth faults Ritschl, however, for bringing 'the Creator and the creature…too close to one another' (618) and for failing to capture the fact that 'God is eternal quite apart from this goal adopted by his will' (619):

> As God's omnipotence is more than his omnicausality, and is not exhausted but merely operative in it, God's eternity is more than the unity of all times with the goal and purpose of his will, and is not exhausted by this unity. It is rather the presupposition of this unity, without which it cannot be believed and known as accomplished and maintained by God. (619)

---

[97] Thomas G. Weinandy, *Does God Suffer?* (Notre Dame: University of Notre Dame Press, 2000), 62 n. 30. Rather oddly, Weinandy later says that 'maybe' Barth is to be included among theologians who 'hold that God is immutable…in himself' (*ibid.*, 163 n. 31). By contrast, see Pannenberg's description of Dorner as 'the most important champion of an essential Trinity in Protestant theology during the second half of the 19th century' in his *Systematic Theology*, 3 vols., trans. Geoffrey W. Bromiley (Grand Rapids: Eerdmans, 1991–1998), 1.295.

[98] Sherman, 'Isaak August Dorner on Divine Immutability', 400, acknowledges that Barth's exposition of constancy is grounded 'in an expressly Trinitarian framework', yet he somehow claims at the same time that it 'completes and makes explicit the shift from a metaphysical to an ethical construal of God's freedom'.

If Barth is not to be charged with attempting to pass off as an explanation of divine constancy what he rejects as an explanation of divine eternity, he must by implication have intended to include in his own definition what he finds lacking in Ritschl's: a dimension in God's being, even beyond the created order. God's metaphysical liveliness transcending the created order is the presupposition of his liveliness within it.

Following his reference to Dorner, Barth picks up his exposition with a clarification of his critique of the tradition. Its fault, once again, was the old inversion of interpreting God's immutability in light of an assumed concept of strict motionlessness, rather than the assumed concept in light of God (493). The implications of such a procedure, in Barth's widely quoted lines, are dire:

> For we must not make any mistake: the pure *immobile* is – death. If, then, the pure *immobile* is God, death is God....And if death is God, then God is dead. (494)[99]

In fact, by ascribing this kind of immutability to God, Protestant orthodoxy, according to Barth, unwittingly paved the way for modern atheism (494).

This reference to modern atheism recalls Barth's earlier analysis (287–97) of the way in which nineteenth-century Hegelian theologians – with 'the collusion of the older orthodoxy' (289) – lapsed into idolatry with their denial of the personality of God. As in that earlier discussion, so here Barth again emphasises that God's immutability is that of the divine life. Both in itself and in its interaction with the created order, it is the constancy of the divine person:

> This immutability includes rather than excludes life. In a word, it is life. It does not, therefore, need to acquire life from the impulse of the created world, or above all from the emotions of our pious feeling....God's constancy – which is a better word than the suspiciously negative word 'immutability' – is the constancy of his knowing, willing and acting and therefore of his person. (495)[100]

As Barth argued previously, the divine person is the One who loves, one who is himself fellowship and therefore capable of fellowship (285–6; cf. 641).

---

[99] Cf. Dorner, *Immutability*, 137: 'The divine being could not be living, but could only be rigid dead substance or equally lifeless law, if it were motionless in itself, without real distinction of the positing and the posited life.'

[100] It is, thus, misleading when Berkhof claims that, for Barth, God's changes *ad extra* 'are eternalized in God' (*Christian Faith*, 153), for this suggests that God does in fact acquire his liveliness 'from the impulse of the created world'. Barth's logic clearly moves in the other direction. It would be better to say that God's liveliness *ad intra* is 'temporalised' in the created order.

One particular aspect of the fellowship God has with his people Israel, an aspect which both marks it as that of a person and also serves as a standard test-case for a doctrine of divine immutability, is the matter of Scripture's testimony to God's repentance, regret, and changing his mind (495–9). What Barth asserts is both that God really does partake in created alteration, and that 'there is something corresponding to that alteration in his own essence' (496). This 'holy mutability' of God is such that:

> He is not prevented from advancing and retreating, rejoicing and mourning, laughing and complaining, being well pleased and causing his wrath to kindle, hiding or revealing himself. And in all these things he can be always himself, and therefore he can be them seriously, yet still according to the order of his essence, and therefore in a definite sequence and gradation. (498–9)

Barth's reference to the 'order' and the 'definite sequence and gradation' of God's essence may indicate specifically the triune relations; at the very least, it means that all of these economic acts have some counterpart in the divine life. It is admittedly difficult to conceive what aspect of God's eternal and blessed liveliness might be revealed in events such as God's mourning or complaining or wrath. Without fuller consideration of the implications of election for the divine life, Barth might even concede that this is impossible to determine.[101] Barth affirms nevertheless that all of God's dynamic involvement with the created order is somehow revelatory of God's eternal liveliness.

The very existence of a created order serves as another standard test-case for divine immutability, which Barth addresses in transitioning to a second stage of argument (499–512). On Barth's account, because God creates in the freedom of his constant vitality, and because creation has no other basis than God himself, 'Creation cannot bring him any increase, decrease or alteration of his divine being and essence' (499). The very novelty and otherness of creation are simply a manifestation of the eternal newness and otherness in God himself:

> It is by him that there is the new thing of a reality distinct from himself, and it is by him that all the new things in this reality exist. But all these novelties can and do exist by him because it is in him himself that they have their ground, because he is immutable in the fact that he is the One who is eternally new, and because it was in this immutability that he chose to be the Creator and Lord of the world and to manifest his love in freedom. (500; cf. 317)

---

[101] Recall Barth's assertion of the 'incomprehensible' form which grace takes in God's own life (CD II/1, 357).

Creator and creature exist, therefore, neither in monistic conflation nor in dualistic separation; the two are distinct in God's freedom but inseparable in his love (500–2).

Barth then picks up on this idea of God's eternal newness in a first, general discussion of God's constancy in his history with a fallen creation. Sin, human opposition to God, is a new event, one grounded neither in God himself nor in creation (503–4). God's response to it, however, both in the execution of his eternal election and in the maintenance and assertion of the eternal peace of Father, Son and Spirit, 'is simply a confirmation that he is unalterably alive with a life to which sin cannot oppose anything new, strange or superior' (505):

> Newer than the novelty that man has sinned is the new fact that becomes visible and active in the work of his opposition to it in his essence. This is the divine mercy and the divine wrath in which he does not become different, but confirms himself anew as the one he has been from all eternity and from the creation of the world. (506 rev.; *KD* 569)[102]

Even beyond his self-confirmation in the general act of creation, it is in this new and particular self-confirmation of God in reconciliation, in all its historical dimensions, that we see the true nature of the divine immutability (506). As Barth puts it, flirting with the logic of the *felix culpa*, 'The God of Genesis 3 is more living, because more definite, than the God of Genesis 1–2' (507). In God's choice of and partnership with specific people, in the miraculous nature of his working and the light this casts on creation's future, and in his response to prayer, God freshly and more clearly shows who he unchangeably is (507–12).

Barth's discussion of prayer in particular is striking, and it contains in short compass a number of elements which characterise the whole subsection on constancy. The thrust of the passage is simply to affirm that God hears, that is, responds to prayer:

> We need not hesitate to say that 'on the basis of the freedom of God himself, God is conditioned by the prayer of faith'. The basis is his freedom. It is thus a form of his sovereignty, and therefore of his immutable vitality, that he is willing not merely to hear [*hören*] but to hearken [*erhören*] to the prayer of faith, and that he not only permits

---

[102] Cf. *CD* II/2, 175. Cf. Hermann Cremer, *Die christliche Lehre von den Eigenschaften Gottes*, ed. Helmut Burkhardt (1897; Gießen: TVG/Brunnen, 2005), 118: 'While [God's] will to create becomes a will to redeem, this does not bring about any change in his being, nor even in his attitude toward the world. It only means that he remains like himself in his love, and that he remains the same for us precisely in this love.'

to faith the prayer which expects an answer but has positively commanded it. The Bible is completely unambiguous about this: 'he heareth the prayer of the righteous' (Prov 15:29). (510–11; *KD* 574)[103]

Although Barth qualifies his affirmation of God's responsiveness with reference to the divine freedom and concurrence (512), his emphasis is by no means on these qualifications, but rather on the affirmation. Scripture is 'completely unambiguous' on this point. This recalls Barth's earlier claim that 'biblical thinking about God would rather submit to confusion with the grossest anthropomorphism [*Anthropopathismus*]' than to any formulation that might appear to restrict the fulness of the divine life (496; *KD* 558). What this shows is not simply a confidence in the testimony of Scripture (cf. 521), but also something of the practical orientation of Barth's theology. Here is seasoned pastoral sensitivity to the fears and questions of those who would respond to the command to pray, who would take up what Barth, following Calvin, will later identify as the 'normal action', the 'central thing', 'the basic meaning of all human obedience': the invocation of God.[104]

This discussion of prayer is also of interest in light of the persistent charge of determinism in Barth's theology. Sheila Greeve Davaney, for example, makes the following claim about Barth's neighbouring account of the divine omnipotence:

Barth's central conviction is clear: divine knowing and willing (i.e. divine power) are to be interpreted as essentially independent, unconditioned and causative in nature. They are never to be understood as even partly responsive to or dependent upon their objects.[105]

In fact, Barth says otherwise. Not only in his distant discussions of the invocation of God in *The Christian Life*, but even here in the midst of a discussion of so traditionally abstract a divine attribute as immutability, Barth is 'completely unambiguous' in affirming the mysterious mutuality of the communication between God and humankind.[106]

The final stage of Barth's exposition consists of a second, more focussed treatment of God's constancy in the history of reconciliation (512–22). As generally in creation and more clearly in God's history with Israel and the

---

[103] Cf. *CD* III/4, 108–9.

[104] *ChrL*, 43–4.

[105] Sheila Greeve Davaney, *Divine Power: A Study of Karl Barth and Charles Hartshorne*, Harvard Dissertations in Religion 19 (Philadelphia: Fortress, 1986), 48; cf. 59–60 and Case-Winters, *God's Power*, 113.

[106] Cf. George Hunsinger, *How To Read Karl Barth: The Shape of His Theology* (Oxford: Oxford University Press, 1991), 221–3.

church, so with final clarity and particularity God's immutable vitality is manifest in Jesus Christ (512–13).

> God is constant, he does not alter, when he becomes and is one with the creature in Jesus Christ.... He does this *as the One he is* because the incarnation is as such the confirmation of the triunity of God. Without abrogation of the divine unity, there is revealed in it the distinction of the Father and the Son, and also their fellowship in the Holy Spirit. He does it *as the Creator* because the incarnation is as such the confirmation of the distinctive reality of creation; for in the fact that God becomes one with creation there is revealed that God and creation as such are two distinct realities, and that the creature has its own reality over against God. He does it finally *as Reconciler and Redeemer*, because the incarnation as such confirms and explains the fact that God has befriended and continually befriends fallen creation, and will lead it on to a full redemption. (515 rev.; *KD* 579)

In other words, the incarnation does not change God but confirms the eternal distinctions in the triune life as well as God's intention for the created order and for his people Israel.[107] In fact, the incarnation, as part of God's eternal, gracious election of Jesus Christ, does not merely confirm God's intention for creation, but is itself the reason why God created in the first place (514–15).

As Barth will spell out at length in his doctrine of election, what he here affirms is a supralapsarian position on the logical order of the divine decrees.[108] According to this position, or rather to Barth's 'purified' version of it,[109] God first decrees the election (and reprobation) of Jesus Christ, in whom God ascribes to man 'election, salvation and life' and to himself 'reprobation, perdition and death'.[110] God then decrees to create and to allow the fall in order to serve the original, redemptive purpose of the decree of election. Creation, then, has no significance independent of redemption. The same logic is expressed in Barth's well-known description of the covenant as the 'internal basis' of creation.[111] According to the infralapsarian position on the logical order of the divine decrees, God decrees first to create the

---

[107] Cf. particularly the discussion of God's immutability in the incarnation in *CD* IV/2, 84–7.

[108] Barth had held this position at least since his latter days in Göttingen, and for many of the same reasons he gives in *CD* II/2; see *The Göttingen Dogmatics: Instruction in the Christian Religion*, vol. 1, ed. Hannelotte Reiffen, trans. Geoffrey W. Bromiley (Grand Rapids: Eerdmans, 1991), 466–8. For what follows, see the brilliant excursus on the supralapsarian-infralapsarian debate in *CD* II/2, 127–45.

[109] *CD* II/2, 142.

[110] *CD* II/2, 163.

[111] *CD* III/1, §41.3, 'The Covenant as the Internal Basis of Creation' (228–329).

world for some purpose other than redemption; second, to allow the fall, qualifying his original purpose for creation; and third, to elect, somehow confirming his original purpose for creation. Barth sees in this position a shifting-of-purpose incompatible with God's constancy. While Barth might conceivably have found a way to reconcile infralapsarianism with divine constancy, there is a more obvious constancy in the singleness-of-purpose envisioned in the supralapsarian position. This is why Barth can affirm so unequivocally God's constancy in the incarnation. It is the beginning, not merely of redemption, but of all the ways and works of God.

In this context, however, the real point to be made about the incarnation is not merely that it does not compromise the immutability of the divine nature, but that it constitutes 'the revelation of it in its perfection' (515). In a short excursus drawing on the Christ-hymn in Philippians 2, Barth maintains that both Christ's self-emptying (incarnation) and even his self-humiliation (crucifixion) do reveal God's 'truly immutable being as free love' (517). While Barth affirms that 'the cross on Golgotha is itself the divine majesty' (517), he remains disappointingly vague about what particularly Christ's dying reveals about the unchangingly lively divine nature.[112]

Having raised the topic of God's gracious election in the context of a discussion of divine immutability, Barth could hardly resist appending several observations on the nature of election and its formulation in Reformed orthodoxy. Barth was at the time in the very midst of working out the more christologically-focused doctrine of election, which would come to full expression in CD II/2.[113] Here Barth claims that what God does in Jesus Christ, as an act of his constancy, must be understood both as a free and, hence, gracious decision [Entschluß], one that 'takes place in the nature of God himself' (518; KD 583), and also as a necessary and binding decree [Beschluß] (518–19; KD 583). What Reformed orthodoxy failed to discern, on Barth's account, is the way in which the interna voluntatis divinae actio (519), because it 'takes place in the essence of God' (520), completely specifies that God's being is the concrete being of Jesus Christ, and that without remainder. God's revealed will must, therefore, be understood without qualification 'as the true and proper revelation' of God's hidden, absolute will (520). By virtue of election, God's nature becomes not different but particular: God wills to become 'unalterably gracious' to man (522).

---

[112] Barth's discussion of the humility and obedience of the Son in CD IV/1 (192–210) offers some retrospective clarity on God's constancy in the incarnation and crucifixion; cf. CD IV/2, 84–5.

[113] Barth first formulated this new focus in his Debrecen lecture of September, 1936. See Bruce L. McCormack, Karl Barth's Critically Realistic Dialectical Theology: Its Genesis and Development 1909–1936 (New York: Oxford University Press, 1995), 455–62.

In a brilliant but troubling essay, Bruce McCormack argues that one implication of Barth's doctrine of election is that God's triunity is actually contingent upon election:

> The *decision* for the covenant of grace is the ground of God's triunity and, therefore, of the eternal generation of the Son and of the eternal procession of the Holy Spirit from Father and Son. In other words, the works of God *ad intra* (the trinitarian processions) find their ground in the *first* of the works of God *ad extra* (viz. election).[114]

What this proposal achieves for McCormack is, among other things, a resolution of the tension between immutability and incarnation. McCormack rightly reads Barth as affirming God's ontological immutability, and so he asks, 'How is it possible for God to *become* ... without undergoing any *essential* (i.e. ontological) change?'[115] The answer, according to McCormack, is that at no point does God the Son exist apart from his determination to become incarnate.[116] There is no *logos asarkos* which is not also *incarnandus*. It is not the case, in other words, that prior to the decree of election the Son might have chosen not to become incarnate. If the Son had had such an option, he could not be understood as essentially ordered toward the incarnation, and the incarnation would thus involve some degree of essential change in him. As, however, the Son's hypostatic telos has always included his incarnate mission, he undergoes no essential change in its execution. Understandably, McCormack's thesis has sparked a lively debate.[117]

---

[114] Bruce McCormack, 'Grace and Being: The Role of God's Gracious Election in Karl Barth's Theological Ontology', in *The Cambridge Companion to Karl Barth*, ed. John Webster (Cambridge: Cambridge University Press, 2000), 103.

[115] McCormack, 'Grace and being', 96.

[116] McCormack, 'Grace and being', 101, 103.

[117] See, for example, Paul D. Molnar, *Divine Freedom and the Doctrine of the Immanent Trinity: In Dialogue with Karl Barth and Contemporary Theology* (Edinburgh: T&T Clark, 2002), 61–4; Kevin W. Hector, 'God's Triunity and Self-Determination: A Conversation with Karl Barth, Bruce McCormack and Paul Molnar', *International Journal of Systematic Theology* 7.3 (2005): 246–61; Edwin Chr. van Driel, 'Karl Barth on the Eternal Existence of Jesus Christ', *Scottish Journal of Theology* 60.1 (2007): 45–61; Bruce McCormack, 'Seek God Where He May Be Found: A Response to Edwin Chr. van Driel', *Scottish Journal of Theology* 60.1 (2007): 62–79; Paul D. Molnar, 'Can the Electing God be God without us? Some Implications of Bruce McCormack's Understanding of Barth's Doctrine of Election for the Doctrine of the Trinity', *Neue Zeitschrift für Systematische Theologie und Religionsphilosophie* 49.2 (2007): 199–222; George Hunsinger, 'Election and the Trinity: Twenty-Five Theses on the Theology of Karl Barth', *Modern Theology* 24.2 (2008): 179–98; Aaron T. Smith, 'God's self-specification: his being is his electing', *Scottish Journal of Theology* 62.1 (2009): 1–25; Bruce McCormack, 'Election and the Trinity: Theses in response to George Hunsinger', *Scottish Journal of Theology* 63.2 (2010): 203–24; Paul D.

Without rehearsing the details of this debate, what might Barth's account of divine constancy have to say to the issues? To begin with, while Barth wrote his doctrine of the attributes (*CD* II/1) before his doctrine of election (*CD* II/2), McCormack himself has pointed out that Barth came to the view of election expressed in *CD* II/2 back in the summer of 1936, before he began lecturing on the attributes.[118] While statements in *CD* I/1 and I/2 which run counter to McCormack's proposal might thus be written off as having been made before Barth came to his mature view of election, the same cannot be said so categorically of such statements in *CD* II/1. McCormack admits that '*CD* II/1 gives testimony at a number of points (in Barth's treatment of the "perfections" of God, especially) to the presence of residual elements of classical theism (and the ancient metaphysics which made it possible).'[119] Nevertheless, even if Barth's thought in *CD* II/1 has not yet arrived at full consistency with McCormack's proposal, it should at least be moving in that direction. In fact, it is not.

First, we have already noted several statements which clearly indicate that, as Barth said near the end of his life, 'behind the doctrine of election stands the doctrine of the Trinity'.[120] For example, 'it was in this immutability that [God] chose to be the Creator and Lord of the world and to manifest his love in freedom' (500). Here, God's triune immutability is prior to election and manifest in it. Or consider the way in which Barth speaks of God's constancy in the incarnation, which is of course the outcome of election:

> The incarnation is as such the confirmation of the triunity of God. Without abrogation of the divine unity, there is revealed in it the distinction of the Father and the Son, and also their fellowship in the Holy Spirit. (515)

For McCormack, God's eternal election logically includes the incarnation. Yet here Barth says that God's triunity is 'confirmed' and 'revealed' in the incarnation, not constituted by it. Many other statements throughout II/1[121] and

---

Molnar, 'Can Jesus' Divinity Be Recognized as "Definitive, Authentic and Essential" If It Is Grounded in Election? Just How Far Did the Later Barth Historicize Christology?' *Neue Zeitschrift für Systematische Theologie und Religionsphilosophie* 52.1 (2010): 40–81.

[118] McCormack, *Dialectical Theology*, 455–8.

[119] McCormack, 'Seek God', 63–5; cf. Gockel, *Doctrine of Election*, 196.

[120] Hunsinger, 'Election and the Trinity', 182; quoting Karl Barth, *Gespräche 1964–1968* (Zürich: Theologische Verlag Zürich, 1997), 293; cf. Eberhard Busch, *The Great Passion: An Introduction to Karl Barth's Theology* (Grand Rapids: Eerdmans, 2004), 127.

[121] For example, Molnar, 'Can the Electing God be God without Us?' 213–16. Cf. *CD* II/1, 305–7, where Barth rejects 'any idea of God taking his origin from himself' and asserts that God's 'being other than he is is ontologically and noetically excluded, ... an

later in the *Dogmatics*[122] have been adduced against McCormack's proposal. McCormack is not unaware of such statements, yet they would appear too numerous to represent a mere inconsistency in Barth's thought.[123]

Second, beyond these individual statements, it should be clear by now that Barth presents the divine attributes without exception as antecedent aspects of God's immanent life, which enable and are revealed in his subsequent interaction with the created order. 'God does not first create multiplicity and movement, but he is one and simple, he is constant, in such a way that all multiplicity and movement have their prototype and pre-existence in himself' (612). In other words, 'What God does in time is...a function of what he is in eternity' – not the other way round.[124] This is one of the most basic themes of Barth's exposition. To claim that it is God's interaction with the created order which determines his immanent life is to run directly counter not merely to isolated inconsistencies or residual elements of classical theism in *CD* II/1, but to its entire flow of thought.[125] In a more recent essay, McCormack claims that 'Most of what is said here [in *CD* II/1] is easily adjusted' to his proposal,[126] only to spend a dozen pages documenting the incompatibility of many specific passages, as well as the logic of the whole. Ultimately, he concedes that 'in Barth's doctrine of God in *Church Dogmatics* II/1 ... Christology does not yet control his theological ontology.'[127] It is only by interpreting certain statements in II/1 as in tension with their immediate context that McCormack can still claim to detect in them 'intimations' of his own proposal.[128] McCormack's is a striking constructive proposal in its own right. But it encounters only resistance from Barth's doctrine of the divine perfections.

What Barth has achieved in this section is a remarkable combination of a traditional affirmation of the changelessness of God and, at the same time, a radical relocation of that changelessness to the triune relations. Against the tradition, though just possibly (as Barth would have it) more true than the

---

absolute impossibility'. McCormack candidly acknowledges that these statements 'cannot be redeemed' for his thesis and therefore 'should be rejected' as not representing Barth's mature thought. McCormack, 'Election and the Trinity', 220–1.

[122] For *CD* II/2, see Matthias Gockel, *Barth and Schleiermacher on the Doctrine of Election: A Systematic-Theological Comparison* (Oxford: Oxford University Press, 2007), 178–9. Hunsinger, 'Election and the Trinity', 180–91, has compiled an extensive list from throughout the *Dogmatics* and elsewhere.

[123] McCormack, 'Grace and Being', 101–2; McCormack, 'Seek God', 77–8.

[124] Gunton, *Act and Being*, 97.

[125] Cf. Van Driel, 'Eternal Existence', 52.

[126] Bruce L. McCormack, 'The Actuality of God: Karl Barth in Conversation with Open Theism', in *Engaging the Doctrine of God: Contemporary Protestant Perspectives* (Grand Rapids: Baker Academic, 2008), 212.

[127] McCormack, 'The Actuality of God', 234.

[128] McCormack, 'Election and the Trinity', 213; cf. 217–18.

tradition to its own better insights, Barth vividly depicts the liveliness and movement of God's essence even and primarily beyond his relations with the created order. Though Jüngel does not cite this treatment of constancy, it fits precisely what he describes as Barth's broader depiction of the divine 'becoming': not 'an augmentation or a diminution of God's being' but rather God's 'trinitarian livingness'.[129] Further, by making this clarification, Barth commends confidence that it really is the changeless God of Scripture who is revealed in the incarnate Jesus Christ and who himself, and not merely in appearance, acts in such varied and responsive ways toward his creation and toward humankind centrally placed within it.

Omnipotence

With the divine constancy, a perfection of God's freedom which indicates particularly this same freedom, Barth pairs omnipotence, also a perfection of God's freedom, but one which indicates in addition the love in which God is free. Perhaps the first feature of Barth's account of omnipotence to strike a reader is its disproportionate length. Such a reader might find cause for misgiving in Barth's observation, on the first page of exposition, that the early creeds saw in God's omnipotence a 'compendium' of all other perfections (522; cf. 544–5). Barth does not rehearse his foregoing exposition, however, but presses on to a consideration of God's power, and this, perhaps unexpectedly, in terms of God's knowing and willing. These three – God's power, God's knowing and God's willing – are traditionally given separate consideration among the divine attributes. Their coordination here helps to explain why exposition extends to roughly three times the space allotted to any of the other individual perfections of the divine freedom. Not only are there effectively three attributes to expound in this one sub-section, but their coordination demands (and Barth supplies) treatment of their several possible permutations and combinations.

But why this coordination in the first place? To begin with, if Barth wanted to preserve the intricate symmetry of §§30–31, he clearly could not have treated God's knowledge and will separately without a corresponding treatment of two additional perfections of the divine loving. The coordination of knowledge and will with omnipotence is not, however, merely or even primarily a formal consideration. From very early in his career, Barth had drawn a close material connection between divine omnipotence and the divine knowing and willing. In a 1913 lecture entitled 'Faith in the Personal God', Barth proposed that any viable concept of God would have to include emphasis both on God's personality, including his thinking and willing,[130] as

---

[129] Jüngel, *God's Being Is in Becoming*, xxv–xxvi.

[130] Karl Barth, 'Der Glaube an den persönlichen Gott', in *idem, Vorträge und kleinere Arbeiten 1909–1914*, Karl Barth Gesamtausgabe 22, ed. Hans-Anton Drewes and

well as on God's exaltation (*das Erhabene*), including such attributes as eternity, omnipresence and omnipotence.[131] This same personality-exaltation polarity is still evident in Barth's Göttingen lectures, where, significantly, omnipotence is associated not with God's exaltation, aseity or hiddenness, but with his personality.[132] By his Göttingen lectures, in other words, God's omnipotence is integrally connected to God's knowledge and will, because these not only distinguish it from impersonal force but also indicate the positive, reconciling goal to which it is directed.[133] In the *Church Dogmatics*, Barth takes up and explores in still finer detail this material connection between God's power, will and knowledge (cf. 209–15).

The unfolding of this connection begins with the very first sentence of exposition. In a deliberately self-referential definition, parallel to that of the divine constancy according to which 'God remains the One he is' (491), Barth now explains that God's omnipotence is that perfection by which God 'is able to do what he wills' (522). A suspicious Christine Kress senses that, with this opening definition, 'Barth is already manoeuvring towards the implicit goal of his exposition: safeguarding the unlimited power of God'.[134] Barth's point is in fact just the opposite. God's power is neither absolute nor infinite in the way that the Protestant scholastics often suggested (523), but materially limited to 'everything that he wills or could will' (522; cf. 423). God himself defines, that is, limits and gives shape to, his own omnipotence.

Barth's exposition of omnipotence continues in three stages. First, Barth gives a series of five 'distinguishing and delimiting' characteristics (543) of God's power (524–43). Here Barth is primarily concerned to rule out what he perceives to be either actual or potential errors in traditional expositions.[135] Second, he develops the material content of omnipotence in terms of God's knowledge and will (543–99). The thrust of this second stage is to affirm that, while God's knowing and willing are themselves God's

---

Hinrich Stoevesandt (Zürich: Theologischer Verlag Zürich, 1993), 511; cf. 527. Cf. Raynal, *Perfections*, 32–3; McCormack, *Dialectical Theology*, 104–6; Claus-Dieter Osthövener, *Die Lehre von Gottes Eigenschaften bei Friedrich Schleiermacher und Karl Barth*, Theologische Bibliothek Töpelmann 76 (Berlin: de Gruyter, 1996), 108–11.

[131] Barth, '*Der Glaube an den persönlichen Gott*', 494, 523, 525.

[132] Barth, *Göttingen Dogmatics*, 404, 409–11. Cf. Ingrid Spieckermann, *Gotteserkenntnis: Ein Beitrag zur Grundfrage der neuen Theologie Karl Barths* (Munich: Chr. Kaiser, 1985), 201.

[133] Christophe Chalamet, *Dialectical Theologians: Wilhelm Herrmann, Karl Barth and Rudolf Bultmann* (Zürich: Theologischer Verlag Zürich, 2005), 169; cf. 233.

[134] Christine Kress, *Gottes Allmacht angesichts von Leiden: Zur Interpretation der Gotteslehre in den systematisch-theologischen Entwürfen von Paul Althaus, Paul Tillich und Karl Barth*, Neukirchener Theologische Dissertationen und Habilitationen 27 (Neukirchen-Vluyn: Neukirchener Verlag, 1999), 208.

[135] Cf. Raynal, *Perfections*, 147–52.

omnipotence, they are also distinct from it and express the personality or spirituality by virtue of which God is also master of his omnipotence (and, by implication, of all of his other perfections, as well). Third, Barth argues that God's omnipotence has its concrete, personal centre in Jesus Christ (599–607).

The first distinguishing and delimiting characteristic of God's omnipotence is that it is not just any power, or power in itself, but the particular power of God (524). Repeating his opening definitions, Barth continues to insist that the reality of God controls what may be understood by subordinate concepts like omnipotence:

> In a word, whatever it may mean that God is almighty, and can therefore do all things, and possesses all possibilities, it is at least certain that we depart from Scripture in any statement which either openly or secretly has any other subject than God the Father, the Maker and Lord of the covenant with Abraham, the Father of Jesus Christ, and with him his Son and his Holy Spirit, or in which we fail to understand the predicates 'mighty' and 'almighty' as wholly filled out and defined by this subject. (526)

As with every other perfection, so with omnipotence: Barth insists that it be understood as that of the triune God of the covenant as attested in Scripture.

Second, in a nod to the Protestant scholastics,[136] Barth argues that God's omnipotence, as God's, is never simply a physical capacity or force (*potentia*), but always also a moral and legal capacity (*potestas*) (526). God's exercise of power is always legitimate. 'What God is able to do *de facto*, he is also able to do *de jure*' (526).

Third, God's omnipotence is revealed in, but not exhausted by, his work *ad extra* (526–8). 'He has not lost his omnipotence in this work,…like a piece of capital invested in this undertaking, and therefore no longer at the free disposal of its owner' (527). That is, while God reveals his power in creation, reconciliation, and redemption, he still has more power in himself. This 'excess' power does not invalidate revelation, as though the more-powerful God of eternity were somehow misrepresented by the less-powerful God active in the created order. We need not fear that God 'will be utterly different, and not the Shepherd of Israel and Lord of the church, in other work not known to us or in his divine essence' (527). On the contrary, it is precisely this 'excess' power which marks creation, reconciliation and redemption as free and gracious acts, in that it points to the fact that God had the capacity to do other than he did.

[136] Cf. Heinrich Heppe, *Reformed Dogmatics*, ed. Ernst Bizer, trans. G. T. Thomson (1857; reprint Grand Rapids: Baker, 1978), §5.42 (103–4).

In this formulation, Barth takes aim both at certain Protestant orthodox theologians, who maintain that God's omnipotence refers not to God's power in himself but only to his capacity to act in the created order (528–9), as well as at Schleiermacher, who, by logical extension from the orthodox, claims that this capacity to act is exhausted in the created order (529–31). Schleiermacher, in other words, reduces God's omnipotence to the mere 'omnicausality' of all created effects.[137] Against both of these claims, Barth maintains:

> God is the omnipotent God as he is the trinitarian God; in his life as this God; in his power to be the Father, Son and Holy Spirit; in the power by which he is the One by and in the Other, all being equal in origin, necessity and glory; in the power in which he is in himself the One whose life consists in the begetting and being begotten, the causing to proceed and proceeding, in which God has and is in himself the reality and therefore the possibility of this divine life. (529)

Once again, the doctrine of the Trinity governs Barth's description of a divine perfection.[138]

Fourth, God's omnipotence consists positively in his specific power to be himself, that is, to be constant (532–8):

> God has the power, as Father, Son and Holy Spirit, to be himself and to live of and by himself. This is his omnipotence. Everything else which he has the power to do, he has the power to do in virtue of this power. (532)

As noted previously, Barth insists that the immutable divine essence be conceived not statically, abstracted from the eternally lively relations between Father, Son and Spirit, but precisely in these relations. Here, in describing God's omnipotence as 'the power of his constant vitality' (532), Barth goes on to describe every act of God in the created order as in fact involving another 'recapitulation' or 'repetition' [*Wiederholung*] of the divine essence:

> If in his omnipotence he is active outwards, in relation to another, all his activity consists simply in a recapitulation [*Wiederholung*] of his own being. ...How can he be active, or active in a better or higher way,

---

[137] Cf. Barth, *Göttingen Dogmatics*, 405–7; Kress, *Gottes Allmacht*, 216–17.

[138] Davaney, *Divine Power*, 34 (cf. 58), acknowledges that Barth grounds divine power in the doctrine of the Trinity, but she then makes the bizarre claim that this trinitarian grounding actually *excludes* 'a relational, other-oriented conception of power'. It is 'ultimately nonsocial power' (*ibid.*, 59).

than by being himself again, and this time fully, in his outward as in his inward relationship? (532; *KD* 598)

Barth is not saying that God gains another mode of being every time he acts in the created order – a misunderstanding which the translators may have been attempting to avoid by using 'recapitulation' rather than 'repetition'. Rather, Barth draws an analogy of sorts, a parallel between the eternal self-repetition of the divine essence in Father, Son and Spirit and the way in which God brings his whole essence to bear in every one of his temporal acts. God's omnipotence is the power active in both.

The primary implication that Barth draws from this is that God himself must be the criterion of what is possible for his power (532). God's power cannot be bounded, as many a theologian has argued, by what is supposedly possible in itself (534), for such a claim involves an idolatrous absolutising of a creaturely and therefore strictly relative confidence concerning 'the possible'. In a passage of some urgency and insistence, including allusion to the Barmen Declaration, Barth warns that this is precisely the kind of divinizing of creaturely reality at work in Hitler's surging 'Third Reich of madness' (536–7).[139]

Fifth and finally, God's omnipotence is absolutely sovereign over, because qualitatively different from, all created powers (538–42). Anticipating his discussion of the divine *concursus* in CD III/3,[140] Barth argues that God's power is 'the power of all powers, the power in and over them all....He is not at any point limited or determined by them, but at every point he limits and determines them' (538). Such overwhelming power is not tyrannical, however, because it is that of the triune God. God's triune omnipotence does not preclude the existence of other powers, for 'it is the power of the eternal love in which before all worlds God is not only full of power in himself, but as Father and Son always has power in another' (538).

To this fifth point Barth appends a discussion of the scholastic distinction between God's absolute and ordained power. God in his absolute power (Luther's *Deus absconditus*) cannot be conceived as other than or only arbitrarily related to the way he appears in the exercise of his ordained power (Luther's *Deus revelatus*). Rather, 'God has finally and definitively revealed his *potentia absoluta* as *potentia ordinata*' (542). More simply, 'We can count on a greater omnipotence, but not on a different one' (542). Barth's concern, once again, is with the simultaneous freedom and validity of revelation.

---

[139] The Nazi glorification of impersonal power (Evans, *The Third Reich in Power*, 210) may also have added to the urgency with which Barth emphasises the personal, that is, the knowing and willing character of divine power.

[140] CD III/3, §49.2, 'The Divine Accompanying' (90–154).

The explicitly trinitarian logic evident in Barth's series of 'delimiting characteristics' and his explicit rejection of Schleiermacher's formulation pose something of a problem for Claus-Dieter Osthövener. Osthövener's thesis is that both Schleiermacher and Barth construct their theologies under the influence of a single, governing principle. For Barth, this supposed principle is absolute divine independence. (As Wolf Krötke wryly notes, Osthövener thus ascribes to Barth a method which Barth himself reviles as 'untenable, and corrupt and heathen'.[141]) How then does Osthövener account for the way in which the doctrine of the Trinity functions here – if anything does – as the single, governing 'principle'? Basically, either by ignoring it or by simply equating it with absolute divine independence. Osthövener devotes several pages of analysis to Barth's comments on God's relation to the possible (532–3) and to Barth's statement that 'we must recognise [God's] capacity, his *potentia absoluta*, only in the capacity chosen by him, in his *potentia ordinata*' (541). Osthövener concludes that, from a creaturely perspective, there is thus 'only a formal difference between God's capacity in itself and his capacity as actualized and accessible to us in the world'.[142] This may be true, but Barth's explicit appeal to the doctrine of the Trinity shows that he held in high importance something well beyond the creaturely perspective. Osthövener, however, cannot maintain his thesis and acknowledge this kind of 'beyond' in Barth, and so he simply ignores it. 'In this respect', he concludes, 'Barth stands in much greater accord with Schleiermacher than he would admit.'[143] Barth would not admit to such agreement with Schleiermacher at this point precisely because he was unwilling to ignore God's triunity. The nearly total absence of engagement with the doctrine of the Trinity in Osthövener's study of Barth is also achieved by reinterpretation, that is, by equating Trinity with absolute independence. One particularly clear example occurs in his discussion of 'modal logic', that is, the analysis of conditions of necessity and possibility. Here, Osthövener asserts that, while Schleiermacher restricts his reflections to the creaturely sphere, 'Barth is obliged by his concept of divine freedom to refuse this restriction and enquire into the function of modal operators in the divine subject itself.'[144] It is not some abstract concept of divine freedom (interchangeable, for Osthövener, with absolute divine independence) which drives Barth to enquire how necessity and possibility ('modal operators') function within the Godhead. Barth does so because he believes that God is triune and that

---

141 Wolf Krötke, review of *Die Lehre von Gottes Eigenschaften bei Friedrich Schleiermacher und Karl Barth*, by Claus-Dieter Osthövener, *Theologische Literaturzeitung* 123.3 (1998): 295, citing *CD* IV/1, 186.

142 Osthövener, *Gottes Eigenschaften*, 193, cited approvingly by Kress, *Gottes Allmacht*, 216 n. 769.

143 Osthövener, *Gottes Eigenschaften*, 193.

144 Osthövener, *Gottes Eigenschaften*, 193.

all of God's acts in the creaturely sphere are animated by and therefore reveal his own triune power.

> God has the power, as Father, Son and Holy Spirit, to be himself and to live of and by himself. This is his omnipotence. Everything else which he has the power to do, he has the power to do in virtue of this power. And further, everything else which he has the power to do is simply a manifestation, revelation and application of this power. (532)

Returning to Barth's exposition, we find that these five points provide merely initial clarification of the divine omnipotence. The second stage of argument, the material development of omnipotence, takes the rather surprising form of a discussion of divine knowledge and divine will (543–99). Much of what Barth wants to say about God's power, it turns out, he wants to say in terms of God's knowledge and will, that is, in terms of what Barth calls the divine personality or spirituality:

> We must now push on…in an attempt to understand the power of God expressly and in detail as the power of the divine knowledge and will. It is in this way alone that the God confronts us whom Holy Scripture attests as the omnipotent God. According to Scripture, his freedom, and therefore the divinity of his love, is the freedom of his personality. (543)

It is actually God's personality, Barth goes on to argue, which underlies the five initial points about the divine omnipotence (544–5). For it is the fact that God is personal, a knowing and willing subject, which expresses for Barth that God is the Lord and wielder of his power, 'the master of his omnipotence and not its slave' (544).

The connections between the divine knowledge and will and the broader context of Barth's chapter on the divine perfections are not to be missed. Mere mention of the knowledge of God recalls Barth's discussion of this theme in the opening chapter of CD II/1, and more specific parallels are not lacking. For example, the earlier discussion of God's primary and secondary objectivity (3–62) is echoed here in the claim that, in revelation, it is 'fellowship *with his own knowledge*' that God gives us (546 rev.; KD 614). The reference to God's will as his 'decision and resolve' [*Entschließens und Beschließens*]' (543; KD 611) looks ahead to Barth's doctrine of election in CD II/2, even as it recalls Barth's earlier assertion, in his treatment of the divine constancy, that what God does in Jesus Christ, and hence God's gracious election, must be understood as both free decision [*Entschluß*] and necessary decree [*Beschluß*] (518–19). The prominent function of God's knowledge and will in the immediately preceding and following chapters of the *Dogmatics* may help to account not merely for the length Barth's account of omnipotence but also for the especial care evident in it.

Barth continues his exposition with five further points concerning the relation between God's omnipotence and his knowing and willing.[145] Before taking up these concerns, however, Barth, in another surprising move, shifts from exposition into meditation. This meditation takes the form of a diptych on God's knowing and willing (545–9), the first panel of which is one of the most sublime and moving passages in all of the *Church Dogmatics*.[146] Here is a portrait of 'God With Us', of the intimate, personal fellowship which lies at the heart of reconciliation.[147] Amidst all the conceptual analysis and polemic and straining for clarity, Barth reminds his readers that the object of the theologian's task is the God who in his grace evokes not merely our dogmatics, but also our awe, our gratitude and our most profound joy.

A delicate and noteworthy feature of both this diptych and the exposition which follows is that Barth has given them their own love-freedom dialectic. These are part of 'the endlessly dovetailing structure' of §§30–31,[148] and they help mitigate the structural anomaly which results from the inclusion of God's knowing and willing as part of the divine omnipotence. In the language of his earlier description of God's love (e.g. 273), Barth says that, knowing us, 'God gives us fellowship with himself' (546); in the language of his earlier description of God's freedom (e.g. 301), Barth says that, because it is God's will to know us, he acts 'in free self-determination' as a 'free person' (547). Like the divine loving, the divine knowing comes first; like the divine freedom, the divine willing follows. Barth further explains the reason for this sequence by associating it with the order between revelation and reconciliation, where revelation comes first in logical sequence and reconciliation follows. It is 'the divine revelation where we meet God as the One who knows' and 'the divine reconciliation where we meet God as the One who wills' (549). While this association is somewhat ad hoc and not to be pressed, it functions here to explain the logical or sequential priority of God's loving knowledge over God's free will. This same dialectic between knowledge and will, patterned on the small-scale dialectic operative within each pair of attributes, is also found in each of the five points which follow. Moreover, while the first four points show the *identity* between God's omnipotence and his knowing and willing, the fifth point moves in the opposite direction, showing the *distinction* between God's omnipotence and his knowing and willing, that is, God's freedom in the exercise of his omnipotence.

---

[145] These bear no direct relation to the previous five.

[146] Cf. de Margerie, *Les Perfections*, 151–3.

[147] Cf. *CD* IV/1, §57.1 (3–21); Hunsinger, *How to Read Karl Barth*, 173–5.

[148] Robert W. Jenson, *God After God: The God of the Past and the God of the Future, Seen in the Work of Karl Barth* (Indianapolis: Bobbs-Merrill, 1969), 135.

The five-point series of this second stage thus exhibits a dialectical structure almost as intricate as that which carries the whole chapter.

God's knowing and willing, then, are omnipotent. How is this so? First, Barth affirms again that God's attributes are God's essence. God's knowledge and will are each his (omnipotent) essence (549–51) – proof, if it were needed, that Barth does view knowledge and will as themselves perfections of God. They are not merely ancillary concepts to round out omnipotence, even though this is formally the place they occupy in Barth's exposition:

> With the statements 'God knows' and 'God wills' we are describing the one total essence of God. God's knowledge is God himself, and again God's will is God himself. (549)

Thus, God's knowing and willing, like and as God's essence, are perfect in themselves even apart from the actual existence of their objects in the created order. As one who knows and wills, it is constitutive of God's essence to be one who confronts others as intending and purposive. Thus, 'we cannot think of God at all without being summoned in the same instant to faith, obedience, gratitude, humility and joy' (550).

Second, Barth reconfigures the equation to read, 'God's knowledge is his will and God's will his knowledge' (551). While remaining distinct and irreducible, Barth's point is that the two are also co-extensive. 'Everything that God knows he also wills, and everything that he wills he also knows' (551). God's knowledge and will include the actual, the possible, and even the logically and ontologically impossible, each in its own way:

> He knows what is real outside him as that which has been raised to reality by himself, and as this he also wills it. He knows the possible as that which has its possibility in and by him, whether as that which he will raise to reality in its own time, or as that which will always be a possibility from him and by him, but only a possibility. And he also wills this possibility as such, whether it is to be realised in the future or not at all. He knows also the impossible, that which from him and by him is not possible. He knows it as that which he has rejected, excluded and denied: sin as sin; death as death; the devil as the devil. And he also wills it to be this, to be what it is in virtue of his rejection of it, in the way which belongs to it as the impossible. (551–2)

Everything, all reality and un-reality, actual and possible, falls within the scope and under the governance of God's knowledge and will.

Third (552–8), God's knowledge, as omnipotent, is omniscience. Likewise God's will, as omnipotent, is 'omnivolence', that is, 'a complete and exhaustive will, embracing and controlling not only being which has no will but all other wills, although without detracting from their character as wills' (555).

151

Nothing escapes God's knowledge and will; not even human disobedience lies outwith their dominion (556–7). Yet, this exhaustive scope does not make them infinite:

> It is the knowledge of God – and with it his will – which defines the limits of being. For this reason God's knowledge, as it embraces all things – all that is – is a knowledge which is finite, not limited from without, but by itself. (553)

God's will, likewise, is 'a will which is finite in its compass' (555). Despite these affirmations, Kress makes the bewildering claim that, according to Barth, 'there is no sense in which God's power can be considered as bounded or limited'. Barth 'makes every effort to think of God's power, knowing and willing as totally unlimited and infinite'.[149] It is as if Kress sees creaturely limitation of God as the only limitation that counts. Since Barth denies that God is 'limited from without', Kress thinks there is no limitation whatsoever. God's self-limitation of his perfections is a crucial affirmation for Barth, however, because it subordinates the human concept of any given perfection to God's own reality.

Fourth, God's knowledge is foreknowledge and his will free will (558–63), by which Barth means that they are absolutely superior to and independent of everything else (559). God does not know a thing because it exists; it exists, even if only as a possibility, because he knows it as such (559) and wills it as such (561). Ultimately, the reason why everything exists and occurs as it does, whether creation, fall or reconciliation, is that God has eternally known and willed it to be so (561).

Fifth, having explained in the first four points how God's knowing and willing are themselves his omnipotence, Barth now considers why these must at the same time be distinguished from omnipotence (563–99). For while God is essentially omnipotent, Barth needs to show that God is also consciously and freely omnipotent. Barth clarifies this difference by taking up again the idea that God's knowing and willing make the 'possessor of his power and the Lord of its use' (564; cf. 589). God's knowing is an act involving 'consciousness and conscious representation of itself and other objects' (564). God's willing is a free, living and purposive act (587). Therefore God does not exert his power unconsciously, without awareness, mechanically, like some physical force (cf. 526), but consciously, freely, purposefully, deliberately (565–6, 587–8, 597–8). God's power, in other words, as governed by and therefore differentiated from his knowledge and will, is spiritual or personal power (589). It is this which expresses for Barth not merely the freedom of God's exercise of power, but also the reality of the love revealed in it:

[149] Kress, *Gottes Allmacht*, 210–11.

It is by ... the knowledge of the true spirituality and personality of God, that ... we can know God genuinely and properly as love, as the One who loves. We could not take or say this seriously if we could speak of God's knowing and willing only figuratively and metaphorically and not with ultimate truth. If God does not know and will, he does not love either. (599)[150]

The 'ultimate truth' of God's knowing and willing lies of course in his triune being. Barth here recalls his earlier discussion (e.g. 16, 49) of God's primary objectivity:

Over all God's knowledge of the heights and the depths of the reality that is distinct from himself there stands, basically and decisively, the comforting and warning knowledge of himself, the Father's knowledge of the Son and the Son's of the Father (Mt 11:27), the Spirit's know-ledge of the deep things of God (1 Cor. 2:10). (555)[151]

The reason there can exist an 'inner differentiation' (566) between God's knowing and willing and his power, even though these are identical with the divine essence, is that there exists the prior and more basic differentiation between Father, Son and Holy Spirit.[152]

Two parallel excursuses round out this fifth point. The first begins with a catalogue of scholastic distinctions on the divine knowledge. It then turns to a fascinating analysis of the Molinist controversy, and, along with it, the

---

[150] Cf. Cremer, *Eigenschaften Gottes*, 90–1, who also speaks of God's omnipotence in terms of love and freedom, and of reconciliation as 'the supreme deed of the Almighty, in his omnipotently free love'.

[151] Osthövener simply dismisses the trinitarian character of God's primary objectiv-ity: 'Barth's reference to the doctrine of the Trinity is hardly persuasive' (*Gottes Eigenschaften*, 156–7 n. 13). Cf. Jüngel, *God's Being Is In Becoming*, 63–4.

[152] Schleiermacher denies a distinction between God's knowing and willing (*The Christian Faith*, §55.1). In his zeal to bring Barth as near as he can to Schleiermacher, Osthövener (*Gottes Eigenschaften*, 193–4) insists that Barth's affirmation of such a distinction is 'totally obscure'. He sees in Barth's parallel development of knowledge and will only evidence for their strict identity. The distinction which Barth draws between God's knowing and willing must simply be an 'unavoidable anthropomorphism' in light of Barth's *a priori* concept of person. 'The only reason Barth gives for their differentiation is that God must be understood as a person ... and so can obviously be thought of only as knowing and willing.' Because Osthövener sees Barth as working not from revela-tion but from overarching principles, he can only account for Barth's insistence on this distinction as follows: 'All in all it appears that this is merely a technical differentiation. On the basis of this distinction between knowing and willing, Barth can present the tradition that is bound to these concepts, yet without having to commit himself from the outset either to affirming or to rejecting it.'

153

nature of Roman Catholic theology as a whole (567–86).[153] According to Barth, the 'fundamental necessity' (581) for rejecting Molinism's *scientia media* along with its qualification of divine foreknowledge lies in the nature of grace. As implied in creation, particularly creation out of nothing (580–1; cf. 562), and in the doctrine of the incarnation, particularly the anhypostasis of Christ's human nature (583, 585; cf. 286), grace can face no competition from the creature, not even from the creature's freedom (580–1). Human knowing and willing, since these cannot compete with or operate at the same level as God's, require no curtailment of God's knowing and willing in order to secure their creaturely freedom and independence. As Barth says later of the divine will:

> Since God is Spirit, he is not *per se* omnipotent in a way which threatens and destroys the independence of his creature. As Spirit, he is omnipotent in the freedom of his creatures....If the knowing and willing of his omnipotence is known as that of his love, the problem of competition, from which all the errors necessarily and constantly derive, withers away of itself. (598)

Here, Barth rehearses a point which he has made several times in his account of omnipotence and which he also explained as an aspect of the divine uniqueness (443). Yet for all this insistence, it remains one of the most consistently overlooked themes in all of Barth's theology, namely, the non-competitive relation between divine and human freedom (cf. 302–4), or 'double agency', as George Hunsinger has described it.[154] God and humanity do not exist in 'a relation of mutual limitation and necessity' (562). Sheila Greeve Davaney, for example, concludes that on Barth's account God's 'absolute power, even though gracious in character, cannot be reconciled with creaturely freedom and accountability except by sheer assertion'.[155] Following Davaney, if not Barth, Anna Case-Winters claims that for Barth, 'Power is still being conceived as the ability to dominate and control.'[156] Compare these claims to

---

[153] In this analysis, Barth appears to have taken his rhetorical cue from Johann Quenstedt, who, in 'a masterpiece of polemic', argued that the Jesuits, though they intended to establish human freedom by the *scientia media*, actually made common cause thereby with the 'extremely Calvinistic determinism' of Quenstedt's Reformed foes (*CD* II/1, 576). Barth's own tactic is to argue that the Thomists, though they intended to establish the divine freedom by rejecting the *scientia media*, nevertheless compromised the divine freedom by virtue of the *analogia entis* at the heart of their theology (*CD* II/1, 579, 583–4).

[154] Hunsinger, *How To Read Karl Barth*, 185–224; cf. Webster, *Barth's Ethics of Reconciliation*, 143–4, 228–30.

[155] Davaney, *Divine Power*, 230; cf. Webster's critique, *Barth's Ethics of Reconciliation*, 7–8.

[156] Case-Winters, *God's Power*, 97.

what Barth said earlier of God's patience:

> We define God's patience as his will, which lies in his nature and con-
> stitutes his being and action, to allow to another…space and time for
> its own existence, thus conceding to this existence a reality side by side
> with his own, and thus fulfilling his will towards this other in such a
> way that he does not suspend and destroy it as this other, but rather
> accompanies it, sustains it and allows it to do as it pleases. (409–10
> rev.; *KD* 461)[157]

This is 'sheer assertion' only on the assumption that God's exercise of power
and freedom is inversely proportional to any corresponding creaturely exercise of the same. Kathryn Tanner has argued concerning Barth (and much
of the tradition as well) that, just as creatures have no existence apart from
'immediate relation' to God's creative and sustaining agency, so creatures
have neither power nor freedom except as, and to the degree that, these
are extended to them by God.[158] In other words, the scope of creaturely
power and freedom, on Barth's account, are to be understood as directly
proportional to the exercise of divine power and freedom. 'There can be a
real world confronting [God], not threatened with destruction by the divine
absoluteness, but, on the contrary, existing as a world precisely because of
it' (309; cf. 313–14). So, however strongly Barth may emphasise the sovereignty of the divine omnipotence, there are simply no grounds for the claim
that this in any way threatens human agency or freedom. Rather, it grounds
them.[159]

The second excursus (590–7) begins with a similar catalogue of scholastic
distinctions on the divine will, many of which Barth either substantially
qualifies or rejects outright. In each case, it is for Barth a matter of affirming
that God's revealed will is not merely virtual, an appearance, a figure, but
one with his hidden will and, therefore, a revelation of it (592–3). In this
context – and in a singularly charged political context – Barth also touches
upon the problem of evil:

> To this our only answer is that God's supreme and truest good for
> creation, and therefore the good determined for and promised to cre-
> ation, is revealed in its full splendour only when its obedience and
> blessedness are not simply its nature, the self-evident fulfilment of its

---

[157] Cf. John Webster, 'Freedom in Limitation: Human Freedom and False Necessity in
Barth', in *idem, Barth's Moral Theology* (Grand Rapids: Eerdmans, 1998), 105.

[158] Kathryn E. Tanner, *God and Creation in Christian Theology: Tyranny or Empowerment?*
(Oxford: Basil Blackwell, 1988), 84–5; cf. 94 on the parallels with the divine *concursus*
in *CD* III/3.

[159] See esp. *CD* III/3, 146–8.

existence, its inevitable course, but when they are salvation from the edge of an abyss, when in its obedience and blessedness creation is constantly reminded of its creation out of nothing and its preservation from nothingness by the menacing proximity of the kingdom of darkness, when its obedience and blessedness are therefore grace and salvation. (595)

With a serenity and measure remarkable for a text whose delivery and publication spanned the outbreak of the Second World War, Barth affirms a traditional, Augustinian theodicy[160] of the unqualified goodness and omnipotence of the divine will for creation.

Following on the complex expansiveness of the second stage of Barth's exposition, the third and final stage, the christological resolution, has admittedly the feel of a hurried afterthought, especially by comparison with the monumental christological paragraphs of *CD* IV. This does not make it a merely 'superfluous appendage', nor should Barth be faulted for not paying more attention to God's revelation in Christ at this point – that is, for not writing more![161] This third stage contains most of the sub-section's exegetical material, yet Kress claims that it lacks 'any real relevance' to the previous argument. She then complains that 'biblical-theological argumentation' has only 'peripheral importance' for Barth's treatment of omnipotence generally in *CD* II.[162] Kress's complaint can be explained in part by her thesis that Barth actually comes to a more exegetically and soteriologically oriented treatment of omnipotence in *CD* IV. She is highly motivated to downplay the significance of exegesis and soteriology throughout *CD* II/1.

Granted that Barth might well have expanded this third stage of his argument, what he has said is highly significant and indicates that his foregoing exposition was by no means constructed independently of Scripture's witness to Christ. In the space of a few pages, Barth argues that the all-important distinction between God and his power, emphasised throughout the first two stages of exposition, is identified in Scripture as that between God and his hand (600–1) or word (602–4), by which God acts, not as an abstract force, but personally in the history of his covenant. This history, Barth continues, has its 'concrete temporal centre' in Jesus Christ (604–5), who is the 'final and decisive ground' (599) for the claim that God's omnipotence is that of his love. As divine, Christ is himself the power and wisdom of God. As both divine and human, Christ both receives from the Father and wields this power and wisdom (605–7). Since Christ, as divine, 'can be known as such only by God himself' (607; cf. 44), even human assent to

---

[160] For example., Augustine, *Enchiridion* 26.100, *A Treatise on Rebuke and Grace* 10.27.
[161] Grell, *Der ewig reiche Gott*, 322.
[162] Kress, *Gottes Allmacht*, 224 and 224 n. 800; cf. 208. Kress does not address instances elsewhere in II/1 where Barth speaks of God's power, for example, 402, 452.

Scripture's testimony, even the faith by which alone Christ is recognised as the power and wisdom of God – this is itself a work of this very concrete, personal power. 'It is, therefore, the knowledge of Jesus Christ the Crucified which is the knowledge of the omnipotent knowing and willing of God' (607). The major themes of this sub-section on omnipotence (God's power and his knowing and willing) are here tied to Christ, and Christ crucified, at that. That Barth leaves his readers to explore further the relevance of this point does not mean that such relevance does not exist.

There remains one final, common critique of Barth's treatment of omnipotence to address. It is implicit in Osthövener, and is expressed by Kress as follows:

> It becomes apparent here [in CD II/1] that, while Barth does formally hold to his trinitarian-christological approach, he cannot maintain it in his exposition in any compelling manner. The result is that, in Barth's doctrine of God…omnipotence is ultimately identified as abstract omnicausality and autocracy [*Allwirksamkeit und Alleinherrschaft*] – as 'Power in and over…all'.[163]

Several aspects of this claim are puzzling, given Barth's explicit denial that God's omnipotence is mere omnicausality and that it in any way compromises the freedom of the creature. The critique of interest at this point, however, is the claim that Barth's exposition does not live up to its trinitarian-christological intentions. According to Kress's own view, God's omnipotence must be understood precisely 'as the omnipotence of love, which includes God's impotence and suffering' as well as 'God's self-abandonment'.[164] Her argument is that a doctrine of omnipotence drawn strictly from revelation, particularly the cross, requires a moment of impotence in God. She assumes, therefore, that any concept of omnipotence which denies such impotence in God must be beholden to abstract principles and cannot be adequately trinitarian-christological.[165] Since Barth denies any impotence in God (e.g. 524) and says nothing about divine suffering and self-abandonment (at least here in his treatment of omnipotence), Kress charges him with abstraction from his trinitarian-christological intentions. It is gratuitous to assume, however, that careful attention to the history of revelation will invariably confirm some kind of impotence in God. Moreover, not only does Kress, like Osthövener, pass over in silence those explicitly trinitarian aspects of Barth's exposition so far noted here, but there is also a more deeply trinitarian logic underlying even this third stage of Barth's argument. It is the logic of Book

---

[163] Kress, *Gottes Allmacht*, 204, citing *KD* II/1, 605 [*CD* 538]; cf. Case-Winters, *God's Power*, 110–13.

[164] Kress, *Gottes Allmacht*, 28–9, 208; cf. 3.

[165] Kress, *Gottes Allmacht*, 211–12.

VII of Augustine's *De trinitate*. For a theologian as acquainted with the tradition as Barth, the implicit appeal to Augustine's reasoning could hardly be clearer. For not only does Barth, like Augustine, focus his exposition on an analysis of 1 Cor. 1:24, 'Christ the power of God and the wisdom of God'. He also draws the same conclusions as Augustine: that the Son, as co-essential with the Father, is himself the divine power and wisdom, and at the same time, by eternal generation, also receives power and wisdom from the Father.[166] Moreover, in that Barth also takes into account 'the creaturely-historical side' of Christ's existence (605), aligning Christ's human reception of power and wisdom with the Son's eternal reception of the same, he makes a significant christological advance over Augustine. Now whether Barth's implicit appeal is to Augustine himself or more generally to the reasoning Augustine embodies (Barth does cite *De trinitate* on 323, 549, 559 and 661), the parallels are too striking to be coincidental, especially considering Barth's explicit handling of trinitarian logic elsewhere in this section. Barth could undoubtedly have made himself clearer still, but given his considered avoidance of technical theological terminology, its absence in this final stage of argument should not be allowed to obscure the underlying logic. Despite Kress's claim, Barth is simply not open to the charge of failing to give a trinitarian and christological account of divine omnipotence, however much clearer his vocabulary might have been, however much more exegetical material he might have included, or however differently his exposition might have turned out.

To sum up, the thrust of Barth's treatment of omnipotence is his insistence that it is God's own, triune power and therefore personal power, specifically, knowing and willing power, and therefore a truly free and truly loving power. What Barth has called the 'essential nature' of God's knowing and willing (563) is the fact that they express God's free, personal lordship over his power. This may be why Barth reports favourably what he sees as the early church's understanding of omnipotence as something of a 'compendium' of all of the divine perfections (522). For the same reason, Barth suggests that omnipotence occupies 'a kind of key position for the understanding...of all the divine perfections whatsoever' (545).[167] God's omnipotence, understood as that of his knowing and willing and, therefore. as personal omnipotence, conceptually safeguards God's freedom in the exercise of all of his attributes. So, although God is essentially gracious and merciful and patient, he is also the free Lord in the exercise of these (553-4, 596). This explains further why, as noted in the analysis of righteousness, Barth's hypothetical universalism[168] cannot be seen as driven by his conception of the divine attributes.

---

[166] Augustine, *The Holy Trinity* 7.1.1–7.2.3.
[167] Barth does not mean by this that omnipotence is inherently more important than any of the other attributes, as rightly noted by Osthövener, *Gottes Eigenschaften*, 190.
[168] *CD* IV/3.1, 477–8.

At the same time, because Barth draws connections between God's knowing and revelation, and between God's willing and reconciliation, God's knowing and willing just as clearly indicate the love in which God is free. For in his knowing and willing omnipotence he both reveals himself to human beings and reconciles them to himself. God, by the knowing and willing omnipotence of his person, emerges yet again as the One who loves in freedom.

§31.3. Eternity and Glory

There is a certain elegance to Barth's having placed eternity and glory as the final perfections of the divine freedom and, therefore, of all of the perfections. Eternity and glory are metonyms for future hope; they point forward to the consummation of redemption and to heaven beyond. While it is thus fitting that they come at the end of Barth's exposition, it is important to emphasise that 'at a pinch' they could have come at the beginning, not of all of the perfections, but of the perfections of the divine freedom. As Barth will argue, what he calls the 'pre-temporal' aspect of eternity requires just as much attention as that given to eternity in its aspect of 'supra-temporality' and 'post-temporality' (631). And glory, too, is primarily an element of the triune life 'before the world began' (John 17:5) (661, 667), that is, before it freely and lovingly overflows to make creation, reconciliation and, ultimately, redemption into reality. Eternity, as first in the pair, is purely a perfection of the divine freedom. Unlike omnipresence, with which eternity is often traditionally paired, Barth did not find in eternity those indications of the divine loving which led Barth to place omnipresence as the second of its pair.[169] Glory, on the other hand, though a perfection of the divine freedom, also indicates the love of God, in that it seeks the creature, reaches it and evokes from it that glorification of God for which it was created.

Eternity

Throughout his career, Barth, like Augustine, found his mind irresistibly drawn by the thought of eternity. From his Romans commentaries through the *Church Dogmatics*, the relation between God as eternal and his creatures as temporal entranced Barth and loosed his pen as few other themes. 'If I have a system', Barth once famously declared, 'it is limited to a recognition of what Kierkegaard called the "infinite qualitative distinction" between time and eternity.'[170] Barth's fascination is reflected in the secondary literature, which has flocked to consider the role of eternity in Barth's thought. One commentator claims that 'God's being-in-act is the ontological

---

[169] Oblau, *Gotteszeit und Menschenzeit*, 122, 173.
[170] Barth, 'The Preface to the Second Edition', in *idem, Romans*, 10.

fundamentum of the *Church Dogmatics*, and the axis of eternity and time the medium through which this ontology is diffused throughout the theological structure of [Barth's] work.'[171] Though overstated and tellingly abstracted from the person of Jesus Christ, such a claim gives something of a feel for the significance often attached to Barth's concept of eternity. Early and now well-known criticisms of Barth's concept of eternity by his Basel colleague Oscar Cullmann,[172] Hans Urs von Balthasar,[173] the French Jesuit Henri Bouillard,[174] American theologian Robert Jenson[175] and others[176] have also given impetus to study of Barth's concept of eternity. This literature is generally concerned with the role of eternity throughout the *Church Dogmatics*[177] and often touches only lightly on the account of eternity as a divine perfection. In light of the many volumes which both Barth and his commentators

---

[171] Richard H. Roberts, 'Karl Barth's Doctrine of Time: Its Nature and Implications', in *idem, A Theology on its Way: Essays on Karl Barth* (Edinburgh: T&T Clark, 1991), 20.

[172] Oscar Cullmann, *Christ and Time: The Primitive Christian Conception of Time and history*, trans. Floyd V. Filson (London: SCM, 1951), 62–3: Though Barth 'lays very strong emphasis...on the temporal quality of eternity', 'the philosophical influence which controls the conception of time in his earlier writings, especially in the Commentary on Romans, is still operative in the *Dogmatik* of 1940; here still, in spite of everything, he takes as his starting point a fundamental distinction between time and eternity...and so as a result there may again intrude that Platonic conception of timeless eternity which Karl Barth in the *Dogmatik* is nevertheless plainly striving to discard'. Cf. Barth, *Table Talk*, 55; James Barr, *Biblical Words for Time*, 2nd ed. (London: SCM, 1969), 158; Pokrifka-Joe, *Redescribing God*, 261–3.

[173] Hans Urs von Balthasar, *The Theology of Karl Barth: Exposition and Interpretation*, trans. Edward T. Oakes (San Francisco: Ignatius, 1992), 371: 'Too much in Barth gives the impression that nothing much really *happens* in his theology of event and history, because everything has already happened in eternity....In short, Barth rejects all discussion of anything in the realm of the relative and temporal that would make for a real and vibrant history of man with his redeeming Lord and God.'

[174] Henri Bouillard, *Karl Barth*, 3 vols. (Paris: Aubier, 1957), 1.238, argues that Barth is ultimately unable fully to capture the temporality of eternity: 'It was the problem of recognising the fullest sense of the incarnation which led Barth to integrate time into revelation. However that may be, does not this concept of revelation still remain too foreign to human time and to history?'; cf. *ibid.*, 2.276–8. According to Bouillard, when Barth acknowledges an aspect of non-temporality in eternity, 'he reintroduces elements of platonic thought fused with the thought of Scripture' (*ibid.*, 2.162, citing Cullmann's critique of Barth).

[175] Jenson, *God After God*, 67: The 'very great difficulties' in Barth's system, both internal and external, all 'result...from a persisting ambiguity in his talk about "eternity"'.

[176] For example, Jürgen Moltmann, *Theology of Hope*, trans. James W. Leitch (London: SCM, 1967), 57–8; Colin E. Gunton, *Becoming and Being: The Doctrine of God in Charles Hartshorne and Karl Barth*, new ed. (London: SCM, 2001), 180–1.

[177] Particularly *CD* I/2, §14, 'The Time of Revelation'; *CD* III/2, §47, 'Man in his Time'; and *CD* III/4, §56.1, 'The Unique Opportunity'.

have devoted to this topic, Barth's exposition here in *CD* II/1 may be said to possess an unexpected directness and simplicity.

Barth's exposition of eternity falls into two stages: a general, first-order description (608–19) followed by an elaboration in terms of pre-temporality, supra-temporality, and post-temporality (619–40). Much of what Barth wants to say is summed up in his opening definition of eternity as 'pure duration' in which 'beginning, succession and end are not three but one, not separate as a first, a second and a third occasion, but one simultaneous occasion as beginning, middle and end' (608). This shows both eternity's relation to time, in that both have beginning, middle and end, as well as eternity's distinction from time, in that eternity is marked by a simultaneity which is lacking to time. Barth's potentially puzzling combination of 'pure duration' and 'simultaneity', which 'appear to be (at least) contraries', is not Barth's 'halting between two positions'.[178] These express his desire to capture both the relation and the distinction between eternity and time. Significantly, it is not the distinction, not the 'negative judgement' on time's lack of simultaneity,[179] but rather the positive relation between eternity and time which Barth emphasises. It is this weighted distinction-in-relation between eternity and time, captured by Barth's concept of 'pure duration', which grounds Barth's rejection of two opposing errors.

The first is the definition of eternity as the 'infinite extension of time both backwards and forwards' (608). 'What could this have to do with God?' Barth asks (608 rev.; *KD* 686).[180] Such a definition clearly fails to capture the *distinction* between eternity and time, and Barth makes quick work of dismissing it. Even though 'in the act of his love God exalts something else to share in his eternity', eternity, as a perfection of the divine freedom, belongs 'exclusively' to God (609–10). It is Barth's insistence on the uniqueness, the 'divinity', of God's eternity – and not because of supposed philosophical influence, as Cullmann argued – that eternity remains distinct from time.

The second and far more alluring error is the definition of eternity as 'the negation of time' (610). Barth argued earlier that such a definition is too indebted to a general concept of infinity as the antithesis of the finite (464–8). Here it is the positive *relation* of eternity to time which is compromised, and much else besides. As will become clear, the relentlessness of Barth's opposition to the concept of eternity as timelessness is due in part to

---

[178] Gunton, *Becoming and Being*, 179–80.

[179] Douglas Farrow, *Ascension and Ecclesia: On the Significance of the Doctrine of the Ascension for Ecclesiology and Christian Cosmology* (Grand Rapids: Eerdmans, 1999), 291; cf. Raynal, *Perfections*, 114–15.

[180] The English rather ineptly reads, 'Time [*diese*] can have nothing to do with God', mistaking 'time' as the referent of '*diese*' rather than 'infinite extension'. This line has led at least one interpreter to claim that, according to Barth, 'God as he is in himself…is non-temporal'; see Alan G. Padgett, *God, Eternity and the Nature of Time* (New York: St. Martin's Press, 1992), 142.

its inherent nominalism (the temporality of revelation could not correspond to anything in a timeless God[181]) and to the problems it creates for understanding the incarnation and reconciliation (618). The problem, as Gotthard Oblau ably expresses it, is that 'infinitum non capax finitum': timelessness is incapable of time.[182] Barth is unremitting in his rejection of this antithetical view of the relation between eternity and time also because (as he confesses in a well-known, autobiographical passage) it was a view of which his own earlier writings could justly be accused (634–6).

God's eternity is not the negation of time because, as pure duration, it both possesses 'beginning, succession and end' without separation and also grounds all other beginnings, successions and endings (610).[183] Here, Barth recalls with admiration Boethius's definition of eternity as 'the total, simultaneous and perfect possession of unlimited life' (611 rev.; *KD* 688). Eternity is, therefore, to be understood not by 'negation of the concept of time' – an expression, perhaps, of 'our dissatisfaction with time'[184] – but positively as a perfection of God's illimitable life and, therefore, as 'the prototype and foreordination of time' (611). Only in this way can 'the time of revelation, the time of Jesus Christ' truly reflect God himself without nominalistic qualification (611–12). Turning the tables on his assumed objectors, Barth charges that 'it is an illegitimate anthropomorphism to think of God as if he did not eternally have time' (612). As Jüngel notes, this means that God's eternal being is also (in its own way) historical. It is this which 'makes revelation possible as historical event'.[185] Oblau explains:

> For all their differences, eternity and time have to have a common denominator which allows both to be defined as the form of a history. Time is the form of the history of God with humanity and human history. Eternity is the form of the history of the inner life of God. The general form of history is a kind of temporality that is common to both eternity and time.[186]

Recalling Barth's account of the divine constancy, it is the divine eternity which gives form both to the actuality and liveliness of God's history *ad*

---

[181] As Barth will argue later, particularly in *CD* III/2, to a timeless God there can correspond only a godless time; see Busch, *Great Passion*, 267–8.

[182] Oblau, *Gotteszeit und Menschenzeit*, 123.

[183] De Margerie, *Les Perfections*, 242, objects to Barth's inclusion of these temporal categories in the divine eternity. 'We cannot admit these. We have said it before in other terms, and now we say again: God is indivisible. He is the absolutely simple.' Barth, too, is a firm believer in divine simplicity, but he does not feel it compromised by such categories.

[184] Jenson, *God After God*, 127, 134; cf. Robert W. Jenson, *Systematic Theology*, 2 vols. (New York: Oxford University Press, 1997–9), 1.94.

[185] Jüngel, *God's Being Is In Becoming*, 112.

[186] Oblau, *Gotteszeit und Menschenzeit*, 22–3; cf. 136.

intra as well as, in the subordinate form of created time, to God's history with humanity *ad extra*. This must be the case. For if God did not possess in himself the prototype of everything he manifests in revelation, revelation would tell us nothing about God (612). It would not be revelation. And 'Nothing less than the assurance of faith and the possibility of trust in the enduring God depends on [this]' (612; cf. 325).

Lest readers take his insistence on this relation between eternity and time too strongly, Barth returns briefly to the distinction between them: 'What distinguishes eternity from time is the fact that there is in him no opposition or competition or conflict, but peace between origin, movement and goal, between past, present and future' (612):

> Eternity is certainly the negation of created time in so far as it has no part in the problematical and questionable nature of our possession of time.... But eternity is not the negation of time *simpliciter*. On the contrary, time is absolutely presupposed in it. (613)

Eternity, then, is related to time as the prototype of all beginning, succession and end, and it is distinct from time in its simultaneity. It is the relatedness of eternity to time which Barth emphasises (613).[187] Eternity, nevertheless, retains its 'superiority' over time, and time only has its 'co-existence' with eternity as the result of divine grace in the act of creation (614–15).

This sketch of the relation between eternity and time elicits from Richard Roberts the following criticism:

> On the one hand [Barth] denies the involvement of true eternity with the dialectic of finite and infinite categories; on the other he affirms eternity as the total time-positing action of God. This position can only be consistently maintained if the temporal categories asserted by the latter at no point identify with the finite-infinite dialectic. This means that the vast and complete temporal system that emerges in the *Church Dogmatics* must never coincide with non-theological temporal categories in identity, only in the so-called dialectic of transcendence.[188]

Roberts's argument is highly compressed but amounts to the claim that, if eternity excludes the finite-infinite dialectic, then in order for eternity to include temporal categories, these temporal categories cannot partake of the finite-infinite dialectic, either. So far, so good. But Roberts takes this to mean that the temporal categories of beginning, succession and ending must have

---

[187] Cf. Oblau, *Gotteszeit und Menschenzeit*, 136.
[188] Roberts, 'Karl Barth's Doctrine of Time', 26.

their distinction and integrity obliterated by the simultaneity of eternity.[189] By thus explaining away Barth's use of categories which describe the relation of eternity to time, Roberts effectively reduces Barth's account of eternity to its distinction from time.[190] It is this absolute, unqualified distinction between eternity and time which, according to Roberts, constitutes a systematic breach in Barth's thought. Time in its theological dimension (i.e. God's eternity) remains 'absolutely undetectable' except in the event of revelation and faith,[191] and Barth's rejection of all natural theology has supposedly become a rejection of all natural reality.[192] Is it really fair, though, to dismiss one side of Barth's argument and then charge him with being one-sided? 'Barth's intention is manifestly...to conceive positively the relation of divine time to created time.'[193]

In light of the clarity of Barth's intentions and material assertions, it is somewhat ironic that the *Church Dogmatics* as a whole has also been accused of holding to an antithetical view of the relation between eternity and time. Robert Jenson, for example, asks:

> But what can possibly be the content of saying that God in eternity is whatever is the prototype of his life in time? Either this sentence is perfectly empty, or the very form of the statement makes some sort of comparison between God's own characteristics and his temporal characteristics. Such a comparison can only be between timelessness and time....[I]f the whole of God's temporal story is to be analogous to something else, what can this something else be – if not a timeless deepest reality of God?[194]

Colin Gunton concurs:

> The upshot of all this is that despite Barth's attempt to see God's eternity as a kind of eminent temporality, the tendency to define eternity in

---

[189] Oblau, *Gotteszeit und Menschenzeit*, 130–1, details Barth's insistence on the order and unsubstitutable integrity of these moments of eternity.

[190] Noted by Pokrifka-Joe, *Redescribing God*, 231–2. Hunsinger, '*Mysterium Trinitatis*', 197 n. 14, suggests that this rather glaring oversight on Roberts's part is the result of his having failed to take into account the trinitarian structure of Barth's exposition.

[191] Roberts, 'Karl Barth's Doctrine of Time', 26.

[192] Roberts, 'Karl Barth's Doctrine of Time', 56. In the same volume in which Roberts's essay was originally published, Rowan Williams questions this judgement; see 'Barth on the Triune God', in *Karl Barth: Studies of his Theological Method*, ed. S. W. Sykes (Oxford: Clarendon, 1979), 152–3.

[193] Gunton, *Becoming and Being*, 180; so Wolf Krötke, *Gottes Klarheiten: Eine Neuinterpretation der Lehre von Gottes »Eigenschaften«* (Tübingen: Mohr Siebeck, 2001), 262.

[194] Jenson, *God After God*, 153–4; cf. 132 for Jenson's acknowledgment of Barth's better intentions.

opposition to time, and therefore as a *negation* of the historical orientation of the understanding of revelation, is very marked. Consequently, the history of God with man is telescoped, for the future is not understood eschatologically, as the era when there will take place new triune events, but seen to be merely the vehicle of the repetition of the timeless past.[195]

These claims are, of course, based on a reading of the whole of Barth's theology. Whether or not they are a valid reading of the whole, the point to be made here – with which Jenson and Gunton would concur – is that Barth's exposition of eternity as a divine perfection cannot be charged with having 'never moved a single step past the *Commentary on Romans*'.[196]

The divine eternity, Barth continues, is 'the eternity of the triune God'. Barth's tantalizing triads – for example, 'beginning, succession and end' (610), 'origin, movement and goal' (612) – may have led readers to anticipate that Barth will map past, present and future onto the respective persons of Father, Son and Spirit. He does not. Rather, the divine eternity is the eternity of the Father, who is 'undividedly beginning, succession and end', the eternity of the Son, who is 'also undividedly beginning, succession and end', and the eternity of the Spirit, who is 'also undividedly beginning, succession and end' (615) – a *'repetitio aeternitatis in aeternitate'*.[197] Barth does not appropriate either eternity or any of its moments to any one person of the Trinity.[198] Though he later speaks of Christ as 'the centre of time' (629) in his discussion of God's supra-temporality, this does not constitute any appropriation of supra-temporality to the Son. God's supra-temporality, rather, is 'the supra-temporality of God the Father, Son and Holy Spirit' (625). Likewise here, in the first stage of argument, it is the one God, Father, Son and Holy Spirit, whose eternity is 'pure duration, free from all the fleetingness and the separations of what we call time' (615). Nevertheless, there exists in the divine eternity, as grounded in God's triunity,[199] an 'order and succession' which is 'without anything arbitrary...or the possibility of its reversal' (615; cf. 639).

The eternity of the triune God, in its relation to and distinction from time, can only properly be grasped on the basis of 'the real fellowship between God and the creature, and therefore between eternity and time', namely, Jesus Christ (616). Though Barth does not emphasise the pneumatological component of this basis, he does acknowledge that 'a correct understanding of the concept of eternity' is a matter of faith and hence of 'the co-existence

---

[195] Gunton, *Becoming and Being*, 183; see 181–4.
[196] Jenson, *God After God*, 67.
[197] CD I/1, 353.
[198] Hunsinger, '*Mysterium Trinitatis*', 198, 205.
[199] Krötke, *Gottes Klarheiten*, 261.

of the creature taken up into fellowship with God by the grace of the Son and the Holy Spirit' (616–17):

> The fact that the Word became flesh undoubtedly means that, without ceasing to be eternity, in its very power as eternity, eternity became time....In Jesus Christ it comes about that God takes time to himself, that he himself, the eternal One, becomes temporal...permitting created time to become and be the form of his eternity. (616)[200]

Thus, what we see of God's eternity in Christ is not 'pure timelessness', if this is understood as 'the negation of time' (617). God is timeless, however, in the sense that 'the defects of our time, its fleetingness and its separations' are healed when he assumes time in Christ (617).[201] In Christ we see that the divine eternity, the ordered simultaneity of past, present and future, is 'the absolute basis of time, and therefore absolute readiness for it' (618).

Barth expands on this idea of eternity as 'absolute readiness' for time in his second stage of argument. God's eternal readiness for time includes moments of 'pre-temporality, supra-temporality and post-temporality' (619). In other words, the God 'who was and is and is to come' (Rev 4:8) is related to time in such a way that:

> He precedes its beginning, he accompanies its duration, and he exists after its end.[202] This is the concrete form of eternity as readiness for time. (619)

Barth insists that this constitutes a more biblical way of speaking about God's eternity because it emphasises eternity's 'positive relationship' to time, while not overlooking the differences between them (619). The relationship is positive, and not antithetical, because God's eternity would be temporal 'even if no time existed apart from it' (620). What Barth faces here is 'the difficulty of having to find a way to express the aseity of eternity over against empirical time, but...always having to take his lead strictly from empirical time in doing so'.[203] Barth rehearses the calamitous consequences of nominalistic failure at this point. If God's temporality as testified to in the Christian message has no actual basis in God's eternity, then the gospel is in

---

[200] Pokrifka-Joe, *Redescribing God*, 240, rightly notes, 'This does not mean that created time...is the *only* temporal form of God's eternity'. He also notes the several parallels to Phil 2:6–11 here; *ibid.*, 253.

[201] Hunsinger, '*Mysterium Trinitatis*', 204–5, argues that the wounds of time healed by the incarnation are not those inflicted upon it by sin, but rather those inherent to it even as God's good creation. Cf. Pokrifka-Joe, *Redescribing God*, 238–9, 242.

[202] Cf. Barth's exposition of God's providential *praecursus*, *concursus*, and *succursus* in CD III/3, §49.2, 'The Divine Accompanying' (90–154).

[203] Oblau, *Gotteszeit und Menschenzeit*, 128.

fact only 'the myth of a pious or impious self-consciousness, the comfortless content of some human monologue which lays no real claim upon us, the substance of a well-meant pastoral fiction' (620). Only if this nominalising of the temporality of the divine eternity is decisively rejected can the gospel speak the truth about God and therefore truly bind and comfort and be believed (620–1).

God's pre-temporality (621–3) means that his existence precedes that of creation and is itself preceded by nothing. Like God's freedom in its aspect of aseity (cf. 301–2), God's pre-temporality means that God 'was no less himself, no less perfect, not subject to any lack, superabounding from the very first even without us and the world' (621). It was 'in this time before time' that everything was 'determined beforehand', 'including every name and the great and the small events of every bearer of every name' (622). This foreordination or predestination of all things occurs in 'pre-time' in God's turning to the world in Jesus Christ (622). It is, thus, Christ himself who is the key to understanding God's pre-temporality.[204]

God's supra-temporality (623–9) expresses the fact that 'eternity faithfully accompanies time on high', or rather 'causes itself to be accompanied by time' (623). In accompanying our time, God in his supra-temporality unites in himself the separation that exists between the beginning and the ending of our time. Time also moves along because eternity moves along above it, preserving and securing it.

> God's eternity is in time. Time itself is in eternity. Its whole extension from beginning to end, each single part of it, every epoch, every life-time, every new and closing year, every passing hour: they are all in eternity like a child in the arms of its mother. (623)

Supra-temporality is, thus, clearly more than an eternal 'now', but includes 'also pre-time and post-time' (624) – something easily forgotten, according to Barth, by 'mysticism, and the existentialism which secretly draws its life from mysticism' (625). Mysticism's 'hypostatising of our "now" between the times [*zwischen den Zeiten*]', and its exclusive concern with our present deci-sions and responsibility, have produced a one-sided and therefore idolatrous account of the divine eternity (624; *KD* 703). It is not merely Bultmann whom Barth has in view in making this qualification, but also his own earl-ier self. In his *Romans* he had written:

> As Christ, Jesus is the plane which lies beyond our comprehension.
> The plane which is known to us, he intersects vertically, from above.

---

[204] Osthövener, *Gottes Eigenschaften*, 201, offers no evidence for his claim that Barth associates grace, mercy and patience with God's pre-temporality, and holiness, right-eousness and wisdom with God's supra-temporality.

Within history, Jesus as the Christ can be understood only as Problem or Myth. As the Christ, he brings the world of the Father. But we who stand in this concrete world know nothing, and are incapable of knowing anything, of that other world.[205]

Barth now rejects any such one-sidedness. 'Any conception of the relation of time and eternity is in error which tries to find eternity *only* in an immediate perpendicular connexion with each moment of time, and does not see that the basis of time is also in the divine "before" and "after"' (624). The event of revelation therefore cannot be conceived as a timelessly eternal moment. T. F. Torrance explains that, because space and time for Barth are 'created forms of rationality', '[a]part from space and time nature would be indeterminable and unintelligible', that is, formless. 'This is why any so-called "demythologizing" that aims at stripping away the spatial and temporal ingredients from our theological concepts and terms...can only lapse into irrationality and meaninglessness.'[206]

As with God's pre-temporality, Jesus Christ is the key to understanding God's supra-temporality, as well. It is Christ who marks disobedience, sin and death as past, and obedience, righteousness and life as future. There is, moreover, no 'equilibrium' or 'endless repetition' between these two, between man as *peccator* and as *iustus*. Rather, though man is both *simul*, there is an order between them: the first destroyed in the crucifixion and the second established by the resurrection (626–7). Time itself has become in Christ 'the way from this past to this future' (627). The only 'Christian' conception of time, says Barth, is 'the conception of human existence moving in Jesus Christ out of the first and into the second sphere. The fact that we have time and live in time means...that we live in this turning' (627). As Douglas Farrow notes, if it is Christ who constitutes time itself, there can obviously be no access to God in time which bypasses Christ.[207] A Christian in particular can therefore neither wish to re-live the past nor worry about the future, for the troubles of both past and future have already been done away with in Christ. Christ, who is 'the centre of time', causes us to live in this turning and, thus, to experience something of God's eternity as supra-temporality (629).

God's post-temporality, finally, captures that aspect of eternity which is after time (629–38). God in his post-temporal eternity is the goal, the perfection towards which all time moves, the 'Sabbath rest after the completion of all his works', 'the absolute, unsurpassable future of all time and of all that

---

[205] Barth, *Romans*, 29–30. See Busch, *Great Passion*, 264, for a sampling of Barth's early assertions of the antithesis between eternity and time.

[206] Torrance, *Space, Time and Incarnation*, 65, 61. Barth speaks of space and time as each a 'form of creation' on 465 and 612.

[207] Farrow, *Ascension and Ecclesia*, 231.

is in time' (629–30). In God's post-temporal eternity lies the final judgement, when God will be revealed always to have been 'all in all':

His *is* the kingdom. He *is* the Last. He *is* the One who is all in all. It is only then, at the goal and end of time, that he will be revealed as this and no longer veiled at all. But he is this already in himself. He was it from the beginning. (631)

At that point, the kingdom will be no longer a matter of faith, but of sight, no longer under a 'veil of hope', but in full peace and blessedness (630–1).

There follows the well-known excursus (631–8; cf. viii)[208] in which Barth insists that God's pre-temporality, supra-temporality, and post-temporality must each receive due emphasis, for 'from him and through him and to him are all things' (Rom. 11:36). According to Barth, there can be no theologically dominating concern with God's pre-temporality (631–2), as was the case with the Reformers' preoccupation with election; nor with God's supra-temporality (632–3), as was the case with liberal theology's preoccupation with man and his present needs and possibilities; nor finally with God's post-temporality (633–8), as was the case with the theology of crisis and its insistence on the 'pure and absolute futurity of God' (634). 'In the attempt to free ourselves...from these early forms of one-sidedness, especially from that of pietistic and Liberal Neo-Protestantism', confesses Barth of his earlier theology, 'we took the surest possible way to make ourselves guilty of a new one-sidedness' (634). It was, therefore, 'most fortunate' when Barth became aware of the pre-temporal emphasis of 'the theology of Luther and Calvin' and took up again, despite 'a dangerous proximity to certain propositions dear to the eighteenth and nineteenth centuries', the issue of church-state relations and the problem of ethics (637–8).

Barth concludes by reminding his readers again that eternity is God himself (638–40):

The Christian knowledge of eternity has to do directly and exclusively with God himself, with him as the beginning before all time, the turning point in time, and the end and goal after all time. This makes it a complete mystery, yet also completely simple. In the last resort when we think of eternity we do not have to think in terms of either the point or the line, the surface or space. We have simply to think of God himself, recognising and adoring and loving the Father, the Son and

[208] Balthasar, *The Theology of Karl Barth*, 367–8, quotes from the passage at length; the editors' preface also draws attention to it (*CD* II/1, viii); see also Busch, *Karl Barth*, 120; T. F. Torrance, *Karl Barth: An Introduction to his Early Theology 1910–1931*, new ed. (Edinburgh: T&T Clark, 2000), 40–1, 78–9, 85; McCormack, *Dialectical Theology*, 288–90.

the Holy Spirit. It is only in this way that we know eternity. For eternity is his essence. (639)

Barth suggests that it was perhaps the failure truly to grasp the fact that eternity is God himself which allowed preoccupation with pre-temporality, supra-temporality or post-temporality or his own earlier preference for geometric imagery in portraying eternity (639–40). If eternity is understood to be that of the living God himself – here Barth recalls again Boethius's definition of eternity as the 'possession of unlimited life' – there can be no such reduction of its full breadth. 'At this point, as in the doctrine of the Trinity itself, we can and must speak of a *perichoresis*, a mutual indwelling and interworking of the three forms of eternity' (640). The *perichoresis* of the three forms of eternity is not that of the three persons but, like it, involves their inseparable unity in distinction.

The divine eternity, then, is neither the infinite extension of time nor abstract timelessness as the tradition often held. Rather, as 'pure duration', it is both related to time, as the prototype of all beginning, succession, and ending, and also distinct from time, by virtue of that simultaneity of past, present, and future which time lacks. The divine eternity, grounded as it is in God's triune nature, is a mutual indwelling of pre-temporality, supra-temporality and post-temporality in God, none to the exclusion or suppression of the others. Like all of the divine perfections, God's eternity is ultimately '*der ewig reiche Gott*'[209] himself. Contrary to much criticism of Barth's view of eternity, its temporality, and hence God's temporality, God's positive relation to time, is very prominent here. 'Barth's explanation of the individual temporal moments of eternity indicates above all eternity's openness and orientation toward created time.'[210]

Glory

The arc of Barth's doctrine of the divine perfections extends from grace to glory, and from gratitude to joy. As Balthasar tells the story, it was partly in rejection of Bultmann's dissolution of 'every possible form of revelation which is objectivised and historically perceptible' that Barth capped his exposition of the divine perfections with a treatment of God's very perceptible glory.[211] Barth captures this particularly by addressing the beauty

---

[209] Busch, *Karl Barth*, 487 n.

[210] Oblau, *Gotteszeit und Menschenzeit*, 127.

[211] Barth may also be paying his respects to Polanus, who concludes his doctrine of the attributes with the divine glory. Rinse H. Reeling Brouwer, 'The Conversation between Karl Barth and Amandus Polanus on the Question of the Reality of Human Speaking of the Simplicity and the Multiplicity of God', in *The Reality of Faith in Theology: Studies on Karl Barth: Princeton-Kampen Consultation 2005*, ed. Bruce McCormack and Gerrit Nevin (New York: Peter Lang, 2007), 82.

of this glory – 'for the first time in the history of Protestant theology'![212] As Balthasar notes, glory is for Barth the 'form of revelation'. Some of this section's broadest implications for Barth's theology derive from the connection it draws between God's revelation and his glory and beauty. One of the most important of these is that Barth's concept of the beauty of God captures that distinctly affective dimension of the divine self-revelation which is often muted by Barth's typical emphasis on revelation's cognitive dimensions.

Glory, the 'last step' in Barth's exposition of the divine perfections (640), is primarily an attribute of the divine freedom, yet it also, secondarily, shows God's love:

> For while the glory of God describes especially his freedom, majesty and pre-eminence, and therefore definitely belongs to the second series of divine perfections dealt with in this section, yet this final and supreme predicate of the divine freedom can be understood as such only if the divine freedom itself and as such is seen to be God's freedom to love. (641)

Barth's exposition proceeds in four stages: an initial definition and survey of glory in Scripture and the tradition (640–5); a fourfold clarification of the divine glory drawn from the insights of Petrus van Mastricht (645–9); a full and famous aside on beauty as the form or manner of the divine glory (649–66); and finally a consideration of the divine glory as it manifests the divine love in awakening the creaturely response of gratitude, joy, praise, and thus the glorification of God (666–77).

Barth begins his exposition of glory by linking it with one of the most prominent themes in his theology: revelation. Glory, says Barth, is what legitimates revelation:

> God's glory is his dignity and right not only to maintain, but to prove and declare, to denote and almost as it were to make himself conspicuous and everywhere apparent as the One he is....To sum up, God's glory is God himself in the truth and capacity and act in which he makes himself known as God. (641)

God, in his glory, is free to 'create recognition for himself' (641). In so doing, he also establishes fellowship with another, the very hallmark of his love. Because God is glorious, 'he is in himself, and therefore to everything outside himself, relationship, the basis and prototype of all relationship' (641). God's glorious creation of fellowship is definitively manifest in Jesus Christ,

---

[212] Hans Urs von Balthasar, *The Glory of the Lord: A Theological Aesthetics*, trans. Erasmo Leiva-Merikakis, ed. Joseph Fessio and John Riches (Edinburgh: T&T Clark, 1982–1989), 1.53–4; cf. 56–7.

who emerges in Scripture as both 'the reflection of the divine glory' as well as 'the prototype of all participation by creation in the glory of God' (643).[213]

> [Glory] is the self-revealing sum of all divine perfections. It is the fulness of God's deity, the emerging, self-expressing and self-manifesting reality of all that God is. It is God's being in so far as this is in itself a being which declares itself. (643)[214]

That Barth calls glory the 'sum of all divine perfections', or later 'the sum of the whole doctrine of God' (671), must not be misread as implying that glory is somehow the 'chief perfection' which 'supersedes' the others.[215] On the other hand, neither is it the case that glory is 'not a...concluding attribute' at all, but merely the harmony of the other perfections.[216] Glory is a divine perfection. Like all of the other perfections, the divine glory is God himself. Recall that Barth can just as readily say of the divine unity, for example, 'All the perfections of God's freedom can be summed up by saying that God is One' (442). With respect to the divine grace, Barth affirms that God's 'whole being, in all the heights and depths of the Godhead, is simply grace' (358). And to the divine omnipotence Barth ascribes 'a kind of key position for the understanding of all the perfections of the divine freedom and therefore indirectly of all the divine perfections whatsoever' (545). This is neither contradiction nor confusion on Barth's part, but rather the descriptive outworking of the dogmatic affirmation that each perfection is itself the whole divine nature and, therefore, identical with all the other perfections. As Barth explains on the very first page of his exposition of the attributes, 'Strictly speaking, in dogmatics and in church preaching every single statement is at once the basis and the content of all the rest' (257). Moreover, if there were a chief perfection on Barth's account, it would be 'the one perfection of God, his loving in freedom' (322), which is itself just another way of describing God's life as Father, Son and Holy Spirit (323).

It is also important to note here that Barth describes not merely God's being *ad extra* as revealing, expressing and manifesting, but also God's being 'in

---

[213] This connection between glory, revelation, and Christ and the use of both vocal and visual metaphors for the divine glory (641–2) anticipates the magnificent opening section of CD IV/3.1 (§69), 'The Glory of the Mediator', and its description of Christ in his prophetic office as 'eloquent and radiant' (IV/3.1, 79).

[214] Cremer (*Eigenschaften Gottes*, 121) also designates God's glory as the unity of his attributes in revelation.

[215] So Christopher R. J. Holmes, *Revisiting the Doctrine of the Divine Attributes: In Dialogue with Karl Barth, Eberhard Jüngel, and Wolf Krötke* (New York: Peter Lang, 2007), 70, 89, 72; cf. 97–8 n. 83, 223–4. Cf. Krötke, *Gottes Klarheiten*, 77 n. 112; John Mark Capper, *Karl Barth's Theology of Joy* (Ph.D. diss., Cambridge University, 1998), 81–2, 101.

[216] Osthövener, *Gottes Eigenschaften*, 202.

itself'. It is God's glory 'in his inner life', and thus 'behind' his self-revelation to sinful man, which constitutes its 'self-sufficiency' (644). Because it is the 'fulness of God's deity', it is not merely our lack of knowledge of God which God's glory supplies.

> Rather, since God's self-declaration is the self-declaration of the God who is sufficient in himself, the supplying of our lack of ability to know God carries with it a supplying of every lack in our life....He who has God has really everything...[and has it] in such a way that he can be satisfied and content. (644)

Here, Barth makes his first mention of that affective, human response which occupies so prominent a place in his description of this perfection:

> To be comforted by God's glory is genuine, Christian contentment....The older theologians were right. God's glory is also the fulness, the totality, the sufficiency, the sum of the perfection of God in the irresistibility of its declaration and manifestation. (645)

At several points in this first stage of argument, Barth describes the manner in which God's glory confronts the creature in terms suggesting domination or coercion. God's glory, says Barth, is his right 'in some sense to impose himself' (641 rev.; *KD* 723), 'forcefully [*bezwingend*] creating...recognition of himself' (642; *KD* 724)[217] in a 'sovereign, irresistible [*unaufhaltsamen*] event' (644; *KD* 726). Barth's intention is both to capture his reading of the Hebrew *kabod* as 'strength [*Mächtigkeit*]' or 'force [*Wucht*]' (642; *KD* 724), as well as to prepare the reader for the dénouement of the third stage of his argument. If such terms appear less than carefully chosen at this point, Barth makes clear at the conclusion of this stage of argument how they are to be understood:

> God's glory is God's love. It is the justification and sanctification of us sinners out of pure, irresistible [*unwiderstehlicher*] grace. (645; *KD* 727)

God's grace confronts 'the resistance with which the creature faces him' (355) not forcibly, not, as he says later, 'ruling, mastering and subduing with...utterly superior force' (650). It does so, rather, as the Reformed tradition has often had to explain, by way of 'opening the eyes' (644),

---

[217] The English 'forcefully' is perhaps too strong. 'Compellingly' might be better, as *bezwingend* can also be used of an attractive or appealing power, for example, an 'irresistible' smile, thus more clearly anticipating Barth's subsequent argument.

persuading and convincing (655), freeing and enabling (669–72), quickening and renewing.[218]

In the second stage of exposition (645–9), Barth both continues his interaction with the tradition and anticipates the third stage of exposition (on beauty) by recasting the fourfold analysis of the divine glory undertaken by Petrus van Mastricht (1630–1706).[219] God is glorious, says Barth, in his absolute pre-eminence over all created beings, in nevertheless seeking and establishing fellowship with his creatures, in reaching us himself (even though he does so through creaturely forms), and in evoking his creatures' response of worship (646–9). In a passage full of spiritual vitality, reflecting that very aspect of the divine glory he expounds, Barth 'expresses magnificently'[220] the wonder of the fact that God's glory creates for itself recognition, attestation, praise and joy in the creature, 'a true if inadequate response in the temporal sphere to the jubilation with which the Godhead is filled from eternity to eternity' (648).[221] All of creation, from angels down to 'even the smallest creatures', has its being and destiny in witnessing to the divine glory (648). This is the case even without man, who, 'when he accepts again his destiny in Jesus Christ...is only like a late-comer slipping shamefacedly into creation's choir in heaven and earth, which has never ceased its praise, but merely suffered and sighed, as it still does, that in inconceivable folly and ingratitude its living centre, man, does not hear its voice...and refuses to co-operate in the jubilation which surrounds him. This is the sin of man which is judged and forgiven in Jesus Christ' (648). It is by virtue of this aspect of the divine glory that fallen humanity becomes, in eternity, proper witnesses to the divine glory, 'rejoicing with the God who himself has eternal joy and himself is eternal joy' (649).

Barth's third stage of argument (649–66), made famous in part by the impetus it gave to the work of Balthasar,[222] focuses on that aspect of the divine

---

[218] E.g., *The Canons of the Synod of Dort*, Third and Fourth heads of Doctrine, art. 12 and 14 in Philip Schaff, *The Creeds of Christendom, with a History and Critical Notes*, 3 vols. (Grand Rapids: Baker, 1977), 3.590 and 3.591–2; cf. Karl Barth, *The Theology of the Reformed Confessions*, trans. Darrell L. Guder and Judith J. Guder, Columbia Series in Reformed Theology (Louisville: Westminster John Knox, 2002), 221.

[219] Cf. C. Holmes, *Divine Attributes*, 77–9; *idem*, 'The theological function of the doctrine of the divine attributes and the divine glory, with special reference to Karl Barth and his reading of the Protestant Orthodox', *Scottish Journal of Theology* 61.2 (2008): 218–21.

[220] De Margerie, *Les Perfections*, 429.

[221] *CD* IV/3.1, 277–81 is a similar passage, coming at the beginning of the final section of his Christology chapter (§69.4), where Barth makes his transition to pneumatology. Here, too, Barth speaks of the way in which 'we are ordained and liberated to take a receptive and active part in his glory' (*CD* IV/3.1, 278).

[222] John Webster, 'Balthasar and Karl Barth', in *The Cambridge Companion to Hans Urs von Balthasar*, ed. Edward T. Oakes and David Moss (Cambridge: Cambridge University Press, 2004), 242.

glory captured by the concept of beauty. Barth's thought is 'positively radiant' here, and his prose 'perhaps the brightest and most cheerful' in all the *Church Dogmatics*.[223] Barth later describes this stage as merely a 'parenthesis' to the main line of his exposition, but nevertheless an 'appropriate' one (666). The irresistibility with which God in his glory evokes creaturely glorification of himself is not merely the 'superior force' of his omnipotence (650). It is also the effect of the fact that God is 'beautiful, divinely beautiful, beautiful in his own way…yet really beautiful' (650). This is the 'shape and form' [*Form und Gestalt*] of God's glory (650; KD 733).[224] God is irresistibly glorious 'as the One who gives pleasure, creates desire and rewards with enjoyment…because first and last he alone is that which is pleasant, desirable and full of enjoyment' (651).[225] Barth notes that, if Protestant piety occasionally entertained the thought of God's beauty, it never did so with a clear conscience. Protestant theology, on the other hand, would have nothing to do with this 'extremely dangerous' concept, so poignantly expressed in Augustine's 'Late have I loved thee, O Beauty so ancient and so new!' (651). In a 1929 lecture, Barth criticised this same passage from the *Confessions* as implying that Augustine knew what beauty was before he encountered it in God.[226] While this danger presumably still threatens, Barth is now more aware that Scripture does not permit us to 'hesitate indefinitely' before affirming God's beauty (651–2).

Having introduced this 'dangerous' concept, Barth immediately hedges it round with both warnings and warrants. God's beauty is subordinate to his glory and, thus, ought not be treated independently as one of the 'leading concepts [*Hauptbegriffe*]' (i.e. perfections) in the doctrine of God, much less as the master concept behind them all (652). On the other hand, the threat of such 'aestheticism' in the doctrine of God is no greater than that posed by conceptual take-over from other directions (652–3). If the medieval concept

---

[223] Michael Trowitzsch, *Karl Barth heute* (Göttingen: Vandenhoeck & Ruprecht, 2007), 318–19.

[224] Krötke, *Gottes Klarheiten*, 108, objects, 'It is not enough…to describe the *doxa theou* as merely the "shape" or "form" of God's revelation', apparently mistaking Barth's talk of 'form' as indicating something merely external and lacking content. It seems, however, that Barth uses 'form' in something like the philosophical sense of *Gestalt*: a vision of a unified whole which is more than the sum of its parts, that is, which has content of its own beyond its formal aspect. 'The form [*Form*] of the perfect being of God is…the wonderful, constantly mysterious and no less constantly evident unity of identity and non-identity, simplicity and multiplicity, inward and outward, God himself and the fulness of that which he is as God' (657; KD 741). Besides, Barth insists that 'There can be no question of distinguishing between the content and the form of the divine being' (658).

[225] Cf. Balthasar, *The Glory of the Lord*, 1.53–4.

[226] Barth, *The Holy Spirit and the Christian Life*, 4–5. Later in the present passage, Barth makes amends for the cheek by commending Augustine's *De vera religione* (A.D. 391, well before the *Confessions*) for rejecting preconceived ideas of beauty (CD II/1, 656).

of the *fruitio Dei* has suffered much abuse, a long catena of biblical passages underscores the indispensability of the concept of God's beauty (653–4).

For while God's glory can certainly 'unleash fear and terror', it nevertheless always includes an element of 'giving pleasure, awaking desire, and creating enjoyment' (653). To rule out talk of God's beauty is, thus, to deny 'the radically evangelical character' of Scripture's testimony to God (654).

But is it really necessary, Barth asks, to speak of God's beauty specifically as radiating joy? 'Why not simply awe, gratitude, wonder, submission and obedience?' (655). Barth reasons that these latter might well describe a glory like Solomon's (664–5), that is 'solemn and good and true' but nevertheless 'gloomy', 'without sparkle or humour, not to say tedious and finally neither persuasive nor convincing' (655). Joy, however, that 'simplest form of gratitude',[227] supplies what these lack. 'Joy, desire, pleasure, the yearning for God and the enjoyment of having him in the fellowship with him which he himself gives us, is all along something which is obviously special and distinctive in all this' (655). 'Joy…is something in God, the God of all the perfections, which justifies us in having joy, desire and pleasure towards him' (655).[228] The concept of joy is entirely necessary to a biblical account of God's glory.

The remainder of Barth's third stage of argument is taken up with a closer investigation of this divine beauty which radiates joy. God's beauty, Barth insists, cannot be ascertained by examination of some 'idea of beauty superior to him' (656). 'On the contrary, it is as he is God that he is also beautiful, so that he is the basis and standard of everything that is beautiful and of all ideas of the beautiful.' It is this consideration of God's beautiful being which makes theology itself 'a peculiarly beautiful science':

> Indeed, we can confidently say that it is the most beautiful of all the sciences. To find the sciences distasteful is the mark of the Philistine. It is an extreme form of Philistinism to find, or to be able to find, theology distasteful. The theologian who has no joy in his work is not a theologian at all. (656)[229]

Thus, as Anselm hinted, the 'proof' of the beauty of God 'can be provided…only by this beauty itself' (656–7).[230] God is beautiful 'with

---

[227] *CD* III/4, 377 (cf. 374–7).

[228] Cf. *CD* III/2, 411–13. The connection between divine and human joy in Barth's thought is brought out ably by Capper, *Karl Barth's Theology of Joy*, for example, 21–4, 83–4, 101–2, 144–6.

[229] Cf. *CD* I/2, 772; III/4, 68; IV/3.2, 802–3, 881.

[230] Cf. Karl Barth, *Anselm: Fides Quaerens Intellectum: Anselm's Proof of the Existence of God in the Context of his Theological Scheme*, trans. Ian W. Robinson (London: SCM, 1960), 15–16.

unambiguous certainty', but that he should be recognised as such is something only God himself can bring about (657).

Following Anselm's hint, Barth does not give criteria which establish God's beauty – criteria which would belie the claim that God's beauty is its own standard. Rather, Barth gives three examples[231] of 'this beauty itself', much in the doxological mode of Anselm's 'proof' or Augustine's prayer. First, God is beautiful in his perfections (657–9). Rehearsing some of the determining features of his exposition, Barth touches briefly on the particularity of the perfections; on their correspondence *ad intra* and *ad extra*; on their expression of both simplicity and multiplicity, both 'movement and peace'; on their ineffable reality commanding and empowering human description, yet 'bursting through every system and relativising from the very first the surveys we try to make' (657–8). The form 'in which God is perfect is also itself perfect, the perfect form' (657). 'And this persuasive and convincing form must necessarily be called the beauty of God' (659).

Second, God is beautiful in his triunity (659–61). Barth notes again some of the crucial distinctions he sees between the doctrine of the Trinity and that of the divine attributes:

> The Christian church has never taught that there are in God three persons and therefore three personalities in the sense of a threefold Ego, a threefold subject. This would be tritheism, which the concept *persona*, understood as *modus subsistentiae*, is in fact meant to avoid. (297)

On Barth's view, the attributes can only be understood as those of the divine essence common to Father, Son and Spirit.[232] A doctrine of the divine attributes cannot venture beyond modest appropriation,[233] because the triune God 'is whole and undivided, and therefore all his perfections are equally the being of all three modes of the divine being' (660).

For all Barth's constant recurrence to trinitarian categories in his doctrine of the divine perfections, it is still criticised for being insufficiently trinitarian. Stephen Holmes, for example, claims that Jonathan Edwards 'is more thoroughly Trinitarian in his discussion of the divine perfections than is Barth'.[234] The reason is that Barth continues to assert 'that the perfections belong to the one essence of God', whereas Edwards considers the

---

[231] Cf. Balthasar, *The Glory of the Lord*, 1.55–6, 7.22–3; C. Holmes, *Divine Attributes*, 80–3.

[232] C. Holmes, *Divine Attributes*, 71–89, is particularly sensitive to the role of divine *perichoresis* throughout Barth's account of glory.

[233] Cf. CD I/1, 375.

[234] Stephen R. Holmes, *God of Grace and God of Glory: An Account of the Theology of Jonathan Edwards* (Edinburgh: T&T Clark, 2000), 66. This charge has a long history: 'Bizarrely enough', even Balthasar claims that the doctrine of the Trinity 'does not play a central role' in the overall shape of Barth's theology, in which the accent falls rather

perfections to be those, not of a common 'essence' but of the 'distinct Divine persons', specifically the Son and Spirit.[235] Clearly, it is not that Barth is less 'rigorously Trinitarian'[236] in his account of the perfections than he might have been; he is simply less pluralistic in his doctrine of Trinity.[237] It is the respective versions of the doctrine of the Trinity which are at issue, not the degree to which Barth's account of the perfections coheres with his own doctrine of the Trinity:

Lastly and supremely, God is beautiful in his incarnation (661–6).

> We are…assuming that the prominent place occupied by this divine work has something corresponding to it in the essence of God, that the Son forms the centre of the Trinity, and that the essence of the divine being has, so to speak, its *locus*, and is revealed, in his work, in the name and person of Jesus Christ. But this work of the Son as such reveals the beauty of God in a special way and in some sense to a supreme degree. (661; cf. 667)

The correspondence or analogy between God's being *ad intra* and *ad extra* applies to the divine beauty as well – and here Barth hints at the surprising use he will make of appropriation in *CD IV*. The beauty of the incarnation reveals to us the fact that 'the Son or Logos of God already displays the beauty of God in a special way in his eternal existence and therefore within the Trinity, as the perfect image of the Father' (661). It is thus supremely in the face of the incarnate Son that we sense 'the beauty of God's being and of the triunity of his being' (662).

This raises again the question of what Barth earlier spoke of as God's concealment and unknowability in his revelation (343). It is on this note of caution that Barth concludes his discussion of God's beauty:

> If it is impossible to over-emphasise the inner unity, the supreme exercise and confirmation of this unity, in which God acts in Jesus Christ, it is equally impossible to over-emphasise the depth with which he here differentiates himself from himself.…What a differentiation in the unity of God emerges at this point! (662)

For God, not in breach but in confirmation of his divine unity, becomes man (662), man with a fallen human nature no less, 'with all the marks of corruption' (663). Barth denies that there is any 'tension, dialectic, paradox

---

on the treatise 'on the *one* God'. See Fergus Kerr, *After Aquinas: Versions of Thomism* (Oxford: Blackwell, 2002), 183; Balthasar, *The Theology of Karl Barth*, 260.

[235] S. Holmes, *God of Grace*, 70, 69.

[236] S. Holmes, *God of Grace*, 68.

[237] Webster, *Barth*, 138–9.

or contradiction' in the 'mystery' of the incarnate Christ, even if to 'our mistaken thinking' this certainly seems to be the case (663, 665). In fact:

> God could not be more glorious as God than in this inconceivable humiliation of himself to man and the no less inconceivable exaltation of man to himself. He is glorious in this very differentiation, this renunciation of himself. And this, his supreme work towards what is outside him, is the reflection and image of his inner, eternal, divine being. In this reflection and image we see him as he is in himself. (663)

Again, this is not the humility and obedience Barth will ascribe to the Son in *CD* IV/1, but it does lean in that direction. Small wonder that Barth insists once again that 'God cannot be known except by God' (665; cf. 44). For it is only in the gift of the divine self-revelation that 'the glory and beauty of God' can be seen in the face of one with no apparent beauty (Isa. 53:2), whose beauty in fact 'embraces death as well as life, fear as well as joy, what we might call the ugly as well as what we might call the beautiful'. 'If the beauty of Christ is sought in a glorious Christ who is not the crucified, the search will always be in vain' (665). Vain also are all artistic attempts to portray the face of Christ – a 'sorry story', an 'unholy undertaking' (666).

One of the most striking aspects of this third stage of Barth's exposition is what it shows about Barth's understanding of revelation. Beauty, the 'form and manner of his glory', is 'the specifically persuasive and convincing element in his revelation' (654). According to Barth, God's glory, because it includes beauty, means that revelation does not conquer creaturely and sinful opposition by force. Rather, it creates desire for God and rewards with enjoyment of God (651, 653). God's beauty expresses in part the affective and non-cognitive aspects of revelation. Criticisms of Barth's doctrine of revelation (and hence his view of salvation) as overly or exclusively epistemic often overlook what Barth says about the beauty of revelation.[238] Admittedly, Barth has relatively little to say elsewhere in the *Dogmatics* about God's beauty. In *CD* IV/3.1, §69, for example, where Barth has much to say about both revelation and 'The Glory of the Mediator', and where Barth even makes explicit reference back to his account of glory here in *CD* II/1,[239] direct reference either to beauty or more generally to the affective

---

[238] E.g., Rosato, *The Spirit as Lord*, 160–6; Alister E. McGrath, *Iustitia Dei: A History of the Christian Doctrine of Justification* (Cambridge: Cambridge University Press, 1986), 2.179–84; A. Torrance, *Persons In Communion*, 117–19. The most prominent early exponent of this line of criticism is Gustaf Wingren, *Theology in Conflict: Nygren, Barth, Bultmann*, trans. Eric H. Wahlstrom (Edinburgh: Oliver and Boyd, 1958), 108–28, esp. 110, 125; cf. Williams, 'Barth on the Triune God', 172–5.

[239] *CD* IV/3.1, 47–8.

element in glory is sparse.[240] However, if Barth might perhaps be criticised for giving this element of revelation insufficient emphasis, he can hardly be criticised for having forgotten it entirely. For Barth, revelation is beautiful; indeed, Christ himself is 'beauty in personal form' (664–5). Because of this, revelation also creates desire, rewards with pleasure and evokes praise. 'The intratrinitarian joy evokes human responses of joy.'[241] It is 'the gift to us of the communicative presence of Father, Son and Spirit',[242] and so it 'involves the total and most intensive conscription and co-operation of all [man's] inner and outer forces, of his whole heart and soul and mind'.[243]

Acknowledgement of this affective dimension of revelation may also assuage concerns about the capacity of a doctrine of the Trinity derived from revelation to describe God's life *ad intra*. Rowan Williams, for example, finds it 'distinctly odd to say' of God in his life *ad intra* 'that he *reveals* himself to himself, and assures himself of his self-revelation'.[244] That is, on the assumption that revelation is a strictly epistemic event of veiling and unveiling, a doctrine of the Trinity derived from revelation cannot accommodate any relational dynamic between Father, Son and Spirit. The reason for this is that God is never veiled to himself and so cannot unveil himself to himself. There is no 'interior divine self-clarification' corresponding to God's self-revelation to us.[245] However, if revelation is also understood as generating desire, delight, gratitude and praise, there is indeed scope for some kind of triune, interpersonal dynamic – which Williams rightly wishes to maintain – yet without resorting to multiple 'centres of volition' or an intensified 'sense of plurality' in God, as Williams suggests.[246]

---

[240] The theological context in which Barth wrote may account for some of this. See John Webster, '"Eloquent and Radiant": The Prophetic Office of Christ and the Mission of the Church', in *idem, Barth's Moral Theology: Human Action in Barth's Thought* (Grand Rapids: Eerdmans, 1998), 128, 131. If explicit reference to God's beauty is muted, the joyful and exultant tone of §69, and its unhesitating praise of God, are not to be overlooked.

[241] Capper, *Karl Barth's Theology of Joy*, 84.

[242] Webster, *Barth*, 58; cf. John Webster, *Holy Scripture: A Dogmatic Sketch* (Cambridge: Cambridge University Press, 2003), 13–17. The knowledge which revelation entails 'is not an objectifying "knowledge about"' but 'a self-involving and self-transforming communion with God as personal Other'; see Trevor Hart, 'Revelation', in *The Cambridge Companion to Karl Barth*, ed. John Webster (Cambridge: Cambridge University Press, 2000), 42; cf. 48–9.

[243] *CD* IV/2, 556.

[244] Williams, 'Barth on the Triune God', 171. Barth does not actually say this. See for example his comments on the immediacy of God's primary objectivity: *CD* II/1, 16, 68. Williams is simply pointing to what he sees as a potential implication of Barth's doctrine of revelation.

[245] Williams, 'Barth on the Triune God', 172.

[246] Williams, 'Barth on the Triune God', 175, 181; cf. Webster, *Barth*, 71–2.

The fourth and final stage of Barth's exposition is a consideration of God's glory as it manifests the divine loving (666–77). The divine glory does so because it is in Jesus Christ that it has its beginning (the triune life *ad intra*), centre (reconciliation), and goal (redemption) (667). It therefore 'belongs to the essence of the glory of God not to be *gloria* alone, but to become *glorificatio*' (667). This *glorificatio*, the glorification of God by the creature – note again the implied non-competitive nature of divine and human agency – is both the work of the divine glory itself and an actual 'supplement' to the divine glory (667–8). God is also glorious, as Christopher Holmes aptly states, 'because the triune event that God is encompasses and encircles the creature…in such a way that the creature can and will participate in God's own self-glorification'.[247] On its own, humanity is both deaf to creation's praise of God and 'sinfully impotent' to join in the same (668). The divine glory, however, evoking as it does the human glorification of God, and thus seeking and establishing fellowship with humanity, manifests the divine love:

> As we look to Jesus Christ we not only profess our faith in the revelation of the divine being in its glory. We also confess that there is a sinner reconciled by him and in him, and therefore a loosing of tongues that were dumb, and therefore a reply awakened to his glory and evoked by God himself, and as awakened and evoked by him having a share in his glory. (668)

Although this *glorificatio* is merely that of the sinful creature, it is yet genuine. 'The divine *gloria* is not ashamed to dwell in it and to shine through it' (669; cf. 647). The creature, on the other hand, 'is free for God's glory, not because it was able or willed to be so on its own account, but because it has been made free for it by God's glory itself' (669). The creature, therefore, exists 'in pure gratitude towards God' (669).

What Barth has been speaking of in terms of desire, pleasure, enjoyment and now the glorification of God can also be described as the subjective dimension of revelation, or as man's response to revelation. It is therefore fitting that, before turning to what may be described as a miniature ethics of gratitude, Barth addresses the role of the Spirit in the human glorification of God. Human response to God is always a gracious and creative gift of the Spirit. God's glory, says Barth, as the glory not only of Father and Son, but also of the Spirit, is 'the divine reality by which the creature has its heart opened to God and is made able and willing to receive him' (669).[248] 'There

---

[247] C. Holmes, *Divine Attributes*, 71–2; cf. 222.

[248] Though critical of Barth's doctrine of the Spirit, Eugene Rogers 'grudgingly…concedes' that, in this passage, God's glory and hence his beauty are 'not only a characteristic of the whole Godhead, but also the *personal* contribution of…the Holy Spirit'. See his

is no glorification of God by the creature that does not come about through this work of the Holy Spirit by which the church is founded and maintained, or that is not itself, even in its creatureliness, this work of the Holy Spirit' (670).

What then does it mean 'that the creature is permitted to thank and serve the glory of God' (670)? Because this is something permitted to the creature, it is not something which can be accounted for merely in terms of creaturely abilities (671). With the permission to glorify God, however, comes the granting also of the 'primary' and 'decisive' thing: the ability to do so (671). This permission of the divine glory is thus the creature's liberation from its powerlessness to praise God (672) and the fulfilment of creaturely existence (673).[249] This, says Barth, is the 'whole point of creation':

> God wills to find again in another the reflection and image which he finds in himself from eternity to eternity in his Son. It was in order that there should be this reflection that the Son of God became flesh. (673)

It is only 'in post-temporal eternity' that this glorification of God will reach its perfection (675). Meanwhile, though humanity is not excluded from the glory and glorification of God, it participates in these only provisionally: by the grateful offering of 'life-obedience' to God (674), in the visible 'form of the church', and thus in 'proclamation, faith, confession, theology, [and] prayer' (676). Because it is only in the church and its faith that God's glory may be seen, the church becomes 'both the indispensable blessing and at the same time the most urgent task in human existence and history' (677). Keeping in mind both the comfort and the chastisement by which God in his grace sustains the church, Barth can even venture to say:

> We can sum up in the confession *Credo ecclesiam* everything that is to be said about God's glory, and doctrinally about his being. He is the God who is glorious in his community, and for that reason and in that way in all the world. (677)

Confession, and therefore doxology, both in this passage and in the closing quotation from Polanus, fittingly concludes Barth's exposition of the divine glory, and with it his entire exposition of the divine perfections.

According to Barth, glory is that enticing and delightful self-reflection of the divine life, as well as its full outshining, by which God displays himself to the creature in all his perfection and thus evokes joyful praise of himself. This glory is ultimately that of the crucified Christ, whose beauty, like the

---

After the Spirit: A Constructive Pneumatology from Resources Outside the Modern West (Grand Rapids: Eerdmans, 2005), 181.

[249] Cf. C. Holmes, *Divine Attributes*, 86–7.

divine beauty and glory generally, is beyond the perception of the sinful creature, but is yet granted to it by the Spirit's gift of faith. Barth does not merely describe here the human response to this perfection, the glorification of the glorious God; he models it himself and appeals to his readers to join him. To the 'self-revealing sum of all divine perfections' there can correspond nothing less than the sum of the Christian life in faith, prayer, confession, theology, proclamation and worship.

5

SUMMARY AND PROSPECTS

'God is.' In drawing the present study to a conclusion, it is worthwhile to recall the opening words of Barth's exposition. Everything Barth has said about God's being-in-act, about God's identity as the one who loves in freedom, about the appropriate method and presuppositions for a doctrine of the divine perfections, and about the individual perfections themselves – all this, according to Barth, is merely the development and explanation of the 'simple statement' that 'God is' (257). Throughout, it is the identity of the subject of this statement, the divine identity, which has occupied Barth. Who is God? Barth's doctrine of the divine perfections, which everywhere presupposes and employs his doctrine of the Trinity, is a provisional answer.

Barth's express goal, as he memorably puts it, is to portray the 'contours' of God's being (336), not arbitrarily, but as these are reflected in Scripture and illumined by the Spirit. It is this quest which drives Barth's exposition, and not, for example, some *a priori* commitment to absolute divine independence. And while Barth would be the first to acknowledge the inadequacy of his exposition – in fact, he has already done so (442) – such inadequacy has not resulted, as has been variously claimed, from a distorting concept of divine personhood, from a dim view of divine power as petty tyranny, or from an impoverished idea of eternity as finally antithetical to created time. While the present study has not attempted any large-scale assessment of the viability of Barth's account, it has attempted what is, in light of much misinterpretation, necessarily preliminary to any such assessment: the clarification of precisely what Barth does and does not affirm.

Keys to Barth's Doctrine of the Perfections?

Assessment of Barth's account, however, cannot begin with the details of what he says. It must begin much further back. This is rightly acknowledged by those interpreters who have sought keys to the interpretation of Barth's doctrine of the divine perfections. Fundamental theological decisions exert a determinative influence over the whole of his exposition of the divine

185

perfections, and it is with these decisions that assessment of his account must begin. The goal of this concluding chapter is simply to identify some of these basic dogmatic moves and to note their effect on Barth's exposition, thereby preparing the way further for assessment.

What are these fundamental decisions? What are the rules or governing presuppositions of Barth's account? What, we might ask, are the theological attributes of Barth's exposition? A number suggest themselves, and from among these, too, selection is somewhat arbitrary. We will focus briefly on three: Barth's decisions (1) to ground everything he says about the perfections exclusively in God himself, (2) to expound the perfections explicitly as those of the very essence of God, and (3) not to abstract these perfections from their implications for the Christian life. While these decisions are announced and their effects apparent in Barth's account itself, Barth's reasons for making these decisions lie elsewhere – but not so far afield as one might expect. This, for example, is Osthövener's mistake – not by any means that he looks back 100 years in an attempt find in Schleiermacher a key to interpreting Barth, for Schleiermacher was as much a contemporary for Barth as was Thurneysen. The problem is that Osthövener overlooks in the process what Barth says in the few hundred pages preceding the account of the perfections.[1] The three decisions identified here as among the keys to this account are virtually announced as such in the first part of *CD* II/1, the chapter on 'The Knowledge of God'. In this chapter Barth argues that, among other things, human knowledge of God (1) comes exclusively from God, (2) consists in a mediated participation in God's knowledge of himself, and (3) expresses itself in every dimension of human life. These three claims concerning the human knowledge of God ground the respective theological decisions to be considered here. Thus, while 'The Knowledge of God', insofar as it repudiates natural theology, is indeed 'a ground-clearing exercise'[2] for 'The Reality of God', in its positive doctrine it is more aptly described as the 'prolegomenon' to the divine perfections (32). Each of the three sections which follow will explain one of these key theological decisions along with its 'prolegomenon', and then note its impact on Barth's account of the perfections. In doing so, these sections also identify the kinds of broad, fundamental questions which need to be answered in assessing Barth's account.

The Knowledge of Faith

Looking back over the whole of *Church Dogmatics* II/1, Barth describes its first chapter, 'The Knowledge of God', as an attempt 'to learn the lofty but

---

[1] See particularly Claus-Dieter Osthövener, *Die Lehre von Gottes Eigenschaften bei Friedrich Schleiermacher und Karl Barth*, Theologische Bibliothek Töpelmann 76 (Berlin: de Gruyter, 1996), 156–7.

[2] Joseph L. Mangina, *Karl Barth: Theologian of Christian Witness* (Aldershot: Ashgate, 2004), 63.

simple lesson that it is by God that God is known'.[3] Barth explains that, as the object of human knowledge, God cannot be considered just one object on a par with others. God possesses a 'particular and utterly unique object-ivity' (14). Because of this, because of God's utter uniqueness, it is exclu-sively through the Spirit's gift of faith that there can arise human knowledge of God. Nothing else could supply such knowledge. Thus, the counterpart to what might be called God's epistemic exclusivity is Barth's rejection of all natural theology. Taken together, these constitute what Barth once described as a purified version of the Protestant Scripture principle.[4] They also capture something of what George Hunsinger has called the motif of particularism in Barth's thought,[5] and they account for a number of features of his expos-ition of the divine perfections.

Methodologically and structurally, it is this exclusivity of the knowledge of faith which governs his solution to 'the problem of the derivation and distribution of the divine attributes' (335). That is, Barth rejects the *viae* (the ways of eminence, negation and causality) insofar as they function as ways of generating, apart from faith, the concepts to be used in the descrip-tion of God. While the *viae* may serve a useful subsequent descriptive func-tion, the initial concepts must be derived from God's self-revelation. For the same reason Barth rejects the various traditional schemes of distributing the attributes. Not only do these tend to nominalise what Barth classifies as the perfections of the divine loving. They also invariably supply, from elsewhere than revelation, the leading conceptual categories for describing God. Once again, Barth's aim is to allow revelation – God's self-revelation and, thus ultimately, God's own being as encountered in faith – to supply these leading conceptual categories and therefore the very structure of his doctrine.

According to Barth, these leading conceptual categories are the divine lov-ing and the divine freedom. What becomes apparent with these two con-cepts, however, is that they are not, strictly speaking, concepts at all. As Barth uses them, they are shorthand descriptors of an identity unique in its immense richness. They attempt to indicate the way in which 'God is'. God's loving, for example, is not simply any 'seeking and creating fellowship', but emphatically God's own, unique seeking and creating of fellowship, fellow-ship with us his elect and sinful people. Such loving, the divine loving, itself

---

[3] CD II/2, 3.

[4] Karl Barth, *The Theology of the Reformed Confessions*, trans. Darrell L. Guder and Judith J. Guder, Columbia Series in Reformed Theology (Louisville: Westminster John Knox, 2002), 38–64, esp. 48. On the functional priority which Barth accords Scripture over other traditional norms of theology, see the concluding summary in Todd Pokrifka-Joe, *Redescribing God: The Roles of Scripture, Tradition, and Reason in Karl Barth's Doctrines of Divine Unity, Constancy, and Eternity* (Ph.D. diss., University of St. Andrews, 2002), 264–5.

[5] George Hunsinger, *How to Read Karl Barth: The Shape of His Theology* (Oxford: Oxford University Press, 1991), 32–5.

encompassing the entire history of God with his people, cannot be captured in its uniqueness by a neat definition, but only very partially indicated by further description. This is precisely the function of the perfections of the divine loving: to capture some of the richness of this loving in its grace and holiness, mercy and righteousness, patience and wisdom. These individual perfections are in turn merely further indications of the divine identity. The same holds for the divine freedom and its associated perfections.

Moreover, it is not only the divine loving and freedom which evade tight conceptualisation in this way. The same concern to indicate the divine identity in its uniqueness, and therefore to adhere exclusively and attentively to revelation as a means to this end, also makes itself felt in Barth's accounts of individual perfections. These, too, resist precise definition. Though Barth often begins with a general description of a divine perfection, this is often so radically expanded and enriched by subsequent exposition as almost (but never entirely) to make it appear obsolete. For those who approach this chapter of the *Dogmatics* expecting to find a series of concepts defined with analytic precision, this can be a source of bewilderment or even frustration. The welcome sharpness of Barth's initial description of a given perfection fades as exposition continues, and one suddenly finds oneself staring yet again at some aspect of how God has reconciled the world to himself in Christ. But this is precisely Barth's point. He has not lost the plot, but brought it to its climax. God's perfections are those of his enacted identity and must remain transparent to it. The conceptual acrobatics involved in identifying the divine perfections would fail of their purpose were these perfections to become objects of independent interest – idolatry, on Barth's account. Barth's entire exposition of the divine perfections, from its leading 'concepts' of loving and freedom to the details of its descriptions of individual perfections, is thus one long exercise in trying to indicate the wealth and irreducible particularity of God's identity:

> Dogmatics, in each and all of its divisions and subdivisions, with every one of its questions and answers, with all its biblical and historical assertions, with the whole range of its formal and material considerations, examinations and syntheses, can first and last, as a whole and in part, say nothing else but this: God is. (258 rev.; *KD* 289)

Even when dogmatics makes such an attempt, Barth knows very well that it is attended by no guarantee of success. As merely a product of human description, the only guarantee it has on its own is one of failure. It possesses no capacity for conveying the knowledge of God. This is not, however, the end of the matter:

> Our inability to perform by our action what is demanded of us is not at all his inability to cause what is demanded to happen by our action.

What we of ourselves cannot do, he can do through us. (212; cf. 46–7)

Theology's incapacity to convey knowledge of God is not God's incapacity. God is fully capable of using such provisional testimony to bring about true knowledge of himself, and 'we have the promise' that God will in fact do so (213).[6]

Barth's insistence on the uniqueness of God, and on the consequent exclusivity of God's self-revelation as the source of human knowledge of God, constitutes one of the fundamental theological decisions of Barth's account. The validity of his account hinges in part on the validity of this decision. Is God's uniqueness such that his perfections require a more narrative description? Or might simpler, clearer, tighter concepts be more appropriate? Is God's uniqueness such as to require so exclusive an adherence to revelation as Barth attempts? Or might there not be, for example, a 'basic transcendental category of religion', something Wolfhart Pannenberg has identified as 'the infinite', the intuition of which constitutes the human person's 'primordial awareness' or 'non-thematic knowledge' of God?[7] For Pannenberg, it is not revelation, but this non-thematic knowledge of God as it develops through reflection and (religious) experience into a sense of the 'true Infinite', which ought to structure theological description of such divine perfections as holiness, eternity, and omnipresence.[8] The differences between these accounts are some indication of the scope of the implications of the exclusivity of the knowledge of faith as well as of the stakes in the ongoing controversy over natural theology.[9]

The Divine Objectivity

According to Barth, the divine perfections are those of the very essence of God. While this may sound less like a key theological decision and more like a tautology, something true by definition, its influence actually extends throughout Barth's exposition. It drives Barth's insistence that God's being is in act and encapsulates the whole of Barth's dispute with the nominalistic

---

[6] Cf. *CD* IV/3.2, 736–8.

[7] Wolfhart Pannenberg, *Systematic Theology*, 3 vols., trans. Geoffrey W. Bromiley (Grand Rapids: Eerdmans, 1991–1998), 1.113–18; Stanley J. Grenz, *Reason for Hope: The Systematic Theology of Wolfhart Pannenberg*, 2nd ed. (Grand Rapids: Eerdmans, 2005), 72–5; Charles E. Gutenson, *Reconsidering the Doctrine of God* (London: T&T Clark, 2005), 40–3, 75–8.

[8] Pannenberg, *Systematic Theology*, 1.397–415; Grenz, *Reason for Hope*, 81–5; Gutenson, *Reconsidering*, 230–1.

[9] E.g., James Barr, *Biblical Faith and Natural Theology: The Gifford Lectures for 1991* (Oxford: Clarendon, 1993); Paul D. Molnar, 'Natural Theology Revisited: A Comparison of T. F. Torrance and Karl Barth', *Zeitschrift für dialektische Theologie* 21.1 (2005): 53–83.

strain in the tradition. This second key theological decision Barth elaborates as follows: 'All that God is in his relationship to his creation…is simply an outward manifestation and realisation of what he is previously in himself apart from this relationship and therefore apart from his creation' (462). This basic relation between God's immanent and economic reality is 'the dogmatic foundation upon which the doctrine of the divine perfections in CD II/1 stands, and with which it falls'.[10] God has his life in all its perfections apart from the created order, but it is precisely this same life, and nothing less, which God displays in his acts within the created order.

This decision too is grounded in Barth's earlier description of the knowledge of God, for to speak of God's perfections as manifest in the created order is, of course, to speak of God as he makes himself available to human knowledge. We have already noted that, because of his view of the divine uniqueness, Barth locates all human knowledge of God strictly in God's self-revelation to faith. Barth also argues that such knowledge consists in a mediated participation in God's own knowledge of himself:

> As he certainly knows himself first of all, God is first and foremost objective to himself.…We call this the primary objectivity of God, and distinguish from it the secondary, i.e., the objectivity which he has for us too in his revelation, in which he gives himself to be known by us as he knows himself. (16)

God's primary objectivity does come to us mediately, 'clothed under the sign and veil of other objects' than God (16). Staggeringly, however, it is God's very own knowledge of himself – 'first-hand information'! – which is conveyed to faith (210). The significance of this for Barth's doctrine of the perfections is that 'in every creaturely work and sign' which God uses to make himself objective to human knowledge, God himself is present in his very essence (51):

> The revelation of God, in which the fulfilment of the true knowledge of God becomes event in man, is the disposition of God in which he acts towards us as the same triune Lord that he is in himself, and in such a way that, although we are men and not God, we receive a share in the truth of his knowledge of himself. (51 rev.; *KD* 55)

God's perfections, for all the sacramental hiddenness of their secondary objectivity to man (53–6), are nonetheless the same as in their primary objectivity to God himself.

---

[10] Jan Štefan, '*Gottes Vollkommenheiten nach* KD II/1', in *Karl Barth im europäischen Zeitgeschehen (1935–1950): Widerstand – Bewährung – Orientierung*, ed. Michael Beintker, Christian Link, and Michael Trowitzsch (Zürich: Theologischer Verlag Zürich, 2010), 90.

It is this fundamental decision concerning the intimate relation between God as he manifests himself to us and as he is in himself, between God's secondary and primary objectivity, which finds expression, for example, in Barth's claim that God's being is in act, that is, in his act of self-revelation. As he explains it in *CD* I/1, the claim that 'God reveals himself' means that 'God, the Revealer, is identical with his act in revelation'.[11] God does not have his being only in this act, of course, for he exists in his primary objectivity and in the perfections of his triune life apart from the created order. But in his act of self-revelation, God is present in all his triune lordship and mediates a knowledge of himself as such. This same decision launches Barth's relentless campaign against nominalism, the implicit or explicit denial that God is, in his very essence, as he reveals himself to be. The doctrine of the Trinity as confessed by the church has already done the really hard work of identifying the mystery of unity and plurality in both God's essence and revelation. With perfections other than the divine unity, Barth has had considerably less help from the tradition in correlating God's being and act. But correlate he does, implicitly in the case of righteousness, famously in the case of eternity, and problematically in the case of grace and mercy. With these latter two, Barth risks falling into nominalism himself in order to affirm, in loyalty to this basic decision, their full reality in the divine life. As noted, this reveals a lack of that kind of confidence in his emerging doctrine of election which would later free Barth to speak uninhibitedly of the humanity of God.[12]

Once again, evaluation of Barth's account of the perfections as a whole is bound up with evaluation of this second key theological decision. In many ways, trinitarian theology since Barth can be described as an attempt at evaluating precisely this decision, particularly as formulated by Karl Rahner.[13] Has Barth rightly related God's action in the economy to his life *ad intra*? Or does there still remain a speculative moment in Barth's conception of God's eternal, triune being, perhaps in its construal of the divine unity or aseity or absolute power, which cannot be justified by closer attention to the work of Son and Spirit in the economy? When it comes specifically to the divine perfections, might such attention warrant a somewhat fuller, more differentiated account of the perfections *ad intra*? To these latter two questions, the response of Pannenberg – returning to him again simply as a point of reference – is yes. Pannenberg suggests that Barth's view of God's unity (God as a single, triune subject) prevents God from also being eternal love (which requires that at least Father and Son each be understood

---

[11] CD I/1, 296.

[12] Karl Barth, 'The Humanity of God', in *idem, The Humanity of God*, trans. Thomas Wieser and John Newton Thomas (Atlanta: John Knox, 1960), 37–65.

[13] Fred Sanders, *The Image of the Immanent Trinity: Rahner's Rule and the Theological Interpretation of Scripture* (New York: Peter Lang, 2005).

as subjects of the divine loving).[14] Pannenberg insists that such a view of the divine unity cannot arise from due consideration of the plurality of Father, Son and Spirit in the economy. Pannenberg's challenge to Barth is that God's secondary objectivity requires further differentiation between the respective roles of Father, Son and Spirit in the divine loving *ad intra*.[15] Once again, evaluation of specific claims in Barth's doctrine of the perfections depends on the prior evaluation of Barth's decision concerning the nature of the divine objectivity.

A Sober Exuberance

The goal of dogmatics, as Barth sees it, in keeping with its task to serve the proclamation of the church, is to make clear what God wills from all people: that 'in great things and small, in whole and in part, in the totality of their existence...they should and must live with the fact that not only sheds new light on, but materially changes all things and everything in all things – the fact that God is' (258). The fact that 'God is' changes everything. Because of this, Barth insists that to talk about God is necessarily and intrinsically to talk also of the Christian life. The two cannot be abstracted from each other. This is the third and final key theological decision to be considered here, and it, too, is grounded in what Barth says about the knowledge of God. Such knowledge, as noted, is a knowledge which comes strictly in faith. Faith, however, indicates more than merely the exclusivity of this knowledge. According to Barth, 'Faith is the total positive relationship of man to the God who gives himself to be known in his Word' (12). Every dimension of human life is involved: 'Knowledge of God is obedience to God' (26); it is love for God and fear of God (32–5); it is gratitude, adoration, and hope (48). Dogmatics, therefore, cannot achieve its goal, even as it goes about describing the divine perfections, if it does not also and at the same time address the entire scope of human response which God in his perfections wills to evoke.

Such response is to be marked in part by what Barth calls a 'sober exuberance' (219). It is *exuberance* because knowing God is a matter of 'prayer and praise and thanksgiving' (207), of giving glory to God in joy, gladness and 'wondering awe' (218–19). It is *sober* because it is ordered not 'according to our own choice...pleasure...humour, fancy or obstinacy' but according to revelation (218–19). In this way, 'in the exuberance of the worship of God in the heart and mouth of the sinful creature, human knowledge of God is an act of gratitude and therefore partakes of the veracity of the revelation of God' (219). We have already noted some of the specific reasons Barth gives for this sober exuberance. For example, our suffering is God's 'own

[14] Pannenberg, *Systematic Theology*, 1.424–5.
[15] Pannenberg, *Systematic Theology*, 1.425–30.

intimate concern' (373); to our chaotic lives God offers a 'human simplicity' corresponding to his own (460–1); our prayers are heard by God (510–11). Again, in his pastoral meditation on the divine knowing and willing (545–9), Barth observes how, in that 'most wonderful' event of revelation (545), we are both confronted with that truth than which there is none 'more moving, terrifying or soul-rewarding' – the truth that God knows us (547) – and also brought to that submission, fear and joy which prays, 'Thy will be done' (548). Finally, in his account of God's glory, Barth invites us to marvel with him at the beauty in which God is 'the One who gives pleasure, creates desire and rewards with enjoyment' (651).

This sober exuberance is merely one aspect of the full scope of human response warranted by revelation and addressed here by Barth. It is not a privileged aspect of such response, nor can it be neatly separated from other aspects of this response such as repentance and obedience.[16] It is, however, a necessary and integral aspect. A dogmatics conceived as a following after God's revelation cannot ignore the 'religious affections', especially in its doctrine of God.[17] In executing his own doctrine of God in this way, Barth shows himself very much an ecclesial theologian. He speaks as a Christian, and he addresses his readers as though they, too, are Christians, exhorting them as a pastor would his congregation.

Returning a final time and by way of contrast to Pannenberg, Pannenberg speaks as a rational theologian, minimizing confessional allegiance[18] and insisting on the inevitable debatability of theological truth-claims this side of the final consummation.[19] While Pannenberg acknowledges the importance of doxology in a doctrine of God,[20] and while he speaks warmly of hope in God's coming kingdom,[21] his doctrine of God contains none of the sober exuberance found in Barth's. The reason, it would seem, is that such exuberance assumes an eschatological certainty which Pannenberg deems inappropriate to the historical and developmental nature of the way in which God is known. The confidence of Barth's sober exuberance Pannenberg considers 'irrational fanaticism'.[22]

Is the scope and certainty of human knowledge of God such as to require of dogmatics, even and perhaps particularly in its doctrine of God, expression

[16] Cf. *CD* I/2, 401–2.

[17] Joseph L. Mangina, *Karl Barth on the Christian Life: The Practical Knowledge of God* (New York: Peter Lang, 2001), 125–64 ('Grace and Gratitude: The Affective Knowledge of God').

[18] Pannenberg, *Systematic Theology*, 1.xiii.

[19] Pannenberg, *Systematic Theology*, 1.48–61.

[20] Pannenberg, *Systematic Theology*, 1.393–4; cf. his earlier essay, 'Analogy and Doxology', in *idem, Basic Questions in Theology*, vol. 1, trans. George H. Kehm (London: SCM, 1970), 211–38, esp. 215–18, 236–8.

[21] Pannenberg, *Systematic Theology*, 1.399, 1.408–9, 1.417.

[22] Pannenberg, *Systematic Theology*, 1.46–8.

of and exhortation to gratitude and praise? Or does the assumption that one's readers already participate in such knowledge, so that they should be called to fitting response, in fact distort this knowledge? The difference between these two approaches is not simply a matter of the style or disposition of the theologian, the one preferring the forthright role of preacher and the other the subtler role of disputant. The difference rests on a theological decision, a decision which for Barth is intimately bound up with the sinfulness of the theologian himself. In striking demonstration that he has indeed learned 'at the feet of Anselm' (4), Barth goes so far as to invite his readers to join him in praying: '"Lead us not into temptation – into the temptation...of wanting to know Thee in Thy objectivity as if we were spectators, as if we could know, speak and hear about Thee in the slightest degree without at once taking part,...without at once beginning with obedience"' (26). Evaluation of Barth's doctrine of the divine perfections rests in part on the validity of his decision that the knowledge of God in faith bears decisively on every aspect of the Christian life, including but not limited to its affective dimensions. Talk of these perfections is therefore incomplete, on Barth's account, without appeal to the human response at which God aims in revealing himself in these very perfections.

According to Barth, human knowledge of God is strictly that knowledge which God himself gives to the believer. Furthermore, since the gift of this knowledge is truly a matter of God's self-revelation, of God granting to human beings a mediated participation in that same objectivity in which he knows himself, it must be that God always reveals himself in the economy as the same one he is in eternity. Finally, the knowledge of this God is something which does not exist and, therefore, cannot be adequately described apart from its goal of human glorification of God. These three decisions, announced and developed in the opening chapter of *CD* II/1, constitute some of the most explicit and determinative theological moves for Barth's account of the perfections. Others could also be mentioned – for example, what Barth describes as the 'divinity' of each given perfection, that is, its utter uniqueness because of its co-inherence, indeed, its identity with every other perfection, and the untraditionally broad impact which this very traditional affirmation has on the way Barth relates the perfections to each other. Barth's theology is undoubtedly influenced by other factors as well, from personal circumstances and faculty dynamics to political and economic concerns. But while all of these have left their mark, it is basic theological decisions such those identified here which hold the most promise as keys to the interpretation and evaluation of Barth's account of the perfections as a whole.

Prospects

Finally, what prospects remain for further research on Barth's doctrine of the divine perfections? The present study is a detailed commentary on Barth's doctrine of the divine perfections in *Church Dogmatics* II/1. As such, it has not had scope to explore, for example, the systematic connections between the divine perfections and other doctrines, though it might provide a basis for doing so.[23] Beyond such exploration, it seems that future research, at least initially, has one central knot to untie: the question of development in Barth's thought. If Barth's sober exuberance in his task as theologian only matured with age, this was in part because he also delved more deeply into the implications of both the exclusivity of Christ for human knowledge of God and the nature of the divine objectivity. Barth's understanding of the divine perfections appears to have matured likewise. To what degree? When Barth speaks later in the *Church Dogmatics* about the divine perfections, does he merely elaborate on his formulations here in *CD* II/1? Or are there significant changes in his approach?

The question of development arises most significantly in the magnificent, opening Christological section of *Church Dogmatics* IV/1. Here, Barth approaches the work of Christ in terms of 'two moments': Christ's humility and Christ's obedience.[24] By the logic of Barth's sharpened sense of the divine objectivity, 'the astounding conclusion' must be that these reveal a divine humility and a divine obedience.[25] What is intriguing about Barth's formulation is that throughout this section he deliberately and explicitly recurs to the language and logic of II/1. Barth speaks of humility and obedience as divine perfections – possibly even a love-freedom pair. At the same time, however, humility and obedience are not merely appropriated to the Son, as they would have to be if they truly were divine perfections. They are exclusively those of God the Son.[26] Why does Barth speak of humility and obedience as divine perfections when dogmatically it seems they must be personal properties of the Son? Does this represent development in his doctrine of the divine perfections, even though Barth continues to insist on the same, traditional definition of a divine perfection as describing the whole essence of God?[27] Or has Barth reconceived the categories of

---

[23] For example, the relation between attributes and atonement in chapter 4 of Adam Johnson, *God's Being in Reconciliation: The Theo-Ontological Basis of the Unity and Diversity of the Doctrine of the Atonement in the Theology of Karl Barth* (Ph.D. diss., Trinity Evangelical Divinity School, 2010). McCormack continues his provocative exploration of the relation between attributes and Christology in 'Divine Impassibility or Simply Divine Constancy? Implications of Karl Barth's Later Christology for Debates over Impassibility', in *Divine Impassibility and the Mystery of Human Suffering*, ed. James F. Keating and Thomas Joseph White O.P., 150–86 (Grand Rapids: Eerdmans, 2009).

[24] *CD* IV/1, 179–92 (humility) and 192–210 (obedience).

[25] *CD* IV/1, 202.

[26] *CD* IV/1, 203.

[27] *CD* IV/2, 86; cf. *CD* I/1, 375.

'essence' and 'person',[28] so that this actually represents development in his doctrine of the Trinity? Does this redeem Barth's doctrine of the perfections for McCormack's proposal or complicate matters further? Does this suggest ways in which Barth might have corrected, or merely extended, what he wrote in II/1?

No doubt the currently flourishing field of Barth studies will yield many an insight on the divine perfections not foreseen here. And how, of course, could it be otherwise, given the rare capacity of Barth's theology to occasion and enliven reflection on *der ewig reiche Gott* himself, as he has made himself known in the glorious face of Jesus Christ?

---

[28] Bruce L. McCormack, 'Karl Barth's Historicized Christology: Just How "Chalcedonian" Is It?' in *idem, Orthodox and Modern: Studies in the Theology of Karl Barth* (Grand Rapids: Baker Academic, 2008), 228–9.

BIBLIOGRAPHY

Augustine. *Confessions*. Translated by Henry Chadwick. Oxford: Oxford University Press, 1991.

Balthasar, Hans Urs von. *The Glory of the Lord: A Theological Aesthetics*. Translated by Erasmo Leiva-Merikakis. Edited by Joseph Fessio and John Riches. Edinburgh: T&T Clark, 1982–1989.

—. *Theo-Drama: Theological Dramatic Theory*. 5 vols. Translated by Graham Harrison. San Francisco: Ignatius, 1988–1998.

—. *The Theology of Karl Barth: Exposition and Interpretation*. Translated by Edward T. Oakes. San Francisco: Ignatius, 1992.

Barr, James. *Biblical Faith and Natural Theology: The Gifford Lectures for 1991*. Oxford: Clarendon, 1993.

—. *Biblical Words for Time*. 2nd ed. London: SCM, 1969.

Barth, Karl. *Anselm: Fides Quaerens Intellectum: Anselm's Proof of the Existence of God in the Context of his Theological Scheme*. Translated by Ian W. Robinson. London: SCM, 1960.

—. *The Christian Life: Church Dogmatics IV/4, Lecture Fragments*. Translated by Geoffrey W. Bromiley. Grand Rapids: Eerdmans, 1981.

—. *Die christliche Dogmatik im Entwurf*. Vol. 1, *Die Lehre vom Worte Gottes: Prolegomena zur christlichen Dogmatik, 1927*. Karl Barth Gesamtausgabe 14. Edited by Gerhard Sauter. Zürich: Theologischer Verlag Zürich, 1982.

—. *Church and State*. Translated by G. Ronald Howe. With an introduction by David L. Mueller. Greenville: Smyth and Helwys, 1991.

—. *Church Dogmatics*. Edited by G. W. Bromiley and T. F. Torrance. Edinburgh: T&T Clark, 1956–1975.

—. *The Doctrine of the Word of God*. Translated by G. T. Thomson. Edinburgh: T&T Clark, 1936.

—. *The Epistle to the Romans*. Translated by Edwyn C. Hoskyns. Oxford: Oxford University Press, 1968.

—. *Evangelical Theology: An Introduction*. Grand Rapids: Eerdmans, 1979.

—. 'Der Glaube an den persönlichen Gott'. In *idem, Vorträge und kleinere Arbeiten 1909–1914*. Karl Barth Gesamtausgabe 22. Edited by Hans-Anton Drewes and Hinrich Stoevesandt. Zürich: Theologischer Verlag Zürich, 1993.

—. *The Göttingen Dogmatics: Instruction in the Christian Religion*. Vol. 1. Edited by Hannelotte Reiffen. Translated by Geoffrey W. Bromiley. Grand Rapids: Eerdmans, 1991.

—. *The Holy Spirit and the Christian Life: The Theological Basis of Ethics*. Translated by R. Birch Hoyle. Forward by Robin W. Lovin. Louisville: Westminster John Knox, 1993.

—. *The Humanity of God*. Translated by Thomas Wieser and John Newton Thomas. Atlanta: John Knox, 1960.

—. *Karl Barth's Table Talk*. Edited by John D. Godfrey. Scottish Journal of Theology Occasional Papers 10. Edinburgh: Oliver and Boyd, 1963.

—. *Die kirchliche Dogmatik*. Munich: Chr. Kaiser, 1932, and Zürich: Evangelischer Verlag Zürich, 1938–1967.

—. *The Knowledge of God and the Service of God according to the Teaching of the Reformation: Recalling the Scottish Confession of 1560*. Translated by J. L. M. Haire and Ian Henderson. London: Hodder and Stoughton, 1938.

—. *A Letter to Great Britain from Switzerland*. Translated by E. H. Gordon and George Hill. London: Sheldon, 1941.

—. *Offene Briefe 1935–1942*. Karl Barth Gesamtausgabe 36. Edited by Diether Koch. Zürich: Theologischer Verlag Zürich, 2001.

—. *Predigten 1935–1952*. Karl Barth Gesamtausgabe 26. Edited by Harmut Spieker and Hinrich Stoevesandt. Zürich: Theologischer Verlag Zürich, 1996.

—. *Protestant Theology in the Nineteenth Century: Its Background and History*. New ed. Translated by Brian Cozens and John Bowden. London: SCM, 2001.

—. *Theological Existence Today! A Plea for Theological Freedom*. Translated by R. Birch Hoyle. London: Hodder and Stoughton, 1933.

—. *Theology and Church: Shorter Writings 1920–1928*. Translated by Louise Pettibone Smith. New York: Harper and Row, 1962.

—. *The Theology of John Calvin*. Translated by Geoffrey W. Bromiley. Grand Rapids: Eerdmans, 1995.

—. *The Theology of the Reformed Confessions*. Translated by Darrell L. Guder and Judith J. Guder. Columbia Series in Reformed Theology. Louisville: Westminster John Knox, 2002.

—. *Unterricht in der christlichen Religion*. Vol. 3, *Die Lehre von der Versöhnung, Die Lehre von der Erlösung, 1925/1926*. Karl Barth Gesamtausgabe 38. Edited by Hinrich Stoevesandt. Zürich: Theologischer Verlag Zürich, 2003.

Benz, Meinrad. Review of *Die kirchliche Dogmatik, Die Lehre von Gott*, by Karl Barth. *Divus Thomas: Jahrbuch für Philosophie und spekulative Theologie* 3.21 (1943): 213–23.

Berkhof, Hendrikus. *Christian Faith: An Introduction to the Study of the Faith*. Rev. ed. Translated by Sierd Woudstra. Grand Rapids: Eerdmans, 1986.

—. 'The (Un)Changeability of God'. In *Grace Upon Grace: Essays in Honor of Lester J. Kuyper*, ed. James I. Cook, 21–9. Grand Rapids: Eerdmans, 1986.

Berkouwer, G. C. *The Triumph of Grace in the Theology of Karl Barth: A Scriptural Examination and Assessment*. Translated by Harry R. Boer. London: Paternoster, 1956.

Bettis, Joseph D. 'Is Karl Barth a Universalist?' *Scottish Journal of Theology* 20.4 (1967): 423–36.

Bloesch, Donald G. *God the Almighty: Power, Wisdom, Holiness, Love*. Carlisle: Paternoster, 1995.

Bouillard, Henri. *Karl Barth*. 3 vols. Paris: Aubier, 1957.

Bromiley, Geoffrey W. *Introduction to the Theology of Karl Barth*. Edinburgh: T&T Clark, 1979.

Brouwer, Rinse H. Reeling. 'The Conversation between Karl Barth and Amandus Polanus on the Question of the Reality of Human Speaking of the Simplicity and the Multiplicity of God'. In *The Reality of Faith in Theology: Studies on Karl Barth: Princeton-Kampen Consultation 2005*, ed. Bruce McCormack and Gerrit Nevin, 51–110. New York: Peter Lang, 2007.

Brown, Robert. 'On God's Ontic and Noetic Absoluteness: A Critique of Barth'. *Scottish Journal of Theology* 33.6 (1980): 533–49.

Brunner, Emil. *Dogmatics*. Vol. 1, *The Christian Doctrine of God*. Translated by Olive Wyon. London: Lutterworth, 1949.

Brunner, Emil and Barth, Karl. *Natural Theology: Comprising 'Nature and Grace' by Professor Dr. Emil Brunner and the Reply 'No!' by Dr. Karl Barth*. Translated by Peter Fraenkel. With an introduction by John Baillie. 1946. Reprint Eugene: Wipf and Stock, 2002.

Buckley, James J. 'Christian Community, Baptism, and the Lord's Supper'. In *The Cambridge Companion to Karl Barth*, ed. John Webster, 195–211. Cambridge: Cambridge University Press, 2000.

Buckley, Michael J. *At the Origins of Modern Atheism*. New Haven: Yale University Press, 1987.

Busch, Eberhard. *The Great Passion: An Introduction to Karl Barth's Theology*. Translated by Geoffrey W. Bromiley. Grand Rapids: Eerdmans, 2004.

—. *Karl Barth: His Life from Letters and Autobiographical Texts*. Translated by John Bowden. Grand Rapids: Eerdmans, 1994.

Calvin, John. *The Institutes of the Christian Religion*. 2 vols. Edited by John T. McNeill. Translated by Ford Lewis Battles. Library of Christian Classics. Philadelphia: Westminster, 1960.

Camfield, F. W. 'Development and Present Stage of the Theology of Karl Barth'. In *idem*, ed., *Reformation Old and New: A Tribute to Karl Barth*, 47–71. London: Lutterworth, 1947.

Capper, John Mark. *Karl Barth's Theology of Joy*. Ph.D. diss., Cambridge University, 1998.

Case-Winters, Anna. *God's Power: Traditional Understandings and Contemporary Challenges*. Louisville: Westminster John Knox, 1990.

Cave, Sydney. Review of *Die kirchliche Dogmatik II/1, Die Lehre von Gott*, by Karl Barth. *The Congregational Quarterly* 19.2 (1941): 170–1.

Chalamet, Christophe. *Dialectical Theologians: Wilhelm Herrmann, Karl Barth and Rudolf Bultmann*. Zürich: Theologischer Verlag Zürich, 2005.

Colwell, John. 'The Contemporaneity of the Divine Decision: Reflections on Barth's Denial of "Universalism."' In *Universalism and the Doctrine of Hell: Papers Presented at the Fourth Edinburgh Conference on Christian Dogmatics, 1991*, ed. Nigel M. de S. Cameron, 139–60 Carlisle: Paternoster, 1992.

Courth, Franz. *Trinität: In der Schrift und Patristik, Trinität: In der Scholastik*, and *Trinität: Von der Reformation bis zur Gegenwart*. Handbuch der Dogmengeschichte II.1a-c. Edited by Michael Schmaus et al. Freiburg: Herder, 1985–1996.

Cremer, Hermann. *Die christliche Lehre von den Eigenschaften Gottes*. Edited by Helmut Burkhardt. 1897. Gießen: TVG Brunnen, 2005.

Cross, Terry L. *Dialectic in Karl Barth's Doctrine of God*. New York: Peter Lang, 2001.

Cullmann, Oscar. *Christ and Time: The Primitive Christian Conception of Time and History*. Translated by Floyd V. Filson. London: SCM, 1951.

Davaney, Sheila Greeve. *Divine Power: A Study of Karl Barth and Charles Hartshorne.* Harvard Dissertations in Religion 19. Philadelphia: Fortress, 1986.

de Margerie, Bertrand. *The Christian Trinity in History.* Translated by Edmund J. Fortman. Studies in Historical Theology 1. Still River: St. Bede's, 1982.

—. *Les Perfections du Dieu de Jésus-Christ.* Paris: Cerf, 1981.

Dorner, Isaak August. *Divine Immutability: A Critical Reconsideration.* Translated by Robert R. Williams and Claude Welch. Fortress Texts in Modern Theology. 1856–8. Minneapolis: Fortress, 1994.

Driel, Edwin Chr. van. 'Karl Barth on the Eternal Existence of Jesus Christ'. *Scottish Journal of Theology* 60.1 (2007): 45–61.

Dupré, Louis. *The Enlightenment and the Intellectual Foundations of Modern Culture.* New Haven: Yale University Press, 2004.

Evans, Richard J. *The Third Reich in Power: 1933–1939.* New York: Penguin, 2005.

Farley, Edward. *Divine Empathy: A Theology of God.* Minneapolis: Fortress, 1996.

Farrow, Douglas. *Ascension and Ecclesia: On the Significance of the Doctrine of the Ascension for Ecclesiology and Christian Cosmology.* Grand Rapids: Eerdmans, 1999.

Fiddes, Paul S. *The Creative Suffering of God.* Oxford: Clarendon, 1988.

Ford, David F. 'Jesus Christ the Wisdom of God (1)'. In *Reading Texts, Seeking Wisdom: Scripture and Theology*, ed. David F. Ford and Graham Stanton, 4–21. London: SCM, 2003.

—. 'Knowledge, meaning, and the world's great challenges'. *Scottish Journal of Theology* 57.2 (2004): 182–202.

Ford, David F. and Stanton, Graham. 'Introduction'. In *Reading Texts, Seeking Wisdom: Scripture and Theology*, ed. David F. Ford and Graham Stanton, 1–3. London: SCM, 2003.

Franks, Christopher A. 'The Simplicity of the Living God: Aquinas, Barth, and Some Philosophers'. *Modern Theology* 21.2 (2005): 275–300.

Gibson, David. *Reading the Decree: Exegesis, Election and Christology in Calvin and Barth.* London: T&T Clark, 2009.

Gockel, Matthias. *Barth and Schleiermacher on the Doctrine of Election: A Systematic-Theological Comparison.* Oxford: Oxford University Press, 2007.

—. 'On the Way from Schleiermacher to Barth: A Critical Reappraisal of Isaak August Dorner's Essay on Divine Immutability'. *Scottish Journal of Theology* 53.4 (2000): 490–510.

Grell, Mitchell. *Der ewig reiche Gott: Die Erkenntnis, Gewinnung und Bestimmung der Eigenschaften Gottes nach Isaak August Dorner, August Hermann Cremer und Karl Barth mit besonderer Berücksichtigung des Einflusses der Theologie Dorners und Cremers auf die Gotteslehre Barths.* Ph.D. diss., University of Tübingen, 1992.

Grenz, Stanley J. *Reason for Hope: The Systematic Theology of Wolfhart Pannenberg.* 2nd ed. Grand Rapids: Eerdmans, 2005.

Gunton, Colin E. *Act and Being: Towards a Theology of the Divine Attributes.* London: SCM, 2002.

—. *The Barth Lectures.* Edited by P. H. Brazier. London: T&T Clark, 2007.

—. *Becoming and Being: The Doctrine of God in Charles Hartshorne and Karl Barth.* New ed. London: SCM, 2001.

—. 'Introduction'. In Karl Barth, *Protestant Theology in the Nineteenth Century: Its Background and History*. Grand Rapids: Eerdmans, 2002.

—. 'Salvation'. In *The Cambridge Companion to Karl Barth*, ed. John Webster, 143–58. Cambridge: Cambridge University Press, 2000.

Gutenson, Charles E. *Reconsidering the Doctrine of God*. London: T&T Clark, 2005.

Härle, Wilfried. *Sein und Gnade: Die Ontologie in Karl Barths Kirchlicher Dogmatik*. Berlin: de Gruyter, 1975.

Hart, Trevor. 'Revelation'. In *The Cambridge Companion to Karl Barth*, ed. John Webster, 37–56. Cambridge: Cambridge University Press, 2000.

Hector, Kevin W. 'God's Triunity and Self-Determination: A Conversation with Karl Barth, Bruce McCormack and Paul Molnar'. *International Journal of Systematic Theology* 7.3 (2005): 246–61.

Hendry, George S. 'The Freedom of God in the Theology of Karl Barth'. *Scottish Journal of Theology* 31.3 (1978): 229–44.

Heppe, Heinrich. *Reformed Dogmatics*. Edited by Ernst Bizer. Translated by G. T. Thomson. 1857. Reprint Grand Rapids: Baker, 1978.

Heron, Alasdair I. C. *The Holy Spirit in the Bible, the History of Christian Thought, and Recent Theology*. Philadelphia: Westminster, 1983.

Hill, William J. *The Three-Personed God: The Trinity as a Mystery of Salvation*. Washington, DC: Catholic University of America Press, 1982.

Holmes, Christopher R. J. *Revisiting the Doctrine of the Divine Attributes: In Dialogue with Karl Barth, Eberhard Jüngel, and Wolf Krötke*. New York: Peter Lang, 2007.

—. 'The Theological Function of the Doctrine of the Divine Attributes and the Divine Glory, with Special Reference to Karl Barth and His Reading of the Protestant Orthodox'. *Scottish Journal of Theology* 61.2 (2008): 206–23.

Holmes, Stephen R. *God of Grace and God of Glory: An Account of the Theology of Jonathan Edwards*. Edinburgh: T&T Clark, 2000.

—. '"Something Much Too Plain to Say": Towards a Defence of the Doctrine of Divine Simplicity'. *Neue Zeitschrift für systematische Theologie und Religionsphilosophie* 43.1 (2001): 137–54.

Horton, Michael S. *Lord and Servant: A Covenant Christology*. Louisville: Westminster John Knox, 2005.

Hume, David. *An Enquiry Concerning Human Understanding*. Edited by Tom L. Beauchamp. The Clarendon Edition of the Works of David Hume 3. Oxford: Oxford University Press, 2000.

Hunsinger, George. 'Election and the Trinity: Twenty-Five Theses on the Theology of Karl Barth', *Modern Theology* 24.2 (Apr 2008): 179–98.

—. *How to Read Karl Barth: The Shape of His Theology*. Oxford: Oxford University Press, 1991.

—. 'The Mediator of Communion: Karl Barth's Doctrine of the Holy Spirit'. In *The Cambridge Companion to Karl Barth*, ed. John Webster, 177–94. Cambridge: Cambridge University Press, 2000.

—. '*Mysterium Trinitatis*: Karl Barth's Conception of Eternity'. In *idem, Disruptive Grace: Studies in the Theology of Karl Barth*, 186–209. Grand Rapids: Eerdmans, 2000.

Hurtado, Larry W. *Lord Jesus Christ: Devotion to Jesus in Earliest Christianity*. Grand Rapids: Eerdmans, 2003.

Jenson, Robert W. *Alpha and Omega: A Study in the Theology of Karl Barth.* 1963. Reprint Eugene: Wipf and Stock, 2002.

—. *God After God: The God of the Past and the God of the Future, Seen in the Work of Karl Barth.* Indianapolis: Bobbs-Merrill, 1969.

—. *Systematic Theology.* 2 vols. New York: Oxford University Press, 1997–9.

—. 'You Wonder Where the Spirit Went'. *Pro Ecclesia* 2.3 (1993): 296–304.

Johnson, Adam. *God's Being in Reconciliation: The Theo-Ontological Basis of the Unity and Diversity of the Doctrine of the Atonement in the Theology of Karl Barth.* Ph.D. diss., Trinity Evangelical Divinity School, 2010.

Johnson, William Stacy. *The Mystery of God: Karl Barth and the Postmodern Foundations of Theology.* Louisville: Westminster John Knox, 1997.

Jowers, Dennis W. 'The Reproach of Modalism: A Difficulty for Karl Barth's Doctrine of the Trinity'. *Scottish Journal of Theology* 56.2 (2003): 231–46.

Jüngel, Eberhard. *God's Being Is in Becoming: The Trinitarian Being of God in the Theology of Karl Barth: A Paraphrase.* Translated by John Webster. Grand Rapids: Eerdmans, 2001.

Kerr, Fergus. *After Aquinas: Versions of Thomism.* Oxford: Blackwell, 2002.

Kooi, Cornelis van der. *As in a Mirror: John Calvin and Karl Barth on Knowing God: A Diptych.* Translated by Donald Mader. Leiden: Brill, 2005.

Kress, Christine. *Gottes Allmacht angesichts von Leiden: Zur Interpretation der Gotteslehre in den systematisch-theologischen Entwürfen von Paul Althaus, Paul Tillich und Karl Barth.* Neukirchener Theologische Dissertationen und Habilitationen 27. Neukirchen-Vluyn: Neukirchener Verlag, 1999.

Krötke, Wolf. *Gottes Klarheiten: Eine Neuinterpretation der Lehre von Gottes »Eigenschaften«.* Tübingen: Mohr Siebeck, 2001.

—. *Sin and Nothingness in the Theology of Karl Barth.* Edited and translated by Philip G. Ziegler and Christina-Maria Bammel. Studies in Reformed Theology and History ns. 10. Princeton: Princeton Theological Seminary, 2005.

—. Review of *Die Lehre von Gottes Eigenschaften bei Friedrich Schleiermacher und Karl Barth,* by Claus-Dieter Osthövener. *Theologische Literaturzeitung* 123.3 (1998): 293–5.

—. Review of *Die Realisierung der Freiheit: Beiträge zur Kritik der Theologie Karl Barths,* ed. Trutz Rendtorff. *Theologische Literaturzeitung* 105.4 (1980): 300–3.

LaCugna, Catherine Mowry. *God For Us: The Trinity and Christian Life.* New York: Harper Collins, 1993.

Letham, Robert. 'Amandus Polanus: A Neglected Theologian?' *Sixteenth Century Journal* 21.3 (1990): 463–76.

Luther, Martin. *Luther's Works: American Edition.* Edited by Jaroslav Pelikan and Helmut T. Lehmann. St. Louis: Concordia, 1957–86.

Macken, John. *The Autonomy Theme in the Church Dogmatics: Karl Barth and His Critics.* Cambridge: Cambridge University Press, 1990.

MacKenzie, Iain. *The Dynamism of Space: A Theological Study into the Nature of Space.* Norwich: Canterbury, 1995.

Malysz, Piotr J. 'Hegel's Conception of God and its Application by Isaak Dorner to the Problem of Divine Immutability'. *Pro Ecclesia* 15.4 (2006): 448–71.

—. 'Storming Heaven with Karl Barth? Barth's Unwitting Appropriation of the *Genus Maiestaticum* and What Lutherans Can Learn from It'. *International Journal of Systematic Theology* 9.1 (2007): 73–92.

Mangina, Joseph L. *Karl Barth on the Christian Life: The Practical Knowledge of God*. New York: Peter Lang, 2001.

—. *Karl Barth: Theologian of Christian Witness*. Aldershot: Ashgate, 2004.

Marga, Amy. *Karl Barth's Dialogue with Catholicism in Göttingen and Münster: Its Significance for His Doctrine of God*. Tübingen: Mohr Siebeck, 2010.

McCormack, Bruce L. 'The Actuality of God: Karl Barth in Conversation with Open Theism'. In *Engaging the Doctrine of God: Contemporary Protestant Perspectives*, ed. Bruce L. McCormack, 185–242. Grand Rapids: Baker Academic, 2008.

—. 'Divine Impassibility or Simply Divine Constancy? Implications of Karl Barth's Later Christology for Debates over Impassibility'. In *Divine Impassibility and the Mystery of Human Suffering*, ed. James F. Keating and Thomas Joseph White O.P., 150–86. Grand Rapids: Eerdmans, 2009.

—. 'Election and the Trinity: Theses in response to George Hunsinger', *Scottish Journal of Theology* 63.2 (2010): 203–24.

—. 'Grace and Being: The Role of God's Gracious Election in Karl Barth's Theological Ontology'. In *The Cambridge Companion to Karl Barth*, ed. John Webster, 92–110. Cambridge: Cambridge University Press, 2000.

—. *Karl Barth's Critically Realistic Dialectical Theology: Its Genesis and Development 1909–1936*. New York: Oxford University Press, 1995.

—. *Orthodox and Modern: Studies in the Theology of Karl Barth*. Grand Rapids: Baker Academic, 2008.

—. 'Seek God Where He May Be Found: A Response to Edwin Chr. van Driel'. *Scottish Journal of Theology* 60.1 (2007): 62–79.

McGrath, Alister E. *Iustitia Dei: A History of the Christian Doctrine of Justification*. Cambridge: Cambridge University Press, 1986.

Meijering, E. P. *Von den Kirchenvätern zu Karl Barth: Das altkirchliche Dogma in der 'Kirchlichen Dogmatik'*. Amsterdam: Gieben, 1993.

Metzger, Paul Louis. 'The Migration of Monism and the Matrix of Trinitarian Mediation'. *Scottish Journal of Theology* 58.3 (2005): 302–18.

Migliore, Daniel L. *Faith Seeking Understanding: An Introduction to Christian Theology*. 2nd ed. Grand Rapids: Eerdmans, 2004.

Molnar, Paul D. 'Can Jesus' Divinity be Recognized as "Definitive, Authentic and Essential" if it is Grounded in Election? Just How Far Did the Later Barth Historicize Christology?' *Neue Zeitschrift für Systematische Theologie und Religionsphilosophie* 52.1 (2010): 40–81.

—. 'Can the Electing God be God without Us? Some Implications of Bruce McCormack's Understanding of Barth's Doctrine of Election for the Doctrine of the Trinity'. *Neue Zeitschrift für Systematische Theologie und Religionsphilosophie* 49.2 (2007): 199–222.

—. *Divine Freedom and the Doctrine of the Immanent Trinity: In Dialogue with Karl Barth and Contemporary Theology*. Edinburgh: T&T Clark, 2002.

—. *Karl Barth and the Theology of the Lord's Supper: A Systematic Investigation*. New York: Peter Lang, 1996.

—. 'Natural Theology Revisited: A Comparison of T. F. Torrance and Karl Barth'. *Zeitschrift für dialektische Theologie* 21.1 (2005): 53–83.

Moltmann, Jürgen. *Theology of Hope*. Translated by James W. Leitch. London: SCM, 1967.

—. *The Trinity and the Kingdom of God: The Doctrine of God*. Translated by Margaret Kohl. London: SCM, 1981.

Muller, Richard A. *Post-Reformation Reformed Dogmatics: The Rise and Development of Reformed Orthodoxy, ca. 1520 to ca. 1725*. Vol. 3, *The Divine Essence and Attributes*. Grand Rapids: Baker Academic, 2003.

Norgate, Jonathan. *Isaak A. Dorner: The Triune God and the Gospel of Salvation*. London: T&T Clark, 2009.

Oblau, Gotthard. *Gotteszeit und Menschenzeit: Eschatologie in der Kirchlichen Dogmatik von Karl Barth*. Neukirchen-Vluyn: Neukirchener Verlag, 1988.

O'Neil, Michael. 'Karl Barth's Doctrine of Election'. *Evangelical Quarterly* 76.4 (2004): 311–26.

Osthövener, Claus-Dieter. *Die Lehre von Gottes Eigenschaften bei Friedrich Schleiermacher und Karl Barth*. Theologische Bibliothek Töpelmann 76. Berlin: de Gruyter, 1996.

Padgett, Alan G. *God, Eternity and the Nature of Time*. New York: St. Martin's Press, 1992.

Pannenberg, Wolfhart. *Basic Questions in Theology*. Vol. 1. Translated by George H. Kehm. London: SCM, 1970.

—. *Systematic Theology*. 3 vols. Translated by Geoffrey W. Bromiley. Grand Rapids: Eerdmans, 1991–1998.

Pelikan, Jaroslav. *Acts*. Brazos Theological Commentary on the Bible. Grand Rapids: Brazos, 2005.

Pinkard, Terry. *German Philosophy 1760–1860: The Legacy of Idealism*. Cambridge: Cambridge University Press, 2002.

Pokrifka-Joe, Todd. *Redescribing God: The Roles of Scripture, Tradition, and Reason in Karl Barth's Doctrines of Divine Unity, Constancy, and Eternity*. Ph.D. diss., University of St. Andrews, 2002.

Rahner, Karl. 'Remarks on the Dogmatic Treatise "*De Trinitate*."' In *idem*, *Theological Investigations*. Vol. 4. Translated by Kevin Smyth, 77–102. Baltimore: Helicon, 1966.

—. *The Trinity*. Translated by Joseph Donceel. New York: Herder and Herder, 1970.

Raynal, Charles Edward, III. *Karl Barth's Conception of the Perfections of God*. Ph.D. diss., Yale University, 1973.

Roberts, Richard H. 'Karl Barth's Doctrine of Time: Its Nature and Implications'. In *idem*, *A Theology on its Way: Essays on Karl Barth*, 1–58. Edinburgh: T&T Clark, 1991.

Rogers, Eugene. *After the Spirit: A Constructive Pneumatology from Resources Outside the Modern West*. Grand Rapids: Eerdmans, 2005.

Rosato, Philip J. *The Spirit as Lord: The Pneumatology of Karl Barth*. Edinburgh: T&T Clark, 1981.

Russell, John M. 'Impassibility and Pathos in Barth's Idea of God'. *Anglican Theological Review* 70.3 (1988): 221–32.

Sanders, Fred. *The Image of the Immanent Trinity: Rahner's Rule and the Theological Interpretation of Scripture*. New York: Peter Lang, 2005.

—. 'The Trinity'. In *The Oxford Handbook of Systematic Theology*, ed. John Webster et al., 35–53. Oxford: Oxford University Press, 2007.

Schaff, Philip. *The Creeds of Christendom, With a History and Critical Notes*. 3 vols. Grand Rapids: Baker, 1977.

Schleiermacher, F. D. E. *The Christian Faith*. Edited by H. R. Mackintosh and J. S. Stewart. London: Continuum, 1999.

Sherman, Robert. 'Isaak August Dorner on Divine Immutability: A Missing Link between Schleiermacher and Barth'. *Journal of Religion* 77.3 (1997): 380–402.

Smith, Aaron T. 'God's self-specification: his being is his electing'. *Scottish Journal of Theology* 62.1 (2009): 1–25.

Sonderegger, Katherine. 'The Absolute Infinity of God'. In *The Reality of Faith in Theology: Studies on Karl Barth: Princeton-Kampen Consultation 2005*, ed. Bruce McCormack and Gerrit Nevin, 31–49. New York: Peter Lang, 2007.

Spieckermann, Ingrid. *Gotteserkenntnis: Ein Beitrag zur Grundfrage der neuen Theologie Karl Barths*. Munich: Chr. Kaiser, 1985.

Steen, Marc. 'Jürgen Moltmann's Critical Reception of K. Barth's Theopaschitism'. *Ephemerides Theologicae Lovanienses* 67.4 (1991): 278–311.

Štefan, Jan. 'Gottes Vollkommenheiten nach KD II/1'. In *Karl Barth im europäischen Zeitgeschehen (1935–1950): Widerstand – Bewährung – Orientierung*, ed. Michael Beintker, Christian Link and Michael Trowitzsch, 83–108. Zürich: Theologischer Verlag Zürich, 2010.

Tanner, Kathryn E. *God and Creation in Christian Theology: Tyranny or Empowerment?* Oxford: Basil Blackwell, 1988.

Torrance, Alan J. *Persons in Communion: An Essay on Trinitarian Description and Human Participation with Special Reference to Volume One of Karl Barth's Church Dogmatics*. Edinburgh: T&T Clark, 1996.

—. 'The Trinity'. In *The Cambridge Companion to Karl Barth*, ed. John Webster, 72–91. Cambridge: Cambridge University Press, 2000.

Torrance, T. F. *Karl Barth: An Introduction to His Early Theology 1910–1931*. New ed. Edinburgh: T&T Clark, 2000.

—. *Space, Time and Incarnation*. Oxford: Oxford University Press, 1969.

Trowitzsch, Michael. *Karl Barth heute*. Göttingen: Vandenhoeck & Ruprecht, 2007.

Turretin, Francis. *Institutes of Elenctic Theology*. Translated by George Musgrave Giger. Edited by James T. Dennison, Jr. Phillipsburg: Presbyterian and Reformed, 1992–1997.

Van Til, Cornelius. *Christianity and Barthianism*. Philadelphia: Presbyterian and Reformed, 1962.

Vanhoozer, Kevin J. 'Introduction: The Love of God – Its Place, Meaning, and Function in Systematic Theology'. In idem, ed., *Nothing Greater, Nothing Better: Theological Essays on the Love of God*. Grand Rapids: Eerdmans, 2001.

Vischer, Wilhelm. 'Esther'. *Theologische Existenz heute* 48 (1937): 1–29.

Warfield, Benjamin B. 'Calvin's Doctrine of God'. *The Princeton Theological Review* 7 (1909): 381–436.

Weber, Otto. *Foundations of Dogmatics*. 2 vols. Translated by Darrell L. Guder. Grand Rapids: Eerdmans, 1981–1983.

—. *Karl Barth's Church Dogmatics: An Introductory Report on Volumes I:1 to III:4*. Translated by Arthur C. Cochrane. Philadelphia: Westminster, 1953.

Webster, John. 'Balthasar and Karl Barth'. In *The Cambridge Companion to Hans Urs von Balthasar*, ed. Edward T. Oakes and David Moss, 241–55. Cambridge: Cambridge University Press, 2004.

—. *Barth*. Outstanding Christian Thinkers. London: Continuum, 2000.

—. *Barth's Ethics of Reconciliation*. Cambridge: Cambridge University Press, 1995.

—. *Barth's Moral Theology: Human Action in Barth's Thought*. Grand Rapids: Eerdmans, 1998.

—. *Confessing God: Essays in Christian Dogmatics II*. London: T&T Clark, 2005.

—. *Holiness*. Grand Rapids: Eerdmans, 2003.

—. *Holy Scripture: A Dogmatic Sketch*. Cambridge: Cambridge University Press, 2003.

Weinandy, Thomas G. *Does God Suffer?* Notre Dame: University of Notre Dame Press, 2000.

Williams, Robert R. 'I. A. Dorner: The Ethical Immutability of God'. *Journal of the American Academy of Religion* 54.4 (1986): 721–38.

Williams, Rowan. 'Barth on the Triune God'. In *Karl Barth: Studies of his Theological Method*, ed. S. W. Sykes, 147–93. Oxford: Clarendon, 1979.

Wingren, Gustaf. *Theology in Conflict: Nygren, Barth, Bultmann*. Translated by Eric H. Wahlstrom. Edinburgh: Oliver and Boyd, 1958.

Yocum, John. *Ecclesial Mediation in Karl Barth*. Barth Studies. Aldershot: Ashgate, 2004.

INDEX OF SUBJECTS

INDEX OF NAMES

Lightning Source UK Ltd.
Milton Keynes UK
UKOW050858220313

208004UK00003B/33/P